Muḥammad's Ascension in Muslim Spain

Muḥammad's Ascension in Muslim Spain

Elaborations and Contestations of the Miʿrāj in the Eleventh- to Twelfth-Century Maghrib

Frederick S. Colby

SUNY
PRESS

Published by State University of New York Press, Albany

Printed in the United States of America

For information, contact State University of New York Press, Albany, NY
www.sunypress.edu

Library of Congress Cataloging-in-Publication Data

Names: Colby, Frederick Stephen, 1969- author.
Title: Muḥammad's ascension in Muslim Spain : elaborations and contestations of the Mi'raj in the elventh- to twelfth- century Maghrib / Frederick S. Colby.
Description: Albany, NY : State University of New York Press, [2025] | Includes bibliographical references and index.
Identifiers: LCCN 2024022492 | ISBN 9798855800746 (hardcover) | ISBN 9798855800760 (ebook)
Subjects: LCSH: Muḥammad, Prophet, -632--Isrāʾ and Miʻrāj.
Classification: LCC BP166.57 .C649 2025 | DDC 297.6/3--dc23/eng/20241011
LC record available at https://lccn.loc.gov/2024022492

For Penny, with all my love

CONTENTS

Acknowledgments ix

Introduction 1

Chapter One. Antecedents, Commentaries, and Fragments 21

Chapter Two. Shared Discourses and Polemics of Ascent 35

Chapter Three. Emerging Andalūsī Mālikī Traditions 51

Chapter Four. Intertextual Qur᾽ān and Prophetic Reports: Ibn Barrajān 67

Chapter Five. Contemplation of the Visionary Experience: Ibn Qaṣī 95

Conclusion 113

Appendix: Translation of Real Academia de la Historia MS Codera 241 119

Notes 125

Bibliography 157

Index 165

ACKNOWLEDGMENTS

This book would not have been possible without the strong support of friends and colleagues at the University of Oregon. To each of them, I offer my profound thanks (you know who you are). A portion of this book was completed during a term in residence at the Oregon Humanities Center, a truly peaceful environment in which to write. My thanks go to Dr. Paul Peppis and his staff for their support of my work during that period. Sincere thanks are due to Dr. Maribel Fierro for her advice and encouragement about this project that she gave me in 2018, and to Cristina Álvarez Millán, who helped me to access the original MS Codera (Gayangos) 241 at the Real Academia de la Historia in Madrid that summer. Deep thanks to the editor in chief at SUNY Press, James Peltz, and to his wonderful staff at every level who helped to shepherd this manuscript through the stages of production. Finally, this work would not have been possible without the steadfast love and support of my wife, Penny, throughout the research and writing that kept me busy in my office or on research trips when I might have otherwise have been with her at home. I have received help from countless individuals over the more than a decade that this work has been in process, but any mistakes that remain in this work are, of course, my own.

Introduction

The History of the Night Journey and Ascension Narratives

Since the rise of Islam, many Muslims have loved to recount stories of journeys to other worlds beyond this one, especially narratives that describe Muḥammad's fabulous trip through the heavens during his night journey (*isrāʾ*) and ascension (*miʿrāj*). A tale full of significance to elite scholars — from traditionists and theologians to exegetes, philosophers, and mystics — as well as common believers, Muḥammad's journey from the earliest years served as a heavenly canvas on which subsequent Muslim writers of the premodern period could paint tangible images of angels, gardens, fires, oceans, veils, the divine throne, and even at times God himself. These "ascension narratives" spread wherever Muslims lived and traveled, weaving together anecdotes, storylines, and narrative fragments from the wealth of competing versions that have been passed down in both oral and written accounts. In each case, the telling of the tale engaged and interacted with the languages, tropes, and concerns of the local contexts in which those who transmitted the stories articulated their accounts. This book is the tale of select strands of the fabric of the particular history of Muslim ascension narratives in the western Mediterranean, among those arising out of medieval Spain and North Africa, and especially those of scholars whom contemporary specialists would later come to categorize as "contemplatives."[1] These western Mediterranean authors approached the ascension tale from a particular direction, interacting and competing with otherworldly narratives among their Jewish and Christian contemporaries. A few of them also co-opted some of the messianic and apocalyptic discourses of the Muslim reformist regimes that ruled much of the region of what is now southern Spain and Morocco. As a whole, these "Maghribī" (meaning "western" in the sense of the western lands of Islamdom) Muslim contemplative authors came to play a decisive role in shaping the contours of the beloved legend of Muḥammad's ascension as it was popularly circulated for centuries thereafter.

The history and development of Muslim ascension narratives has been the subject of increasing scholarly attention in recent decades.[2] Nevertheless, most studies to date have focused on the accounts composed by a single individual author, or delved into a narrow range of ascension-related themes. Many presume that there is one standard mainstream canonical story of Muḥammad's ascension that can be identified and classified, with other tellings and interpretations measured by their faithfulness to or divergence from this allegedly "orthodox" version. By examining the creativity and expansiveness of written accounts and commentaries about the night journey and ascension in scholarly works in the Muslim West, primarily from the region known as the "Maghrib" from the eleventh through the twelfth centuries of the Common Era, this study builds on the insights of recent methodological works in the field of Islamic studies to argue that previous conceptions of orthodoxy and heterodoxy as applied to the *miʿrāj* tales deserve our reconsideration, and the role of Maghribī commentators in the development of key versions of the tale merit much greater attention.

Specifically, one begins to see how the discussions in this period regarding Muḥammad's heavenly journey that originate with some of the most profound premodern contemplative thinkers in what is modern-day Spain, such as Ibn Barrajān (d. 536/1141), Ibn Qasī (d. 546/1151), and the "Grand Master" Ibn ʿArabī (d. 638/1240), creatively reflect and are in dialogue with debates that were salient at the time: Who enjoys divinely sent leadership of the community? How do religious communities relate to one another and to God's angelic hosts? How do such issues relate to the imminent expectation of the coming End of Times? This work seeks answers to such questions by surveying a range of Maghribī sources from different genres, from Qurʾān commentaries, prophetic biographies (*sīra* literature), and works dedicated solely to the sayings of the Prophet Muḥammad (reports called in Arabic *hadith* in the singular, *āḥādīth* in the plural; hereafter: "hadith" for both) to broader learned mystical treatises and allegorical tales, to show how a variety of Muslims in this specific cultural context debated, delved into, and told competing versions of the story of Muḥammad's ascension. The sources considered in this study narrate in whole or in part the story of this extraordinary journey that the Prophet was said to have experienced in the middle of his prophetic career, adapting it to their present needs and creatively exploring its boundaries.

The present work thus builds on my previous work,[3] as well as Pieter Coppens's more recent groundbreaking study of foundational Sufi Qurʾān commentaries in the eastern lands regarding the theme of the "vision of God" among members of a nascent movement that could more properly be called "Sufi" arising in the city of Nishapur and the wider Iranian Plateau — Sulamī (412/1021), Qushayrī (d. 465/1072), Maybūdī (fl. first half of sixth/twelfth century), Daylamī (d. 587/1191?), and Ruzbihān Baqlī (d. 606/1209).[4] It remains an open question the degree to which the ideas of these eastern Sufis related to, affected, or engaged with the works of western contemplatives who were in some cases contemporaries of these eastern Sufis but who moved in different scholarly circles and environments.

Through the analysis of the Maghribī ascension narratives that are the main focus of our attention, this study illustrates the merits of examining ascension literature through the lens of "explorative authority,"[5] a view that makes claims about delimiting what deserves to be classified as part of the western Muslim ascension discourse while simultaneously extending that discourse by showing it to be in conversation with other related narratives that circulated in the same cultural context. For instance, the Maghribī discussions of Muḥammad's ascension creatively engaged in dialogue and debate with polemical works by other Muslims as well as non-Muslims, not to mention semiautobiographical mystical treatises, esoteric teaching sessions, et cetera, that all circulated around the same period in the western lands of Islamdom. It quickly becomes clear that a fuller understanding of the present topic is possible only by widening the scope of our inquiry and the types of sources we examine.

What Is Islam? What Is an Islamic Ascension Narrative?

In his important work *What Is Islam?*, Shahab Ahmed proposes that in order to account for the diversity of, and frankly contradictory nature of, ideas and practices that Muslims embody and articulate in different times and different periods of history, contemporary scholars need to move beyond previous attempts to define Islam simply as a "religion," a "civilization," a "cultural system," a "discursive tradition," or even as an empty signifier. Rather than following Talal Asad's prescriptive approach which suggests that "Islam" might best be defined as a discursive tradition that engages directly first and foremost with the Qur᾿ān and hadith in order to instruct followers about the boundaries of "orthodoxy," and thus to delimit and to police what counts as truly "Islamic," Ahmed argues that such a restrictive view of Islam neglects to account for what he describes as the more creative "explorative authority" of many Muslim authors and transmitters from a variety of backgrounds. This explorative authority appears in the wide range of Muslim teachings and practices that base their hermeneutics not on narrowing the scope of what may be considered "Islamic" but rather, in contrast, expanding it.[6] Prime examples for Ahmed are the Muslim philosophers and their use of Aristotelean and Platonic-inspired forms of reasoning, as well as the Muslim "mystics" (the famous Ibn ʿArabī, who will be discussed in the conclusion of this work, serving as a major case in point for Ahmed) and their engagement with mystical experiences of existence. Ahmed labels such epistemological approaches with his neologism "Pre-Text," defined as such because they draw on the premise of a wider Universal Reality and sources of authority before and beyond the sacred "Texts" of divine revelation to Muḥammad.[7] He also insists that in addition to such hermeneutical Pre-Text, any approach to defining the slippery concept we call "Islam" inevitably is situated not only in time and space (what one might term a "context") but also in engagement with the "entire lexicon of means and meanings of Islam that has been historically generated and recorded up to any given moment," a lexical source that Ahmed defines with his neologism "Con-Text," standing for "the full historical vocabulary of Islam at any given moment."[8] Before delving even more deeply into this technical theoretical approach to our subject, it is worth recognizing what makes it relevant to the study of western contemplative commentaries on Muḥammad's ascension.

The merit for contemporary readers in considering not only what Shahab Ahmed describes as Text (such as the sacred sources in the Qur'ān and hadith) but also Pre-Text and Con-Text (in the way that Ahmed defines them, summarized in the briefest of fashions, above) is that viewing ascension discourses in such a fashion helps one to take a very expansive and inclusive view of Islam in general, and the wide variety of Muslim ascension discourses circulating in the Maghreb in particular. Concerning the narratives that are the central focus of this study, for example, rather than sidelining "explorative" works such as those of Ibn ʿArabī or of Ibn Qaṣī with labels such as "heterodox" or even "esoteric," Ahmed demonstrates that at least in the "Balkans to Bengal" complex of the late middle and early modern periods of Islamic history,[9] such creative and expansive explorations enjoyed a certain authority and widespread popularity among Muslims of vastly different backgrounds. This book argues that a similar type of cultural complex could be found in the earlier middle periods of Islamic history in the Maghrib or Islamic West. In this environment, one finds an abundance of creativity and what Ahmed calls "explorative authority," seen for example in the diverse ways that Muslim contemplative authors mine a rich source of meaning in their transmitting and analyzing tales of heavenly ascent, whether those connected to the Prophet of Islam or, by extension, those emerging out of their own contemplative / spiritual experiences. In other words, while the present study examines works outside the temporal and geographical range that Ahmed highlights in his pivotal methodological intervention, nonetheless the conceptual tools he offers in his work remain extremely useful when taking an expansive view of the range of Muslim retellings and reinterpretations of the night journey and ascension tales. Therefore, this work will endeavor to elucidate key aspects of the Pre-Text, Text, and Con-Text that inform different western Muslim writers who treated the theme of ascension, especially in the eleventh and twelfth centuries CE, and endeavor to analyze some of their most profound and creative explorations into this rich subject matter.

As alluded to above, the specific history of social and political disruption that took place in the western portions of the ʿAbbasid lands during these particular centuries led to messianic claims among several Muslim leaders in the Mediterranean region. This environment, along with a Neoplatonic worldview that became prevalent among many of the educated elites in the region, had an undeniable effect on the way that important scholars framed their presentations of Muḥammad's otherworldly journey, as well as their discussions of the otherworldly journeys of later spiritually gifted individuals. These presentations, in turn, came to have a transformative impact on subsequent elaborations of the Islamic ascension legend, not only in the Muslim West but all across the world. Before we can trace those developments, however, it will first be essential to take a brief look into the "Pre-Text" that historically precedes the rise of Muslim ascension discourses, for briefly perusing the contours of these works will help to establish some of the basic vocabulary that our authors will go on to employ and develop in new ways.

"Pre-Texts": Ancient Greeks, Jews, and Christians on the Theme of Ascension

Narratives of a hero's ascension to the heavens stretch back for countless years in human history, creating the parameters for what could be part of the vast prehistory of Muslim engagement with the theme of otherworldly journeys, one that provides the common terms and tropes for many such stories. In the region of the lands surrounding the Mediterranean basin, engagement with this language world was particularly long-lasting and deep. Just because many storytellers and authors in the premodern Mediterranean often implored a common idea of the structure of the universe and/or a common vocabulary of heavenly ascent, one should not assume as a consequence that those who drew on this well of terms, symbols, and concepts all used them in a similar fashion, or that they shared an identical understanding of their broader meaning or significance. Importantly, just as Ahmed insists that different Muslims articulate mutually exclusive and in fact contradictory definitions for the question "What is Islam?" while simultaneously contributing to the larger "Con-Text" of Muslim discourses, so, too, writers who explore the theme of ascension do not necessarily agree on the meaning or interpretation of ascension narratives. In fact, rather than agreement, the theme of heavenly ascension more often than not becomes the site of disagreement, debate, and contest among different writers who describe otherworldly journeys drawing on this shared set of symbols and assumptions. Put simply, shared vocabulary does not necessarily lead to shared meanings or interpretations. Within and beyond the narratives that Muslims tell around Muḥammad's night journey and ascension, one should expect (and, in fact, one finds) remarkably distinct — and even contrasting and/or contradictory — readings and uses of these accounts of journeys to other worlds.

Of course, since early in human history, people have told stories of a hero's journey to the heavens, or the related idea of the soul's return to its divine origin during or after one's life on Earth. Focusing on the Mediterranean region, one finds that ancient Egyptians, Greeks, and Romans, as well as Jews, Christians, and "Gnostics" of the first millennium CE, each circulated hundreds if not thousands of versions of such stories.[10] The idea of ascending through the spheres was an important dimension of Neoplatonic thought as articulated, for example, in the *Enneads* of Plotinus, and it is worth noting that such ideas widely circulated in Arab scholarly circles in the early ʿAbbasid era under the guise of a work that was translated and widely circulated as the *Theology of Aristotle* (*Uthūlūjiyā arisṭāṭālīs*).[11]

Jewish texts touching on the theme of ascension over time spread to diverse audiences. Examples include those that emerged out of biblical commentaries on the book of *Ezekiel*, together with expansive stories of the otherworldly journey of the biblical hero Enoch, who was said to have "walked with God; then he was no more, for God took him" (Gen. 5:24), as well as other apocalyptic works that include a vision of the journey to the divine chariot (*merkavah*) or throne that come to be associated with the rubric Hekhalot (palace) literature.[12] These wide-ranging narratives of apocalypse and ascent play an important role in widening the angelology and broadening the parameters of the way Mediterranean writers especially came to envision the heavenly realms and their inhabitants. By the period that is the focus of this study, centered around the eleventh and twelfth centuries in the Islamic West, Jewish Hekhalot texts had circulated in al-Maghrib in general and al-Andalus in particular, and were brought into conversation with Christian discussions of heaven, hell, and the End of Times. Moreover, authors such as Judah Halevi and Abraham ibn Ezra engaged with both Neoplatonic thought as well as Muslim literature and philosophy in their own discussions of the theme of heavenly ascent.[13]

Christian ideas about the potential for humans to ascend through the heavens, beyond ideas about Jesus's descent into hell and ascent into heaven after his crucifixion, also circulated widely in the premodern Mediterranean. Jesus and his mother Mary were not the only "heroes," of course, who were the focus of stories among Christians about being taken up into the heavens. To provide just one famous example, the Apostle Paul of Tarsus came to be associated with a heavenly journey based on the vision mentioned cryptically in his New Testament epistle 2 Corinthians 12:1–9, describing someone "taken up" into the "third heaven." In late antiquity, one first hears of a text allegedly discovered under the floorboards of a house in Damascus, presumably documenting Paul's firsthand account of his own experience of being "taken up," a story that in subsequent centuries spread throughout the Mediterranean via a version that came to be known as "The Apocalypse of Paul." One could recount many similar but less famous examples of otherworldly apocalyptic journeys from the early and middle periods of Christian history.[14]

Although it is beyond the scope of this work to examine the specifics of these earlier ascension narratives in greater detail, for our purposes in this study, the key element that can hardly be stressed enough is that many of these otherworldly ascension narratives remained "in the air" in al-Andalus and part of the broader "Pre-Text" environment in which western Mediterranean authors' writings about Muslim ascension literature lived, breathed, and wrote. These broader collections of largely Mediterranean-originating ascension-related discourses make up the language world in which narratives of Muslim ascent could be imagined and articulated, and they provide some of the basic vocabulary (such as the notion of multiple upperworldly "heavens," beyond which one may find God's throne) for later explorations into these higher spheres.

Islamic Origins and Foundational Muslim Texts

From the qur'ānic perspective, Muḥammad's "night journey" (*al-isrā'*) and heavenly ascension (*al-mi'rāj*) could be understood as two separate events in Muslim sacred history. The opening verse of the chapter in the Qur'ān known variously as "The Night Journey" or "The People of Israel" (Q 17:1) apparently was interpreted in the earliest Muslim historical sources as referring to a single circular journey from Mecca to Jerusalem and back, mainly across land, without much of a sense of Muḥammad rising above the earth through the heavenly spheres.[15] Drawing on a different passage from the Muslim sacred text, a heavenly journey through the spheres remained one way, but not the only way, to understand some of the references in the opening eighteen verses of the "Star" chapter of the Qur'ān, especially the second portion of this opening sequence (Q 53:13–18) that entails a sublime vision at a mysterious site described as the "Lote Tree of the Boundary" that early commentaries identify as an upperworldly tree. The early historian Ibn Sa'd (d. 230/845) significantly gives two distinct dates on the Muslim calendar for these two separate, albeit equally remarkable, prophetic journeys.[16]

While this potential separation between two different journeys associated with the Prophet Muḥammad, labeled "night journey" (*al-isrāʾ*) and "ascension" (*al-miʿrāj*), respectively, may appear rooted in the Qurʾān and the earliest Muslim oral traditions and historical writings, it is equally clear that this separation was quickly superseded by a countervailing movement to treat the two journeys together as the events of one single night in Muḥammad's life. For example, by the time of the compilation of the written accounts of the oral legends of Muḥammad's otherworldly experiences, most of the mainstream collections of which were assembled starting in the second to third century AH (eighth to ninth century CE), the majority of reports demonstrate that in the minds of most Muslims by this time, what earlier appeared to be two separate journeys were woven together as inseparable and deeply intertwined elements of a single journey. That is the case in most of the reports brought together in the major collections that Sunnī scholars would come to consider "sound" hadith, and also in the extended tales of Muḥammad's journey included in some of the earliest Qurʾān commentaries (*tafāsir*, sing. *tafsīr*). By the time of the famous commentaries compiled by eastern Muslim exegetes Ṭabarī (d. 310/923) and Thaʿlabī (d. 427/1035) and thereafter, the Arabic terms *isrāʾ* and *miʿrāj* have become essentially interchangeable in most scholarly contexts,[17] and one may well find discussion of Muḥammad's heavenly ascension in the exegesis of the "Night Journey verse," Q 17:1 (*ayat al-isrāʾ*), as well as the elaboration of the night journey to Jerusalem as part of the broader exegesis of the key verses from opening of the Star chapter, Q 53:1–18.

Further Context: Hadith Literature and Other Oral Traditions

Just as with the brief reference to Enoch walking with God in Genesis that later develops into an extensive and detailed series of versions about Enoch's ascension and transformation, and just as the brief reference in Paul's letter to being taken up into the third heaven that later develops into a long apocalyptic work explaining all the specifics of Paul's journey, so too the concise and elusive qurʾānic references come to be expanded and explained further in oral reports that allegedly originate with Muḥammad himself and were circulated and recorded in what have come to be known as hadith reports. It is beyond the scope of this work to analyze the scores of long and detailed hadith reports of Muḥammad's night journey and ascension that Sunnī and Shīʿī Muslim compilers of the formative period include in their collections. Nevertheless, I present translations of some of the most famous and influential representative examples in what follows.

Taking this textual background for granted, a few observations are in order about the importance of this formative hadith literature to the subsequent development of the ascension narrative in the Islamic West. First, given the predominance of the Sunnī Mālikī approach to Islamic law among the scholars of the Maghrib, and the manner in which this method favored the use of hadith reports and the teachings of the people of Medina for the formulation of jurisprudence, the study of and commentary on Sunnī hadith that the majority of scholars considered most authentic and authoritative flourished in the eleventh through twelfth century Muslim West. The reports remained open to interpretation, however, and we shall see how the reports of Muḥammad's otherworldly journey(s) received disparate and wide-ranging treatments by Muslim scholars in the middle-period Maghrib. Second, although most mainstream scholars came to rely on the chain of transmission (*isnād*) generally attached to the front of any authentic hadith report as a key authenticating device to determine whether or not a report could be considered "sound," one should not overstate the importance of such considerations and formal methods of hadith analysis (called in Arabic *al-jarḥ wa'l-ta'dīl*). The sources we shall analyze in the chapters that follow demonstrate that many mainstream scholars in the western lands did not consistently use this tool in their analysis or studies, and in fact, such critical analytical considerations were often secondary for many of those who drew on these earlier reports in their retellings and reinterpretations of the ascension narrative, even among trained Mālikī experts whom one would presume would take their scrutiny of hadith reports very seriously. While from the perspective of many later Muslim scholars, anyone who omits an *isnād* when transmitting hadith is showing dangerously laxity of precision and/or ignorance of this authorizing device, this study demonstrates that the norms were somewhat different among even the most mainstream scholars writing about Muḥammad's ascension in the eleventh through twelfth-century Maghribī context, despite the resurgence of the Mālikī jurisprudential method during this period.[18] Third and finally, certain night journey and ascension reports, such as different variants of the reports ascribed to Muḥammad's young companion Ibn ʿAbbās, narratives that from the earliest period did not have strong authenticating chains of transmission and were thus rejected by a large number of Sunnī scholars as being "forged" or "spurious" and thus left out of the "sound" collections of hadith, nevertheless became widely circulated by Muslims in every region of the world, as my previous study has shown.[19] A reshaped composite version of the early Ibn ʿAbbās ascension narratives came to have a significant impact on scholarly discussions of the ascension legend in al-Andalus, as this study will demonstrate.

Islamic Spain up through the Twelfth Century CE

Between the Umayyad period of al-Andalus and the rise of the two Amāzīgh ("Berber") dynasties originating from revivalist tribal warriors out of North Africa, the al-Murābiṭūn (Almoravids) and the Muwāḥḥidūn (Almohads), the portion of the Iberian Peninsula that comes to be known as "Islamic Spain" — which by this period was largely confined to the lower half of the Iberian Peninsula, including portions of present-day Spain as well as Portugal — was divided into the rule of multiple Muslim city-states, an era known as the rule of the "Party Kings" (Arabic singular *tā'ifa*, plural *tawā'if*, literally "factions," approximately spanning the years 1009–1091 CE). The different kings, princes, and warlords competed with one another, not only militarily but also scientifically and intellectually. Literature and the arts enjoyed something of a surge of energy and interest in the region, and this may have affected the increased circulation of the Islamic ascension narratives, since they formed a central story in Muslim religious literature.[20] Citing the connection between the political situation and the increase in patronage for the arts, Montgomery Watt writes, "Despite the political upheavals art and letters flourished . . . since each little ruler imitated the splendor of the former caliphal court as far as his resources permitted."[21] As Watt and others have shown, under this quasifeudal system, allegiances in this cultural context were more to a person than to any broader idea of nation or religion, with Muslims and Christians making alliances with one another, sometimes against fellow coreligionists, in whatever way best suited their interests.

One pivotal date during this historical period comes with the fall of the key north-central city of Toledo in 1085 CE to the forces of Alfonso VI of León. The Muslim "Party States" were fully fragmented in this period and "Christian rule" in the north of the peninsula was similarly divided. Therefore, any simplistic conception of a unified Muslim *umma* defending itself against the increasing incursions from a unified Christian "Reconquista" movement coming from the north does not fit the context of the times. It was indeed a period of conflict, tension, and widespread social and cultural disruption, and it is out of this period that one of the earliest Muslim ascension manuscripts currently extant was copied in al-Andalus.[22]

The majority of the Maghribī texts that this study will analyze were composed in the periods that followed on the heels of the Tā'ifa period, firstly that of the Murābiṭūn (literally the partisans in support of the "struggle of religious inspiration,"[23] r. ca.1090–1145).[24] The leader of the Murābiṭūn, Yūsuf ibn Tāshufīn (d. 1107), had been invited from North Africa to al-Andalus to help repel attacks from diverse Christian armies from the northern portions of the peninsula. Despite initial military successes and the eventual conquest of much of the southern portion of the Iberian Peninsula, the Murābiṭūn never seized Toledo from Alfonso VI of León, and attacks of different Christian rulers into southern territories continued throughout this period.[25] Both Yūsuf ibn Tāshufīn and his son ʿAlī b. Yūsuf, who succeeded him (r. 1106–1143), appealed to models of charismatic leadership, drawn partially from Shīʿī models of the role of the *imām* but also mystical ideas about the role of the saintly "friend of God" or *walī*,[26] to help justify their positions of authority. They also promoted the role of Mālikī Sunnī legal scholars in the region as a counterweight to other sources of religious authority.

By the end of the fifth/eleventh century and the rise of al-Murābiṭūn (Almoravids) in al-Andalus, Fāṭimids from the eastern portions of North Africa not only dominated the eastern Mediterranean but their missionaries had undoubtedly made inroads in al-Andalus as they sought to win influence among the elites in the western Mediterranean. Given this situation, one cannot ignore the possibility that esoteric Shīʿī ideas coming from the Fāṭimids may have played a role, directly or indirectly, in helping to shape the rise of diverse approaches to Jamāʿī-Sunnī contemplative practice and/or Qurʾān exegesis in the Islamic West, even though few if any of the prominent scholars in the Islamic West would have officially embraced any form of Shīʿism.[27] As Michael Ebstein rightly points out, the similarities between Ismāʿīlī and/or Brethren-associated esotericism and other western Muslim contemplatives are too numerous to be discounted completely. That being said, as we shall see in what follows, the degree to which Ebstein's hypothesis suggests a deep connection between these two approaches to describing the "inner" meanings of Muslim beliefs and practices, such as one finds in the writings of the twelfth-century Iberian individuals on the subject of Muḥammad's ascension, may be overstated according to the evidence that this study examines.

As mentioned previously, the period of the Murābiṭūn saw the rise of Mālikī Sunnī scholarly revivalism dominating the learned circles of Muslim scholars in both North Africa and al-Andalus. The Mālikī jurists and judges, collaborating with the Murābiṭūn forces from North Africa, helped to displace the "Arabo-Andalusian" aristocracy that had continued to rule in the period of the "Party Kings."[28] As Maribel Fierro has shown, however, it is too simplistic to see the Mālikī scholars of the Murābiṭ era as a monolithic bloc, for although most scholars were indeed Mālikīs, they split into different groupings based on diverse approaches to religious, social, and political issues of the day. For instance, concerning religious matters, claims to messianic divine selection began to be made about certain Murābiṭ leaders, a movement supported by certain Mālikī scholars and opposed by others (such as Qāḍī ʿIyāḍ). In any case, despite such diversity of opinion, it is clear that the general alliance between Murābiṭ leaders and Mālikī scholars during this period served to protect the interests of this dynasty of North African origin against potential rival sources of political power, including those of some prominent contemplatives in the region such as Ibn Barrajān and Ibn Qasī. Despite their success in crushing dissent among charismatic leaders like Ibn Barrajān and Ibn Qasī, such movements may well have "contributed considerably to the beginning of the end"[29] of the rule of the Murābiṭūn.

Claims to messianism also played a role in the rise of the dynasty that followed the Murābiṭūn in the leadership of al-Andalus, after a few decades of hiatus, the Muwāḥḥidūn (literally the "Unitarians" or more loosely "Testifiers to God's Oneness," ruling in al-Andalus ca. 1171–1223 CE). The first Muwāḥḥid leader, Ibn-Tūmart (d. 1130), asserted a claim to be the awaited Mahdi (the messianic "Rightly-Guided One"), and his successor who ruled from al-Maghrib, ʿAbd al-Muʾmin, was appointed to serve as the Mahdi's caliph or viceregent in 1130. The Muwāḥḥidūn came to directly rule much of the southern portion of Iberia beginning with the rule of ʿAbd al-Muʾmin's son, Abū Yaʿqūb (d. 1184), starting around the year 1171.

With the rise of the Muwāḥḥidūn one encounters an increasingly religious rigidity at the center of Maghribī official institutions, corresponding to a rejection of opposing religious points of view as a matter of ruling policy, among both Muslims and non-Muslims. The charismatic model of leadership in this dynasty, which to some degree resembled that of the Ismāʿīlī Fāṭimids who continued to dominate the eastern Mediterranean from their base in Egypt at the time of the Muwāḥḥid rise to power, de-emphasized the allegiance to any particular school of law in favor of allegiance to the teachings of the Muwāḥḥid Mahdi (Ibn Tūmart), his deputies, and the "students" (Arabic *ṭalaba*) who promoted these teachings among the scholarly elite. In the Muwāḥḥid era, inter- and intra-religious polemics were said to have become more pointed and contentious. We shall see how this contentiousness, when applied to the story of Muḥammad's night journey and ascension, pushed the related discourses to grow and expand so that they might meet the needs of different communities in Spain and North Africa in the face of growing rigidity within official circles. We shall also see the growing importance of visions of a charismatic leader or "axial saint" as part of Muslim conceptions of the upper realms.

Major Players of the Iberian Response

Four key authors from this period focus in a concentrated way on not only transmitting but also discussing and analyzing Muḥammad's night journey and ascension in sixth/twelfth century al-Andalus: Qāḍī ʿIyāḍ (d. 544/1149), Ibn Barrajān (d. 536/1141), Ibn Qaṣī (546/1151), and Suhaylī (d. 581/1185). Despite the differences in their approaches and in some of the specific details of the narratives they convey, this study will demonstrate how by analyzing the treatment of the theme of Muḥammad's ascension in the works of these four authors, as well as select works of Jews and Christians in al-Andalus during this key period, we learn something significant about particular Iberian approaches to this discourse. Before turning to the works themselves, it is useful to consider some brief biographical sketches of the figures on whom the following chapters will largely concentrate.

Qāḍī ʿIyāḍ (d. 544/1149) was a judge and hadith scholar who appears to have aimed some of his reflections on Muḥammad's night journey and ascension to challenge theological teachings of the ruling dynasty in al-Andalus that he found objectionable. ʿIyāḍ was a Mālikī traditionist born in Ceuta around 476/1083[30] on the northern coast of North Africa across the straits of Gibraltar from the Iberian Peninsula. After beginning his studies in Ceuta, he traveled to al-Andalus to complete his education in the "east" of Spain, studying with several scholars, including the legalist-minded Qurʾān scholar named Abū Bakr Ibn ʿArabī (d. 543/1149).[31] He began his career as a Mālikī judge (*qāḍī*) in Ceuta, but in 531/1136 he was promoted to the judgeship of Granada, where he served for almost a decade before being dismissed from the post by the al-Murābiṭ leader Tashufīn b. ʿAlī (d. 539/1145), apparently because he was too strict in his rulings, "too censorious."[32] After Tashufīn's death, the latter's son, Ibrahim Ibn Tashufīn, reinstated him as a judge in Ceuta, where he played a role in opposition to the rise of the al-Muwāḥḥid movement. He composed several works,[33] but only a few remain extant, including an important work on Mālikī thought titled *Tartīb al-madārik wa-taqrīb al-masālik li-maʿrifat aʿlām madhhab Mālik*. Unlike the rest of his works, however, Qāḍī ʿIyāḍ's book extolling the merits of the Prophet Muḥammad, known as *al-Shifāʾ bi-taʿrīf ḥuqūq al-muṣṭafā* (*The Cure through Coming to Know the Rights of the Pure [Prophet]*) came to achieve worldwide renown, and it is in this famous work that he examines questions around Muḥammad's ascension in significant detail.

Ibn Barrajān (d. 536/1141) was an important contemplative and Qur'ān exegete, originally from North Africa, who came to serve as the leader of a mystical community based in and around the city of Ishbiliya (in English: Seville). Some considered him "the Ghazalī of al-Andalus," a title that speaks of his importance in al-Maghrib, given the fame enjoyed by Abū Ḥāmid Ghazālī (d. 505/1111), author of the pivotal *Iḥya* 'ulūm *al-dīn* (*Revival of the Religious Sciences*). Ibn Barrajān was the author of two important Qur'ān commentaries that only in the past decade have begun to receive the scholarly attention that they deserve from western academics.[34] Previously, the commentary of Ibn Barrajān was seen as noteworthy mainly because it contained the author's famous prediction of the Muslim recapture of Jerusalem from the forces of Christian Crusaders before the event took place.[35] This being as it may, Ibn Barrajān seems to have composed both of his Qur'ān commentaries in the final two decades of his life[36] in something of an oral fashion as a "teaching" text, aimed first and foremost at providing contemplative esoteric interpretations of the sacred scripture for the instruction of his close followers.

Ibn Barrajān's approach to *tafsīr* (Qur'ān exegesis) focuses to a large degree on two sources, first interpreting the Qur'ān via the Qur'ān, and second offering commentary by way of presenting excerpts from hadith reports, both of which methodologies his disparate discussions of the night journey and ascension illustrate.[37] While other *tafsīr* works draw on similar epistemologies and methodologies, Ibn Barrajān's commentaries are aimed at a specialist audience of western contemplatives who see the Qur'ān as an access point for their "crossing over" (*i'tibār*) from the perception of this world into a perception of the world to come.[38] In neither his longer nor his shorter commentary did he strive to create a comprehensive verse-by-verse *tafsīr* in the traditional form; he instead selected specific qur'ānic passages that he deemed most critical to interpret for the sake of his followers. Ibn Barrajān was a Neoplatonist whose thought may well have been affected indirectly by the teachings of the "Brethren of Purity" (*Ikhwān al-Ṣafā*).[39] Sometimes called a scriptural "hyperliteralist,"[40] Ibn Barrajān related key passages that he understood to refer to Muḥammad's otherworldly journeys, especially Q 17:1 and Q 53:1–18, to surrounding passages that do not on the surface directly relate to this story, justified on the basis of his understanding of the principle of the Qur'ān's miraculous structure (*naẓm*) and the importance of the placement of each verse.

Although a contemplative in the tradition of Ibn Masarra and often seen merely as a forerunner to the more famous Andalusian Sufi who followed a couple of generations after him, Muḥyī al-Dīn Ibn 'Arabī (d. 638/1240), Ibn Barrajān was a unique thinker in his own right. He opposed some of what he considered more extreme forms of esotericism in his day, for instance, the approach he labeled "*bāṭiniyya.*" According to Yousef Casewit, "Ibn Barrajān employed the term *bāṭiniyya* [or "esotericists"] as a catch-all reference to Ismāʿīlīs who trump the divine law, as well as radical Sufis who speak of either union (*ittiḥād*) with God, divine indwelling, incarnation (*ḥulūl*), or physical, this-worldly access to paradise."[41] His vocal rejection of such ideas may have been one of the reasons why Ibn Barrajān came under the official scrutiny of the al-Murābiṭ leadership. Perhaps even more likely, Ibn Barrajān was seen by the ruling dynasty as a potential political threat, given his popularity as a teacher and holy man. Whatever the reason, he and two other Iberian scholars were summoned by the sultan ʿAli b. Yusuf Ibn Tāshufīn (r. first half of the sixth/twelfth century) to appear in Marrakesh (in what is today southern Morocco), where he was commanded to explain passages from his works that his critics deemed potentially heretical. The actual circumstances remain elusive, but he was thrown into prison after being charged with unwarranted religious innovation (*bidʿa*),[42] and he died shortly thereafter in d. 536/1141. Even though José Bellver insists that "the events surrounding his death are better explained by considering his views on Qurʾānic exegesis and the growing tensions produced by the shifting of religious authority from transmitted knowledge to purity of heart and intimacy with God,"[43] it is worth considering whether it is possible to detect in his commentary on Muḥammad's ascension anything that could be considered a rebuke of al-Murābiṭ (Almoravid) doctrines.

Like Ibn Barrajān, his Andalūsī contemporary Ibn Qaṣī (546/1151) was a scholar intrigued by hidden meanings in the Qurʾān, one who was not merely an isolated contemplative but who came to assume the leadership of a large community of devoted followers.[44] He apparently was born neither an Arab nor a North African but rather of "European" origin, given the *nisba* "Rūmī" ("Roman") that is sometimes employed by biographers.[45] He seems to have given away his possessions and led the life of an ascetic, and, according to one biographer, to have begun his esoteric education with a study of the treatises of *al-Ikhwān al-Ṣafāʾ* (the Brethren of Purity).[46] Establishing himself in several small villages not far from the Atlantic coastline in what is now considered Portugal, Ibn Qasī attracted a group of followers who called themselves "aspirants" (*murīdūn*). At some point around 538/1144, he proclaimed himself not only their spiritual master but also the messianic leader known by the title Mahdi, challenging the authority of the al-Murābiṭ (Almoravid) rulers. Most biographical sources cast Ibn Qasī in the role of rebel and revolutionary insurgent, one who initially turned to the al-Muwāḥḥid (Almohad) leaders from North Africa and then some Christian leaders to the north in order to strive for independence from al-Murābiṭ rule.[47] Later Muslim authors come to describe Ibn Qasī as a fraud, a "pretender" who was not a genuine religious leader but rather only interested in cultivating his power. The sole surviving works of Ibn Qasī, *Khalʿ al-naʿlayn wa-qtibās al-nūr min mawḍiʿ al-qadamayn* (*The Removing of the Sandals and the Taking of the Light from the Place of the Two Feet*) and its accompanying section "The Removing of the Removing," offer little evidence to support this later reputation. Instead, the passages from these works that deal with Muḥammad's ascension show him to be a sophisticated contemplative thinker, one who was not afraid to draw on elaborations of upperworldly cosmologies to provide the structural framework for his complex analyses of a wide range of topics, including the nature of Muḥammad's vision near the climax of his heavenly journey.

Unlike our previous authors, Abū al-Qāsim ʿAbd al-Raḥmān b. al-Khaṭīb Suhaylī (d. 581/1185) was born in the Iberian Peninsula and raised in the village of Suhayl in the vicinity of Málaga on the southern coast.[48] He studied the religious sciences of hadith, *fiqh*, Arabic grammar, and Qurʾān commentary in Málaga, Córdoba, and Granada. Like Qāḍī ʿIyāḍ, he was a student of the Mālikī judge and exegete Abū Bakr Ibn ʿArabī (d. 543/1149). Apparently al-Suhaylī lost his sight while in his teens, afterward relying on his students, especially one who himself would become an eminent traditionist (and compiler of scholarly reports on Muḥammad's night journey and ascension), Ibn Diḥya al-Kalbī (d. 633/1236). Suhaylī was something of a specialist in Arabic grammar and genealogy, and also became known for his poetic verse.[49] Suhaylī composed a work on seeing the Prophet in dreams.[50] He became most famous for his commentary on Ibn Hishām's recension of Ibn Isḥāq's *Sīrat Rasūl Allāh*, known as *al-Rawḍ al-unuf fī sharḥ al-sīra al-nabawiyya* (*The Foremost Meadows in the Explication of the Prophetic Biography*).[51] He was received favorably at the al-Muwāḥḥid court of Abū Yaʿqūb Yūsuf b. ʿAbd al-Muʾmin (r. 1163–1184) in Marrakesh, where he made his residence for some thirty years, and where he ultimately died in 581/1185.[52] While Ibn Barrajān, Qāḍī ʿĪyāḍ, and Ibn Qaṣī apparently fought against the prevailing puritanical and neotraditional rule originating out of the Amazigh (al-Murābiṭ and al-Muwāḥḥid) movements arising from North Africa, Suhaylī made his peace with the second of these movements, and as a consequence he flourished. Given these contexts, the question must be raised whether political differences and the passage of one or more generations could be seen to significantly affect the way that these Andalusī scholars represented and discussed the story of Muḥammad's night journey and ascension.

Despite classifying the key Muslim scholars whose biographies were summarized above, Qāḍī ʿIyāḍ, Ibn Barrajān, Ibn Qaṣī, and Suhaylī, as Iberian *ʿulamāʾ*

who all shared something of a "contemplative" approach, it remains premature to classify these scholars as a western "school" of thought that led inexorably to that of the grand master Ibn ʿArabī (d. 638/1240), especially when it comes to the interpretation of Muḥammad's ascension. The contentious debate around the nature of the Prophet's otherworldly journey serves as a case in point. As we shall see in what follows, Qāḍī ʿIyāḍ's discussion appears predicated on the assumption that the Prophet physically ascended into the heavens, an idea that had become a fairly common position of dogma for many Muslims by this time. Nevertheless, Suhaylī attempts to reconcile competing reports by postulating that the Prophet's journey took place twice, first while he was asleep, and then on a second separate occasion while awake and with his physical body. Ibn Barrajān in his later commentary explores disparate levels of metaphorical meanings in the Prophet's ascent, implying at one point an ascent purely of the mind: "The sign of the ascension is that the fancy (*al-wahm*) ascends with the intellect (*al-ʿaql*), and its master is knowledge (*al-ʿilm*)."[53] Meanwhile, Ibn Qaṣī emphasizes the role of the spirit in the Prophet's vision, while insisting that he ultimately looks upon the divine form with his bodily eyes. We are thus quite far from being able to postulate a unified Andalūsī contemplative "school" when it comes to western ascension literature. The most that we can say is that these scholars share an intellectual milieu in which the nature of Muḥammad's ascension and its proper interpretation became a lively focus of debate, at least partially stemming from intra- and interreligious polemic.

As we shall see, versions of Muḥammad's ascension attributed to the early scholar Ibn ʿAbbās served as a lightning rod for anti-Muslim discourses in eleventh to twelfth century Iberia. We find evidence for these polemics that draw on Islamic ascension literature among Iberian Christian scholars beginning with *Liber Denudationis* in the sixth/twelfth century (likely composed between 1085 and 1132 CE) and expanding with *Liber Scalae Machometi* in the middle of the seventh/thirteenth century. We shall also see from this same period that the Jewish Iberian scholar Abraham Ibn Ezra (d. ca. 1167 CE) drew on Muslim ascension themes in his writings to promote the Jewish prior claim to such otherworldly realms. Christian and Jewish polemical use of versions of Muḥammad's ascension help provide one explanation for the proliferation of western Muslim authors who come to discuss many of the details of this subject at great length. In addition to such polemics and scattered fragments, it is an examination of the ascension-related scholarly writings by the four Iberian Muslim authors from the "earlier middle period" mentioned above — Qāḍī ʿIyāḍ, Ibn Barrajān, Ibn Qaṣī, and Suhaylī — that will be the main focus of this study.

Chapter Contents and Main Argument

Chapter 1 analyzes select sources that are crucial to an understanding of the background of Andalūsī ascension literature. It also begins our approach to discourses surrounding Muḥammad's ascension in twelfth-century Maghribī works by exploring several fragmentary narrative contexts, most importantly the acephalous and incomplete Muslim ascension narrative preserved in Madrid Real Academia MS Codera 241. The latter manuscript, preserved and later discovered in a mine somewhere in the vicinity of Granada, Spain, is fully translated from Arabic into English for the first time in the appendix. Taken together with other important early references, these texts suggest that instead of the official hadith-based versions of the Prophet's ascension, it was likely the more detailed and extensive "noncanonical" Ibn ʿAbbās versions of the Islamic ascension discourse that largely set the stage for the rise in intellectual engagement with this subject among Muslim scholars in the eleventh and twelfth century al-Andalus.

Chapter 2 delves into shared discourses of ascent, from references among Ismāʿīlī esoteric writings and the works of early Muslim and Jewish philosophers and contemplatives to Jewish and Christian polemical engagement with the story of Muḥammad's ascension. The former groups include famous scholars such as Ibn Sīnā and Ibn Ezra; the latter explore works authored by figures such as Judah Halevi and others (some of unknown authorship) that sought to prove the falsity of Muslim claims about their Prophet. Chapter 2 analyzes passages from several of these polemical texts, most importantly the anonymous anti-Muslim Christian work titled *Liber Denudationis* that demonstrates a deep knowledge of the details of an ascension narrative fairly similar to the one found in the fragmentary Madrid Real Academia MS Codera 241 that was analyzed in chapter 1.

Chapter 3 examines several key works from this period and geographical context, the hadith-based discussion of Muḥammad's ascension in a portion of the work known as *The Cure* (al-Shifāʾ) by the Andalūsī Mālikī scholar Qāḍī ʿĪyāḍ, and the wide-ranging commentary on the famous *Biography of the Messenger of God* composed by Qāḍī ʿĪyāḍ's contemporary, Suhaylī.

Chapter 4 examines select themes from Ibn Barrajān's two wide-ranging Qurʾān commentaries, focusing especially on his treatment of the idea of Muḥammad's encounter with God at the highest stages of his heavenly ascent. It also delves into Ibn Barrajān's treatment of imamology, the inner journey, and other esoteric subjects that he treats in light of his interpretation of specific words and phrases from ascension texts.

Chapter 5 explores how Ibn Barrajān's contemporary, Ibn Qasī, composes an independent short treatise that supplements his esoteric work *The Removing of the Sandals and the Taking of the Light from the Place of the Two Feet*. This abbreviated treatise, which the author gives the title "The Removing of the Removing," has been inserted into the midst of the aforementioned larger work, but whether it belongs in the present location in the text is a matter of some doubt.[54] The chapter/treatise in question, regardless of its provenance, holds special interest for the present study given that much of its analysis revolves around the question of what Muḥammad experienced near the climax of his journey at the heavenly Lote Tree.

Though the Iberian scholars who are the focus of this study likely are aware of and build on shared technical vocabulary and otherworldly landscapes as Ismāʿīlī Shīʿī and/or Brethren of Purity esoteric treatises circulating at the time, I will argue that there is not sufficient evidence to posit a dependence of the ideas of the western contemplatives studied here on such esoteric authors, with the possible exception of Ibn Qasī. Rather, this study will show how the contemplatives of al-Andalus in the eleventh and twelfth centuries who wrestle with the subject of Muḥammad's ascension are largely in creative dialogue with the ideas of more particularly western "Maghribī"-focused audiences and ideas: the controversies surrounding Muḥammad's heavenly journey that arose at the crux of interreligious debates on the one hand, and diverse Muslim appeals to the ascension discourse as a site for contestation over the legitimacy of contemporary Muslim leaders in the region on the other. These key foundational Maghribī analyses and commentaries on the significance of Muḥammad's ascension paved the way for later western Sufi appropriations of the theme of ascent, such as the ones that in the following century came to appear in the works of the Great Shaykh Ibn ʿArabī. Exploring such ideas and testing out these propositions will be possible only with a consideration of the broader history of engagement with ascension-related themes articulated in the early centuries of Islamic history and within the contexts of medieval Iberia.

CHAPTER ONE.

Antecedents, Commentaries, and Fragments

Jewish Antecedents

Jewish discourses about journeys of an ascending hero to otherworldly realms have a long history, and one finds evidence in both biblical and extrabiblical texts that predate the rise of Islam, including exegetical speculation on the vision of the divinity seated on a throne as appearing, for instance, in the Book of Ezekiel. In recent decades, scholars have engaged in heated debates over whether the so-called Hekhalot texts, some of which describe such an apocalyptic heavenly journey, should be considered as having arisen largely in the rabbinic period in the first centuries CE in Palestine — as was the influential thesis of Gershom Scholem — or whether evidence points to a later provenance, perhaps as late as the seventh to ninth centuries CE, after the rise of Islam.[1] Another contentious issue surrounds whether the central focus of this Hekhalot literature lies in the heavenly journey to the divine throne — again as Scholem postulated — or whether the idea of summoning and commanding angels was instead its key motif.[2] Since these questions do not have a direct bearing on the later Muslim ascension narratives in al-Maghrib, these complex issues will not be taken up here, but beyond questions of the origins of Muslim motifs that occupied early twentieth-century scholars,[3] more relevant to our study are a few related points: First, unlike in many Hekhalot texts, angel adjuration is not a feature of the extant *miʿrāj* works and commentaries, at least not those circulating in the Arabic written sources up through the thirteenth century in the Islamic West that are the primary focus here. Second, despite the differences in these works, clearly, Hekhalot texts were known in Arab lands by the tenth century at the latest, as attested by the joint responsum of Sherira and Hai Gaon (ca. 1000 CE) in

Babylonia, which mentions specific ritual practices that help prepare a qualified person to experience a visionary ascent, and also mentions the names of two prominent works on the subject, a "greater" and "lesser" collection (*Hekhalot Rabbati* and *Hekhalot Zuṭarti*).[4] Versions have been discovered in the Cairo Geniza documents, and many extant modern manuscripts of these and other Hekhalot texts likely bear the imprint of editorial redactions of German pietist Jews (the "Ashkenazi Hasidim") of the twelfth and thirteenth centuries.[5] The Rhineland is not southern Spain, much less North Africa, but scholars for many years have investigated connections between the thought of Jewish and Muslim scholars from eastern lands and different regions to the west, specifically concerning Hekhalot texts and/or visions of God.[6] In addition, as we shall see in what follows, both Jews and Muslims in al-Maghrib include references in their works that make it clear that at the very least certain symbols and tropes, if not entire portions of narratives, were part of the mix of the otherworldly journey accounts that scholars of different religious backgrounds had access to in eleventh- to twelfth-century al-Andalus.

Ascension Traditions from eleventh Century Nishapur: Sulamī, Qushayrī, Khargūshī

In lands further to the east, especially in the city of Nishapur in the Iranian Plateau, members of a movement that came to be identified as "Sufi" formed among a number of the leading scholars, most of whom subscribed to the Shāfiʿī legal method and the Ashʿarī theological orientation. Two such scholars, who became foundational figures in the history of Sufism because of their early contributions to the fields of Sufi Qurʾān exegesis,[7] as well as for their other foundational Sufi works, were Abū ʿAbd al-Raḥmān al-Sulamī (d. 412/1021)[8] and Abū al-Qāsim al-Qushayrī (d. 465/1072).[9] Independent works focusing on the theme of Muḥammad's ascension and treating the sayings of the earliest generations of Sufis on disparate aspects of the Prophet's journey were attributed to both of these scholars, although the authenticity of each remains an open question, and at present, each of these ascension treatises remains extant only in a single manuscript.[10] These works have been studied previously,[11] and it is beyond the scope of this work to explore the ways these eastern Sufis analyzed and passed on specific teachings about the *miʿrāj*, especially since very few of these teachings appear to have had much of an impact on the Maghribī authors that are the focus of this study. Nevertheless, relevant to our study is the fact that these two eastern Sufis of Nishapur, as well as their contemporary, Abū Saʿd Khargūshī (d. ca. 407/1016), in his work in praise of the Prophet,[12] include references to and even extended versions of long and detailed hadith reports describing the Prophet's ascension that are often transmitted in the name of Muḥammad's cousin and companion, Ibn ʿAbbās, even though these versions were later treated as weak if not outright forgeries by later generations of Jamāʿī-Sunnī hadith scholars.[13]

For instance, in the long fantastical report included in Qushayrī's *Kitāb al-miʿrāj*, which this famous Sufi from Nishapur includes after he lists the more typical canonical Sunnī versions of Muḥammad's ascension, one notices that the description of each of the heavens begins not only with an enumeration of the name of the heaven and its elemental substance (e.g., copper, silver, gold, etc.) but also the name of its angelic guardian that more often than not is constructed with a "-yālīl" suffix (e.g., Raqyālīl, Kawkabyālīl, Muʾminyālīl, etc.).[14] This concern with the names of the heavens and guardian angels, together with a description of the pious utterances of the angelic inhabitants of each heaven, merits comparison with the angelology of some of the Hekhalot texts, such as 3 Enoch. It may represent one of perhaps two or three instances of Muslim ascension narratives recorded in the eastern lands that appear to be in direct dialogue with Jewish ascension narratives to the degree that questions of "influence" and/or "borrowing" and/or "common ancestry" deserve to be investigated further.

A similar concern with angels and their pious utterances appears likewise in the work extolling Muḥammad composed by Sulamī's contemporary, Khargūshī, in a chapter titled "The Names of the Seven Heavens and Those . . . in Them."[15] One also observes a parallel between the Ibn ʿAbbās ascension discourse, a report in Qushayrī's *Kitāb al-miʿrāj*, and the chapter of Khargūshī's work dedicated to the "wonders of the ascension" (*ʿajāʾib al-miʿrāj*), which begins with the mention of the Rooster Angel, Half-Fire-Half-Ice Angel, the Angel of Death, and Mālik the Guardian of Hellfire.[16] Khargūshī ends his discussion of the heavenly wonders with a curious narreme about a seated angel who is forced to stand:

> It was said: When [Muḥammad] arrived at the gate to the lowest [first] heaven and it was opened for him, he came upon an angel seated, reclining. The Messenger of God greeted him and he replied without standing up. God revealed to him [saying]: "O Angel, my beloved and my prophet greeted you, and you replied to him sitting. By my might and glory, you will indeed stand and you will indeed greet him, and you will never sit again until the day of resurrection!"[17]

The importance of this short anecdote to later Muslim ascension narratives that this study examines will become clearer when we examine the western Qurʾān commentary of Hūd b. Muḥakkam Hawwārī. In the meantime, however, one cannot fail to notice that it deserves to be directly compared with a scene from

Jewish apocalyptic literature, including a famous instance from the Jewish ascension narrative known as "3 Enoch," chapter 16, which describes the disciplining of the archangel Metatron, who was whipped and forced to stand after Rabbi ʾAḥer saw him sitting on a throne and therefore mistook him for God (or a "second power" in heaven).[18] That parallel context makes it abundantly clear that at stake in such a narreme is not merely bad manners on account of the angel but also the angel's hubris in imitating the divinity sitting on his throne and thus potentially leading the human prophet into heretically worshipping a created being in place of God.

When it comes to the details of the highest heavens, Khargūshī's work remains content with dozens of descriptions of wondrous angels. In contrast, Qushayrī's work in one place narrates how Muḥammad leads the other prophets in liturgical prayer at the Lote Tree in the highest heaven,[19] while elsewhere Qushayrī gives a full account of the intimate colloquy scene in which the Prophet converses with God about the "heavenly host debate," the "seals of Surat al-Baqara" (Q 2:285–286), receiving numerous "favors" from God, including intercession.[20] A report that contains very similar details came to be written down around the same time or in the century that followed in the far western reaches of al-Andalus, the fragmentary textual remains of which will be analyzed at the end of this chapter.

Transmission of the Khudrī Version of Muḥammad's Ascension to the Muslim West

Diverse extended reports of Muḥammad's ascension that the famous eastern hadith compilers Bukhārī, Muslim, and many other Sunnī traditionists chose not to include in their collections of sound hadith or Qurʾān commentaries nevertheless circulated widely in the early centuries of Islamic history.[21] A close examination of the relevant passages in the Qurʾān commentaries of three foundational exegetes, Hūd b. Muḥakkam Hawwārī (a North African ʿIbāḍī Muslim, fl. third/ninth century), Ṭabarī (an eastern Sunnī Muslim, d. 310/923), and Qummī (an eastern Twelver Shīʿī Muslim, d. 307/919), shows that outside the major Sunnī "sound" collections of hadith reports described above — such as those collections that scholars later classified as comprising the "six books" of trustworthy reports — Muslim scholars of the second and third Islamic centuries (eighth–ninth centuries CE) transmitted much longer and more detailed composite narratives of Muḥammad's night journey and ascension that treated these otherworldly legends.

In his commentary on Q 17:1, Ṭabarī records two long composite narratives, one report on the authority of the early companion of Muḥammad from the first generation of Muslims (*ṣaḥāba*) named Abū Hurayra,[22] and the other on another early authority among the *ṣaḥāba* named Abū Saʿīd Khudrī,[23] both becoming widely circulated reports that were influential on the development of the subsequent iterations of Muslim ascension discourses.[24] The Khudrī report shares several features in common with the extensive report transmitted on the authority of the important direct descendent of Muḥammad through the progeny of Fatima and ʿAli, the *imām* and scholar Jaʿfar al-Ṣādiq, a version of which the foundational Imāmī exegete Qummī includes in his early Shīʿī tafsir.[25] While a precise dating of these narratives before the time that they were compiled by Ṭabarī and Qummī is difficult if not impossible to determine, clearly by the beginning of the fourth/tenth century, only a generation after the compilation of Bukhārī and Muslim's sound hadith collections, major Muslim exegetes were explaining the night journey verse (Q 17:1) by conveying long and complex composite narratives that provide details far beyond the rough outlines of the journey described in the major Sunnī sound hadith collections. The ascension narratives that flourished in the western lands in subsequent centuries that will be the focus of this study drew significant tropes and/or inspiration from the Abū Saʿīd Khudrī version of the legend, perhaps because of the way that the early biographies of the Messenger of God (*Sirat rasūl allah*), such as that attributed to Ibn Isḥāq (d. 150/767), similarly rely on it.

Given its emergence in the Muslim West, it is worth recounting a few key details of the Khudrī version of Muḥammad's ascension narrative as recorded by the North African ʿIbādī scholar known as Hūd b. al-Ḥakam Hawwārī.[26] First, one notes that after the initiatic scene in this version during which the angels come and open the Prophet's chest, this report describes the arrival of Burāq, depicting this fantastic beast in the following fashion: "It is a white mount called Burāq, larger than a donkey and smaller than a mule, struck of ears, placing its step at the limit of its sight."[27] This characterization is only slightly more elaborate than that found in Ibn Isḥāq / Ibn Hishām and elsewhere, but the "struck of ears" detail seems especially noteworthy since this description would be taken up as worthy of discussion by later western commentators, as we shall see in subsequent chapters. Also worth noting, this report from Hawwārī contains the narreme about the three distractors on the road to Jerusalem, first a propagandist from the Jews, second a propagandist from the Christians, and third a finely dressed woman who represents the allure of this lower world.[28] One would imagine that this narrative detail would have a particular resonance in the West, where larger populations of Jews and Christians lived among Muslims than in most other parts of Islamdom. Finally, and significantly, one notices that Hawwārī's version leaves out any mention of the prayer with the prophets in Jerusalem, with the appearance of the *miʿrāj* ladder following closely on the heels of the famous "cup test" (where the Prophet is asked to choose between goblets of various drinks) and Gabriel's explanations of the identities of the distractors whom the Prophet encountered on the road to Jerusalem. I would argue that this failure to mention any prayers with other prophets in Jerusalem is especially significant given subsequent western debates over the status of Jerusalem, as well as competing depictions of the status of Muḥammad vis-à-vis the other prophets.

Unlike in the Ibn Isḥāq / Ibn Hishām account in which the night journey and heavenly ascension are potentially separable, and the return journey to Mecca is described before any discussion of the ascent through the seven heavens, in other versions of the Khudhrī report such as the one appearing in Hawwārī's commentary, the description of the heavenly journey becomes collated directly and seamlessly into the rest of the story, with the account of the angelic gatekeeper Ismāʿīl, of Adam presiding over the judgment of souls, and of the punishment of the wicked coming next in the narrative's elaboration of the first heaven. In yet another significant detail, along with the account of Moses congratulating the Prophet on his arrival at the sixth heaven, the Khudrī narrative as transmitted by Hawwārī inserts a brief passage in which Moses says: "The People of Israel claim that I am the most favored of creatures in the eyes of God, but this one [i.e., Muḥammad] is more favored in his eyes than I. Were the Prophet on his own he would have inclined toward me [and my community], but the Prophet and those following him make up his [own] community."[29] This narreme is similar to the passage from the Mālik ibn Ṣaʿṣaʿa hadith from Bukhārī's famous collection of sound Sunnī reports, in which Moses cries when Muḥammad ascends past him, apparently because the former did not know that any other prophet would ever be raised higher in the heavens than he.[30] Unlike in the Mālik report, however, here in Hawwārī's presentation, the emphasis focuses on whether or not Moses and Muḥammad would form part of one community (*umma*), an issue that later Iberian scholars would take up in greater depth, as we shall see. Moreover, in Hawwārī's account, after the encounter with Abraham in the seventh heaven a few new narremes got inserted into the Khudrī report: the appearance of the Muslim community divided into groups depending on the purity of their earthly actions (here symbolically represented by the distinct groups wearing either white or black cloaks), brief tours of Paradise and the Fire, including an encounter in the Garden with the heavenly maiden destined for Muḥammad's foster son, Zayd b. Ḥāritha, and a twice-described visit to the Lote Tree of the Boundary, with the rivers flowing from this tree bringing forgiveness and absolution to those who wash in them.[31] These additional scenes would make an important impression on Maghribī writers in subsequent centuries, as we shall see. Thus, the composite report ascribed to Abū Saʿīd Khudrī — in its multiple variations — needs to be examined as one of the foundational sources that form part of the intellectual background for the authors in this study.

Muslim reports of Muḥammad's ascension, be they conveyed in hadith reports, Qur'ān commentaries, biographies of the Prophet, or other types of sources, served as crucial sources for later scholars in al-Andalus and elsewhere as they engaged in their own interactions with this pivotal tale. Much less obvious, but equally important to acknowledge, are the non-Muslim sources — especially those of Jews and Christians — that may have directly or indirectly informed the way the sixth-/twelfth-century western Muslim scholars understood Muḥammad's otherworldly journey. One final brief anecdote from Hawwārī's Qur'ān commentary, which recalls the short narreme from Khargūshī's work, illustrates this point nicely:

> They recounted[32] that the Messenger of God said: The night I was taken on the Night Journey, I passed a throne before which an angel was standing with a spear in his hand. I said, "Who is that, Gabriel?" He replied, "A prophet was taken on a journey by night before you, and when he passed this one, he found him seated [on the throne] and thought that he was God, so he fell down prostrate, touching his head down [in worship]. God made [that angel] stand ever since in order to demonstrate that he is a servant."[33]

As with the Khargushī narreme, but here even more explicitly, this brief narreme bears a close relationship to the account from the famous scene in the Jewish ascension text 3 Enoch, chapter 16. The interconnection between scenes from the latter Hekhalot text and this narreme, as well as other narrative details that find their way into diverse composite Ibn ʿAbbās ascension narratives of subsequent centuries, is undeniable.[34] Although one only rarely finds a link between the Muslim and Jewish ascension texts as clear as the above anecdote in the writings of western scholars of the sixth/twelfth century,[35] nevertheless, given the contestation between Jews, Christians, and Muslims in al-Andalus over the description of the heavenly realms, non-Muslim sources such as 3 Enoch and others like it deserve to be considered as part of the intellectual context in which our Iberian authors wrote. Furthermore, the discussion of Muḥammad's ascension in the Qur'ān commentary of the North African scholar Hawwārī presents useful background to give one a sense of the types of Muslim oral reports that later western Muslim ascension narratives would come to draw on directly, such as the Khudrī hadith.

A Fragmentary Version from al-Andalus: Real Academia de la Historia MS Codera 241

While the story of Muḥammad's night journey and ascension was well known enough to have come to al-Andalus with the earliest of Muslims who entered the Iberian Peninsula in the second/eighth century, historical evidence for in-depth scholarly discussion and formal transmission of the narrative would have to wait until the sixth/twelfth century. Anti-Muslim polemics among some of the Christians of al-Andalus were known from the previous century or two, as the next chapter of this study will describe, but it is likely not an accident that the discourse around the Prophet's miraculous otherworldly journey began to flourish in the sixth/twelfth century, the same period in which Christian forces in the north of the peninsula began to enjoy significant victories against Muslim forces, and in which news of crusading victories in the eastern Mediterranean brought the concept of the sanctity of Jerusalem to the minds of Jews, Christians, and Muslims throughout the region. The "Favors of Jerusalem" genre of Arabic literature began to circulate, and the idea of Muslim forces "reconquering" Jerusalem from the control of the Crusader Kingdoms must have percolated in the imaginations of some Muslims in the Mediterranean basin, as Ibn Barrajān's famous prophetic prediction of the date in which the latter event would take place bears witness. Significantly, according to several Muslim historical narratives, after a long siege of Jerusalem, the famous general Salah al-Din Ayyūbī (known to Europe as Saladdin) was able to finally enter that city on the very day that commemorated the anniversary of Muḥammad's night journey and ascension, a fitting date according to Muslim sensibilities given that this event represents one of the key reasons that they would come to lay claim to Jerusalem as Islam's "third-holiest" city. While many Iberian Muslims in the premodern period would hardly have concerned themselves with such a faraway backwater town (that was not connected to the rites of the *hajj* in any fashion, for instance), especially given the much more local tumults that shook their lands, it appears that starting in the sixth/twelfth century, some of the Muslim western scholarly elite began paying more attention to Jerusalem, and by extension Muḥammad's journey to and from Jerusalem, in this period.

One should keep that broader context in mind when approaching the primary source that this chapter will analyze, a noncanonical report of the Prophet's heavenly journey that owes much to the Ibn ʿAbbās ascension narrative, that was recorded around this same time (the sixth/twelfth century), and that has come down to us today in a fragmentary form. It relies not on formal scholarly discourses as would circulate in official hadith reports circulated in Sunnī Muslim elite learned circles but rather on the types of stories that would have appealed to a much broader and less scholarly audience because of its valuation of dramatic "tellability" over scholarly rigor and precision (e.g., note the absence of scholarly apparatuses such as chains of transmission).

At the time, the question of Muḥammad's status as a true prophet and his relative merit in comparison with Jesus and others is an active subtext of the discussion of the Prophet's ascension.[36] I would conjecture that the mode of storytelling used to discuss anecdotes from this famous legend serves as a basis for Muslim scholars to articulate a case for Muḥammad's exalted status over and above previous figures such as Moses and Jesus that other groups in the region revered, and likewise it serves as a tool for anti-Muslim polemicists to suggest that Muḥammad did not deserve a place among the "real" heroes descending from Abraham since he was nothing but an impostor.[37] Thus, from the beginning of the history of the Muslim ascension discourse in al-Andalus, interreligious debate and polemic appear to have played a major role, and the significance of this fact to the mystical interpretations of Muḥammad's journey that will come to emerge out of this broader context will become a theme that this book will continue to analyze and examine in the chapters that follow.

The "Primitive Version" of the Ibn ʿAbbās ascension narrative[38] probably originated in the eastern lands of Islamdom in the eighth or ninth century CE, and Hawwārī's exegesis provides evidence to indicate that a more developed version circulated in North Africa (al-Maghrib) not much later. In what follows, we shall see that this same type of Islamic ascension discourse — a detailed and widely circulated telling of the tale of Muḥammad's ascension often ascribed to the very early scholarly authority named Ibn ʿAbbās — came to al-Andalus by no later than the eleventh or twelfth century CE, that is, the period that is the focus of this study, and around the same time that Qushayrī flourished in the East. Such dating was first suggested by Asín in his pivotal work *La escatalogía musulmana en la Divina Comedia*. Commenting on the narrative and the subsequent history of the discourse that he labels "Cycle 2C" (and which I call the Ibn ʿAbbās "Primitive Version"), Asín writes,

> La popularidad y divulgación de este fantástico hadit, durante la Edad Media (siglo XII a lo menos) en España, se comprueba por el ms. 241 de la colección Gayangos, que lo contiene (aunque incompleto).
>
> [The popularity and spread of this fantastic hadith, during the Middle Ages (12th century at least) in Spain, is proven by manuscript 241 of the Gayangos collection [now in the *Real Academia de la Historia* of Madrid], which contains it (although incomplete)].[39]

Although this fragmentary early written text is unparalleled in twelfth-century al-Andalus, the fact that this and other noncanonical hadith reports on Muḥammad's ascension must have been in fairly broad circulation in the western Islamic lands in the middle periods of Islamic history cannot be disputed, for there is ample evidence that even mainstream Sunnī scholars in the Islamic West discussed such reports among the issues and questions that they debated, even as some of them questioned the authenticity of these popular accounts, as we shall see in future chapters. Given the importance of this particular fragmentary ascension narrative[40] as a physical record of early western versions of the Ibn ʿAbbās ascension narrative, and given that several other scholarly discussions of Muḥammad's journey from the time presuppose this very type of narrative, a full translation of this important text will be given in the appendix to this work, which the reader is urged to consult in conjunction with the analysis that follows.

The fragmentary Arabic text presented in this fascinating document shows evidence of having been copied in North Africa rather than Iberia, likely sometime between the fifth/eleventh and sixth/twelfth centuries.[41] This same type of extracanonical Ibn ʿAbbās–style ascension narrative must have been recounted orally throughout Islamdom, as is suggested by the fact that a parallel version appears in Qushayrī's *Kitāb al-miʿrāj*. I contend that the same general storyline was likely known to some if not all of the western authors whose work we will examine in this study, whether or not they accepted it as an authentic report from the Prophet Muḥammad. Further evidence for this conjecture will appear on closer analyses of the specific Iberian Muslim texts under consideration in the chapters that follow.

The extant portion of the fragmentary manuscript under consideration here opens with Muḥammad's first-person account of his experiences in the fourth heaven, beginning with his encounter with Azrāʾīl, the Angel of Death, and his learning about Azrāʾīl's methods of harvesting souls at the time of death. After describing what Muḥammad learns in this encounter, the text turns to describing his brief meeting with the prophet Idrīs / Enoch, whom he finds sitting on a throne (*kursī*) of light, and who defers to Muḥammad's priority as exalted prayer leader for of all of creation. That is, in a trope that recurs at the end of the description of each of the heavens, Muḥammad serves as the *imām* directing prayers for Enoch and for all the angels of the fourth heaven as they collectively pray two cycles of liturgical prayer.[42]

Making use of a formulaic transition phrase interjected between each of the heavens, after praying with the prophet and angel that reside in the fourth heaven, Muḥammad speedily transverses the immense distance of what is otherwise measured as a five-hundred-year journey between each of the heavens.[43]

Although the account is missing in this fragmentary text, the pattern of other similar texts suggests that Muḥammad goes on to meet Mālik, the Guardian of Hellfire, while passing through the fifth heaven.[44] He next encounters in the sixth heaven a massive polycephalous angel bearing the proper name Dardaya'īl (Bearer of the Light of God?), followed by his meeting the very handsome prophet Aaron. Note that both Aaron and Dardaya'īl are found sitting on thrones of light, a common trope in this fragmentary text, established after the initial meeting with the prophet Enoch. In the seventh heaven, another unnamed angel takes over the conveyance and guidance of Muḥammad, and while Gabriel accompanies them past the massive heavenly sea they encounter next, Gabriel is then forced to stop at the Lote Tree of the Boundary, for he explains to the Prophet that this spot is none other than his "known station" (Q 37:164) where he must await Muḥammad's return from more exalted locales.[45] A green *rafraf* (a term drawn from Q 55:76, explained elsewhere as either some form of cushion or else some type of celestial creature) carries Muḥammad past several more seas: waters that are first yellow, then black, then a massive sea of regular water.[46] Approaching closer and closer to the divine throne while riding on the *rafraf*, Muḥammad meets and converses with several of the highest of the heavenly host, including some of the most wondrous of all of God's angels: Mikā'īl (Michael), Isrāfīl (Seraf / Rafael), the Rooster Angel whose call compels all the earthly rooster to crow in God's praise and glorification, and the unspeakably enormous snake that God creates to wrap around his throne ('arsh) to teach the massive throne a lesson in humility.[47] Finally, after having been ushered past a series of veils, some made out of material substances but others made out of more abstract divine qualities,[48] and thousands of rows of angels fixed in one of the positions of liturgical prayer in the worship of God,[49] the divine voice calls out to Muḥammad, telling him not to be afraid but instead to continue forward and to ask what he wills of God's mercy. In response to this call, the Prophet advances into the divine presence and begins the intimate colloquy scene, only the first part of which remains extant in this fragmentary manuscript.

The Prophet's encounter with God in Madrid Real Academia MS Codera 241 contains rich and extensive detail, despite the narrative being cut off mid-sentence at the end of the final folio of the extant document (folio 8v). In what we possess of this intimate colloquy scene, all of the narremes follow the pattern that comes to be standard in the more developed composite versions of the Ibn 'Abbās ascension discourse: God and Muḥammad exchange greetings with words that God inspires the Prophet to say; the two of them discuss whether or not the Prophet can or even wishes to see God physically with his eyes; God quizzes Muḥammad on the details of the Heavenly Host Debate; and, finally, at the divine invitation, Muḥammad petitions for divine mercy on behalf of creation that God replies to while also enumerating other gifts that God reveals as special favors for the Prophet himself. Although it remains difficult to determine with precision given that the rest of the manuscript has been lost, this scene of intercession appears to play an especially prominent role in the narrative as a whole, as does God's clear proclamation to Muḥammad about his station as the very best of all the prophets that have ever been sent to the world. In the context of the interactions and interreligious competitions between Jews, Christians, and Muslims in North Africa and Spain during the period under consideration, these types of explicit arguments on behalf of Muḥammad's high status vis-à-vis other prophets, and this clear proof of the general efficacy of Muḥammad's intercession, are themes that Muslim audiences might well have been especially interested in hearing about and transmitting to others.

Concerning these final elements, two features deserve special attention here. First, it is worth noting that this fragmentary manuscript contains one of the earliest appearances in a Sunnī ascension narrative of the narreme I have elsewhere called "the Hanging Sword" anecdote, a brief narreme that perhaps gets included to attempt to explain and/or justify the internal strife and bloodshed afflicting the Muslim community, or else as an explanation of God's justice in the form of destruction inflicted on Earth that may otherwise remain inexplicable to humans.[50] Given the civil strife in al-Andalus during the period in which this text was copied, the anecdote about the "Sword of Strife" may well have been collated into the ascension narrative in this specific context by one or more Sunnī scholars who saw it as a commentary on their contemporary bloody situation of communal strife afflicting Spain and North Africa in the fourth/tenth to fifth/eleventh centuries. While the balance of these final narremes go on to emphasize God's mercy to the Muslim community as revealed to Muḥammad during his heavenly ascent, this "Hanging Sword" narreme simultaneously insists that violence and destruction will still play a role in God's plan, that God's mercy does not mean that the Muslims will not face trials, difficulties, and strife here on Earth.

Even more importantly, the text ends with an elaboration of the narrative element I have labeled the "Favor of the Prophets" narreme, one in which the Prophet Muḥammad and God at the climax of the ascension together discuss the relative status and favor of Muḥammad vis-à-vis the other prophets. Early versions of this narreme place the Prophet's "favors" that the text describes on the same level as other prophets, with God recounting how Muḥammad's prophetic career contains blessings "just as" noteworthy as those of each of the other prophets. In the version of the trope appearing here, in contrast, each of the merits that God has given to other prophets is not only met with something similar but exceeded by the favors that God has granted to Muḥammad.[51] In this version that was recorded in the Muslim West, God assures Muḥammad that God has not forgotten or neglected him, and that each of the special gifts that previous prophets have been given fall short of the totality of gifts that Muḥammad himself has or will receive. This trope would have especially resonated in the context of Muslim rivalry with Jews and Christians in the Iberian Peninsula and North Africa, the narrative assuring the Muslim community that God himself acknowledges Muḥammad's superiority over all the rest, thus defending the Muslims and their prophet from polemical attacks and missionary efforts of others.

CHAPTER TWO.

Shared Discourses and Polemics of Ascent

The Theme of Ascension in Isma'īlī Esoteric Writings, and Those of the "Brethren of Purity"

Having originally sprung up in the western lands of North Africa, the Fāṭimid dynasty set up a successful new regime centered on the city of Cairo in Egypt beginning in 297/909. The majority of the population continued to be Jamāʿī-Sunnī in orientation, and the masses continued to believe and worship largely as before, unaware of any significant shift in religious orientation among the rulers. Nevertheless, the elites that ruled in Cairo were Ismāʿīlī-Shīʿī Muslims, deriving authority from the charismatic leadership of their *imām*, a descendent of ʿAlī and Fāṭima (hence the claim to the title "Fāṭimid"). Among the small inner group in control of the empire, the Fāṭimī leader was thought to possess legitimacy not only to rule but also to represent the living embodiment of Islamic revelation.[1] Still, among the Jamāʿī-Sunnī majority of the population, guidance from the Sunnī ʿulamāʾ in the empire continued to be sought and provided as before.

The Fāṭimids went on to conquer not only the eastern Mediterranean but also much of the Arabian Peninsula, including the holy cities of Mecca and Medina in 359/969–970. Thus, anyone passing through this central region on journeys to or from the west, be they merchants carrying goods, pilgrims engaged in the sacred hajj to Mecca and its environs, or scholars traveling in search of knowledge of prophetic traditions, would undoubtedly have directly or indirectly been subject to Fāṭimid authority, and the spread of esoteric teachings was a distinct possibility, even given the care with which the Ismāʿīlī elites guarded their secrets. The Fāṭimids were a rival source of authority vis-à-vis the Jamāʿī-Sunnī ʿAbbasid caliph in Baghdad, as well as the breakaway Jamāʿī-Sunnī Umayyad caliphs that emerged in al-Andalus, Córdoba. With the coming of the "Party Kings" period in the Maghrib and the breakup of centralized authority, Fāṭimid influence also expanded in the southern Iberian Peninsula, and esoteric ideas and hermeneutics spread both through the secret work of missionaries as well as the sharing of ideas (in texts and scholarly exchanges).

Shlomo Pines and Alfred Ivry separately argue that during the period of the Fāṭimids, and even in the decade after their fall, Ismāʿīlī terms and concepts had spread among philosophically-minded Jewish thinkers in North Africa and al-Andalus.[2] Ivry writes, "The 'wide reach' of Ismāʿīlī philosophical and theological concepts may be seen as extending vertically as well as horizontally. We may assume Ismāʿīlī teachings were known to Jewish thinkers in the Maghrib and Egypt from the beginnings of the Fāṭimid dynasty there in the tenth century."[3] Further, the works of Judah Halevi (d. 1141, about whom more later in this chapter) offer proof that such teachings extended into the sixth/twelfth century al-Andalus, as Pines demonstrates.[4]

Although not a direct product of Fāṭimid Ismaʿilism, during the same period of the rise of Fāṭimid power, the esoteric writings that came to be known as the "Epistles" (Rasāʾil) of a likely Baṣran-centered group calling itself the "Brethren of Purity" (al-Ikhwān al-Ṣafāʾ) had likely made their way to al-Andalus sometime during the fourth/tenth century.[5] Bringing Neoplatonic ideas about emanation together with Aristotelean teachings about the soul such as those adapted by Ibn Sīnā (d. 428/1037),[6] one of the most significant passages for the purposes of our study appears in the 39th Epistle, part of the discussion of the sciences of the soul involving a vision of God:

> As for the Friends and the Pure of God, the learned gnostics endowed with insight, they see and witness Him in all their states and functions, night and day; He is not absent from them, not even for an instant . . . as He said . . . *only he who bears witness to the Truth, and they who know (him) . . . for we are nearer to him than (his) jugular vein.*[7] When the comprehension of these verses by the Friends of God had been confirmed and they knew them in their profundity, God opened their hearts, gave light to their vision, and removed covering from them, so that they saw and witnessed Him with their sight, as they had known Him in their hearts, without doubt or suspicion.[8]

The epistles describe the goal of a perfected soul as ascending through the spheres on a return journey to God, and this one describes how the spiritually elect — such as the Friends of God (*awliyāʾ Allah*, which is a broad qurʾānic category and need not specify the "Sufis," though eventually Sufis will often claim this term for themselves) and those who know (*al-ʿārifīn*) — come to enjoy a never-ending vision of God through the eye of inner sight (*biʾl-ʿayn al-baṣīra*).

Ibn Masarra and Early Muslim Maghribī Contemplatives

The main thrust of this study focuses on the ascension-related discourses of Muslim contemplatives from al-Andalus composing works in the sixth/twelfth century, investigating the common threads that tie these thinkers and their works together, including a Neoplatonic worldview and a commitment to an esoteric interpretation of the Qurʾān and hadith literature based on a specific type of symbolic interpretation. Both of these common elements are already present in a school of thought championed by the early Andalūsī contemplative, Ibn Masarra (d. ca. 319/931). Basing his analysis solely on the works of heresiographers, since extant works of Ibn Masarra were unknown to him, Spanish Orientalist Miguel Asín Palacios theorizes by these "indirect channels" that Ibn Masarra and his followers were adherents of a "pseudo-Empedoclean" school that he considered common to Andalūsī Sufi thinkers.[9] This claim has been largely rejected by contemporary scholars.[10] More recently, Michael Ebstein argues that Ibn Masarra deserves to be classified as a "Neoplatonic mystic-philosopher,"[11] and not a Sufi, since "the terms *sufi* or *taṣawwuf* do not appear in Ibn Masarra's works and there is nothing distinctly Sufi in them; rather, the mystical conceptions in Ibn Masarra's thought and the terminology he employs point to a type of Neoplatonical mystical philosophy that is found in Ismāʿīlī literature as well, especially (but not only) in the *Rasāʾil ikhwān al-ṣafāʾ*."[12] While influence from *Ikhwān al-ṣafāʾ* and/or Ismāʿīlī sources should not be discounted, Sarah Stroumsa and Sara Sviri assert that "the neoplatonic world-view of Ibn Masarra is typically Andalusī,"[13] and that, "far from being simply an eclectic thinker, Ibn Masarra integrates these elements into something original and perhaps new."[14] They thus argue for the recognition of his "pioneering position in the history of what [they] refer to as Andalusī mystical philosophy."[15] Yousef Casewit agrees that it might be best to consider this approach as a movement of Neoplatonic "contemplation" (*iʿtibār*) followed by a group of Iberian "contemplatives" (*muʿtabirūn*) beginning with Ibn Masarra and running through Ibn Barrajān and others, separate from the eastern Sufi movement and even from other esoteric "*bāṭinī*" thinkers.

Especially key for our examination of the Maghribī treatment of the theme of ascension in this study is the way that Ibn Masarra conceptualizes the idea of "contemplation" (*iʿtibār*) in his treatise dedicated to this subject, which begins with the general thesis that one who "seeks indication by contemplation finds nothing by contemplating the world from below upward other than what has been indicated by the prophets from above downward."[16] In other words, here our author treats the intellectual ascension through contemplation, from the lowest levels of creation up through the highest level of the Neoplatonic schema (the original One), arguing that this journey of upward contemplation fully agrees with the revealed truths of prophetic scripture. In this sense, his ideas anticipate the work of Muslim philosophers such as Ibn Sīnā (d. 1037) and especially the philosophical allegory "Ḥayy ibn Yaqẓān" that he wrote that was later developed further by Andalusians such as Abraham ibn Ezra (d. 1167) and Ibn Ṭufayl (d. 1185).[17]

In sharp contrast to the later Muslim philosopher in the east known as Ibn Sīnā (Avicenna),[18] Ibn Masarra does not in his extant work refer directly to the theme of Muḥammad's ascension, whether as a philosophical allegory or otherwise. Nevertheless, one can detect in his "Treatise on Contemplation" some indirect exploration of this broader theme. As he explains near the beginning of his treatise, "The world in its entirety is . . . a book, whose letters are [God's] speech. Those who seek to behold (*al-mustabṣirūn*) read them by the light of true thinking (*al-fikra al-ṣādiqa*), according to their perception (*abṣār*) and the scope of their contemplation (*iʿtibār*), while the eyes of their hearts (*abṣār qulūbihim*) are turned around the manifest and hidden marvels."[19] He cites a series of qurʾānic passages to support the idea that contemplation of God's signs in creation reflects a divine command,[20] claiming that through such a "ladder" (*daraja*) of the contemplation of the signs in the world, "those who contemplate (*al-muʿtabirūn*) ascend to the great signs of God (*ayāt Allah al-kubrā*) on high."[21] This last reference offers an unmistakable echo of the language from a passage from the Star chapter of the Qurʾān (Q 53:13–18), where the vision at the Lote Tree results in the visionary — usually understood to be the Prophet — seeing "among the greatest signs of his lord" (*min ayāt rabbihi al-kubrā*, Q 53:18). It should not be a surprise, then, that Ibn Masarra concludes this portion of his treatise with the statement that this way of contemplation, which he claims perfectly aligns with prophetic revelation, leads the contemplative philosopher to ascend by means of it into the divine presence and to enjoy a vision of the Truth in his heart:

> In this way, which the Book indicates and to which the messengers guided, the light that is never extinguished is acquired and truthful insights are gained. By these insights, those who approach their Lord come close to Him, and, unlike others, attain the praiseworthy station (*al-maqām al-maḥmūd*, Q 17:79) in this world and the Hereafter. They behold the hidden (*al-ghayb*) with the eyes of their hearts (*abṣār qulūbihim*); they come to know the science

> of the Book, while their hearts bear witness that it/He is the truth (*fa-shahidat qulubuhum lahu innahu al-ḥaqq*).[22]

The final three-quarters of the treatise explores in more depth the specifics of this type of contemplative journey, which by a combination of observing the signs in the created universe and using the exercise of reason leads to a step-by-step realization of and ultimate return to the highest divine truth.

While it remains beyond the scope of this work to explore Ibn Masarra's treatise on the esoteric "Properties of Letters," it is crucial to note Stroumsa's persuasive demonstration that this treatise demonstrates clear engagement with Jewish letter speculation — particularly meditations on the Hebrew alphabet from the extremely popular esoteric text known as *Sefer Yeẓirah*[23] — as well as other ways that it reflects the "impact of Jewish thought," such as in the image of the throne carriers that is clearly biblical.[24] Summing up her argument, Stroumsa reminds us that beyond questions of unidirectional "influence," we need to focus on the shared intellectual environment of this period in Maghribī history: "Despite all the differences, and although one cannot draw a continuous line that describes the direction of development and transmission, there is a similarity of atmosphere which presupposes a common ground of ideas, nourished by direct contacts between Muslims (both Sunnis and Isma'ili Shi'is) and Jews. These contacts allowed for the free flow of ideas *in both directions*."[25]

Ibn Sīnā, Ibn Ezra, and "Dialogue" in the Treatment of Philosophical Ascent

As alluded to in the previous section, eastern peripatetic philosopher Ibn Sīnā (d. 980/1037) composed an Arabic ascension treatise (*mi'rājnāma*) that effectively interprets an extended base narrative account of Muḥammad's heavenly journey as an allegory, with each of its actors, encounters, and settings representing little more than a symbol for some aspect of the philosophical path of Aristotelean intellection. For instance, the Angel Gabriel or "Holy Spirit" (*al-rūḥ al-quddus*), who comes via the divine command (*amr*) to collect the Prophet and lead him on his journey, is understood by Ibn Sīna as nothing less than a symbolic representation of what the philosophers call the Active Intellect, the agent of higher inspiration. Peter Heath studies in depth this type of allegorical imagination as applied to Ibn Sīnā's ascension text, so the details of this philosophical text need not concern us here.[26] Aaron Hughes argues that this type of allegory serves as a tool to help make "foreign" philosophical terms and concepts more acceptable to a religious Muslim mindset, and goes on to apply this same logic to other allegories of the "journey" of intellection that are not as transparently based on the *mi ʿrāj* frame narrative. Hughes shows how Ibn Sīnā's Persian work titled *Ḥayy ibn Yaqẓān* (literally "Living, Son of Awake"), in which the title character plays the role of the heavenly guide / Angel Gabriel / Active Intellect for the unnamed protagonist, follows the same general allegorical pattern that one finds in Ibn Sīnā's *Mi ʿrājnāma*. The fact that this same philosophical allegory captured the imagination of diverse thinkers in sixth/twelfth century al-Andalus, both Muslim and non-Muslim, shows that such ideas were in the air and part of a common philosophical dialogue in the western Mediterranean during the period of our study.

For instance, Abraham ibn Ezra (d. 1167) composed his Hebrew version of *Ḥayy ibn Yaqẓān*, titled *Ḥay ben Meqitz*, to be in direct competition with Ibn Sīnā's version, and, according to Aaron Hughes, to argue for a biblical "priority" concerning the theme of ascension.[27] Peppered with biblical allusions, both direct and indirect, Ibn Ezra's account describes a terrestrial journey that eventually leads to the border of the heavens in which the protagonist becomes overcome with fear until steadied by the encouragement of his otherworldly guide (in a manner reminiscent of Gabriel calming Muḥammad in the Ibn ʿAbbās ascension):

> After this boundary there is a consuming fire (Deut. 4:24)
> To the heavens in reaches.
> Coals burn (cf. 2 Sam. 22:9; Psalm 18:9)
> Sparks rage. (cf. Song 8:6)
> Its blades are like swords (Nahum 3:3)
> Its sparks like stars . . . .
> I envisioned it
> Staring into its likeness.
> My hands were weak
> My knees trembled. (cf. Psalm 109:24)
> My eyes smoked over from fear (cf. Psalm 6:8)
> I fell onto my face. (cf. Daniel 8:17)
> I was unable to stand
> My whole being was stricken with terror. (cf. Psalm 6:4)
> He came to me
> Set me upon my feet. (cf. Ezekiel 2:2)
> He said, "Do not be afraid,
> do not lose heart. (Isaiah 7:4)
> When you walk through the fire, you will not be burned
> Though a flame, it will not burn you." (Isaiah 43:2)
> He passed before me and said

"Come in, O blessed of the Lord."[28] (Genesis 24:31)

Passing through eight heavenly kingdoms, the ascending hero ultimately reaches the divine realm of the divine Necessary Existant, who remains beyond intellectual conception or description:

After these kingdoms there is a boundary
Its foundation unformed and void. (Gen. 1:2)
Long and wide its land
Like the desert and barren prairie. (cf. Deut. 1:1, Jer. 50:12)
Empty of inhabitant or dweller
In it neither occupant nor resident.
Its circumference is immeasurable
The size of its stature unknown.[29]
Everything within is structured
Arranged and perfect.
It happened that when we came to its borders
We approached to cross it.
I saw wonderful forms
Awesome visions. (cf. Daniel 10:7–8)
Angels stood guard
There were mighty ones.
Cherubim
Enormous and many.
Seraphim standing
Praising and announcing His unity
Angels and ofanim (cf. Ezekiel 1:16)
Lauding and singing.
Souls
Consecrating.
Spirits
Glorifying.
I was afraid and said
"How awesome is this place that I see." (cf. Gen. 28:17)
He replied: "From your feet
Remove the sandals." (Exod. 3:5)
From the matter of your corpse
Lift your soul.
Forsake your thoughts
Relax your eyelids!
See by the eyes of your interior

The pupils of your heart.[30]

One finds a striking resemblance between this description of the entry into the divine audience and those of some later versions of the Ibn ʿAbbās *miʿrāj* narrative in which the ascending hero, on entry into the highest realm, becomes terrified.[31] Recalled to his senses, he experiences the heavenly liturgy as all of the highest and most exalted classes of angels worship God in the divine presence.

Concluding our discussion of Ibn Ezra's poetic references to ascent, we see that they combine allusions to Jacob's dream of a ladder to the heavens (with God descending to him and proclaiming to him that the land he lies on will be destined for him and his descendants)[32] together with references to Moses and his conversation with God at the burning bush.[33] Ibn Ezra thus evokes several biblical precursors to this poetical exploration of a heavenly hierophany, underscoring its roots in the biblical tradition. This particular colloquy begins with an exchange about the possibility of seeing God with one's eyes, which in both the Islamic tradition and in the Jewish philosophical tradition as exemplified in the work of Judah Halevi (d. 1141) that we will turn to shortly, becomes displaced by the idea of perceiving divine realities with the eyes of the heart. Nearing the end of this otherworldly encounter, the ascending hero petitions the divinity and thus plays the role of intercessor: "I said, 'Please, my Lord, listen to my plea for mercy (cf. Ps. 130:2) / To you I turn my eyes (Ps. 123:1) / Upon you I cast my troubles / To your hand I entrust my spirit' (Ps. 31:6)."[34] After asking for the appropriate path to approach the divinity, God responds with a type of commission to the seeker: "Uphold my words / Keep my teaching / Walk in my path, and do not depart from me / You will know your spirit / As is fitting to your ability and your strength / Then you will be able to know Him / To apprehend Him."[35] As one might expect from a philosophical allegory, the ultimate "revelation" conveyed through this divine encounter at the climax of the journey is that following the path of the philosopher, as taught by and ordained by God, leads to the apprehension of one's spirit, and thus apprehension of the divinity.[36]

These brief excerpts from Abraham Ibn Ezra's *Ḥay ben Meqitz* help to demonstrate and support Hughes's wider argument that this Jewish philosophical allegory draws on and engages with the symbolic language of the *miʿrāj* in order both to adapt some of its themes and also to contest its claims. Rather than extolling the merit of the Prophet Muḥammad as the hero who uniquely earns an audience with God in the heavenly realms, the *Ḥayy ibn Yaqẓān / Ḥay ben Meqitz* allegories suggest that such an ascent is open to all people who possess the proper philosophical tools and discipline. Further, Abraham Ibn Ezra's version demonstrates how some Jewish writers of the sixth/twelfth century in al-Andalus sought to deploy this motif not only as a philosophical treatise but also as an interreligious polemic that counters some of the claims of the Islamic ascension narratives, such as certain versions of Muḥammad's ascension attributed to Ibn ʿAbbās, that must have been circulating in similar cultural contexts.

The Jewish Polemical Treatise of Judah Halevi

As Ehud Krinis argues in his study of the Judeo-Arabic theological polemical treatise known as *Kuzari* by Judah Halevi (d. 1141), this work draws "terms, concepts, and basic patterns" directly from Shīʿī Muslim literature, and also those from "other literature incorporating the ideas and subject matter associated with that stream in Islam."[37] One of the themes that Krinis deems worthy of exploration concerning cross-fertilization between Jewish and Shīʿī literature is that of the "apotheosis" of select heroes, "manifested in the stages of ascension to the upper world, [crowning] the ascending chosen individuals as having earned a special status above that of the angels."[38] Turning to the specificity of Halevi's *Kuzari*, Krinis cites a very brief reference that touches on the theme: "There will be those among you who will come into My presence and ascend to heavens (*yaṣʿadu ilā al-samāʾ*), [like] those whose souls move about freely among the angels."[39] This reference to a heavenly journey remains on the level of generalities, for it never specifies who "among you" gains the privilege of ascending into the divine presence, nor whose souls "move about freely among the angels." Is the latter to be understood merely as the ability to "come and go in the heavens" (one thinks of the opening of *Hekhalot Rabbati*, which suggests that learning its techniques is akin to having a ladder in one's house and thus the ability to ascend and descend at will), or should one read into it something about being able to participate in the divine liturgy along with the angels? Be this as it may, in addition to this tantalizingly brief and fairly vague passage, one finds many more specific connections between Hekhalot references and the works of Halevi (including his poems). For instance, it is worth considering the references explored in an article by Elliot Wolfson, including an analysis of the phrase apparently common among Jewish writers in al-Andalus at the time, the "vision of the heart,"[40] that appears in Abraham Ibn Ezra's poem, and that also features in Muslim discussions of Muḥammad's ascension (especially given the key qurʾānic phrase "the heart does not lie in what it saw" from Q 53:12).

Tracing key Arabic terminology and themes in Halevi's *Kuzari*, Diana Lobel points out how the author subtly adapts and transforms language such as "union" or "connection" (*ittiṣāl*), divine "command" (*amr*), revelation/support (*taʾyīd*), and even witnessing/vision (*mushāhada*) from the manner in which they are used by earlier Aristotelean and Neoplatonic philosophers, Shīʿī thinkers, Sufis, et cetera, to represent Halevi's own particular views about prophecy and Israel's unique relationship with God.[41] And he is not alone among western Jews of this period wrestling with such issues, of course; creative engagement with and in some cases arguing against the philosophical approaches of al-Farabī and Ibn Sīnā, among others, can be found in the teachings of figures such as Rabbi Hai ben Sherira (d. 1038), Rabbi Ḥushiel of Kairouan (d. 1056), and Rabbi Nissim ben Jacob of Kairouan (d. ca. 1062).[42] The Jewish thinkers of Kairouan, of course, would most probably have come into direct contact with Muslim ascension discourses, and perhaps other dimensions of Ismāʿīlī Shīʿī thought. According to David Kaufmann's study, Rabbi Nissim of Kairouan "singles out the prophets of Israel and the Jewish people collectively (specifically at the Sinaitic theophany) as possessing certain knowledge of God through direct experience, whereas the other nations acquire this knowledge only indirectly,"[43] an argument that one also finds in *Kuzari* (I, 87).[44] In other words, we have once again an argument for Jewish priority and superiority, which is the main goal of the *Kuzari* but not unique to such overtly polemical works. Even though entire texts dedicated to the theme of ascension are less common among Maghribī Jews of the sixth/twelfth century, then, it also remains the case that numerous Jewish thinkers in both North Africa and Iberia engaged productively with this theme, both directly and indirectly, and in doing so they were in conversation not only with those inside but also beyond their Jewish communities.

As far as I am aware, we do not find extant from the sixth/twelfth century Maghribī context a Jewish text that directly attacks the validity of Muḥammad's heavenly journey or uses reports of the latter to attack the legitimacy of Islam, such as one finds in a Christian text that will be discussed shortly titled *Liber Denudationis*. However, a passing reference in a famous Muslim work known as *al-Shifāʾ* by Qāḍī ʿIyāḍ (d. 544/1149) suggests that some Jews did, in fact, use Muslim references to the Prophet's night journey and ascension as a proof text for anti-Muslim polemical attacks. Qāḍī ʿIyāḍ writes, "If the Satanic Verses were true, the Jews would have used [such verses] against the Muslims in the same way that they did with the night journey (*al-isrāʾ*)."[45] While this Muslim author is speaking about something else entirely while making this remark, and he, unfortunately, does not offer any subsequent details about which particular Jews may have used references to Muḥammad's night journey to attack Muslims, the fact that this sixth/twelfth century Andalūsī Muslim author could make this remark as if knowledge of the Jewish use of such polemics did not require further explanation should give us pause to consider the way the accounts of

Muḥammad's otherworldly journey served as something of a lightning rod for interreligious debate in this cultural context.

A Christian Anti-Muḥammad Polemic Based on Details from an Islamic Ascension Text

The *Liber Denudationis*, which was composed by an anonymous Christian author circa 1085–1132 CE according to modern editor and translator Thomas Burman,[46] offers a good example of an anti-Muslim polemical text originally written in Arabic and later translated into Latin. Burman conjectures that the author was likely a Christian who had lived among the Muslims of al-Andalus (thus a "Mozarab"), probably flourishing in or around Toledo in the decades following the Christian conquest of that city in 1085 CE. The author apparently intended the work not only for a Christian audience but also, or even primarily, for a Muslim audience.[47] Its polemical purpose becomes clear in the way the work seeks to expose the alleged lies told about Muḥammad and the falsity of his prophetic claims. The twelfth and final chapter of *Liber Denudationis* appears to be fully devoted to the theme of the night journey and ascension of Muḥammad, which, after the initial citation and paraphrased interpretation of Q 17:1 and a "setting of the scene" narrative frame, consists exclusively of a single paraphrased telling of the tale that draws on details generally stemming from the Ibn ʿAbbās ascension discourse.

In Arabic ascension narratives from the early to middle periods of Islamic history, certain narremes commonly appear in the versions of the story often ascribed to Ibn ʿAbbās, Ibn Isḥāq, or one of Ibn Isḥāq's alleged followers, a storyteller by the name of Abū Ḥasan al-Bakrī. I would contend that *Liber Denudationis* draws on these noncanonical but widespread Arabic sources for its base narrative, rather than relying on a hypothetical Qurʾān commentary as Burman theorizes.[48] Evidence for this hypothesis can be seen by the following common details: (1) Burāq speaks to Gabriel after shying away from Muḥammad, asking to be included in the latter's intercession as a condition for serving as Muḥammad's mount for the night journey to Jerusalem;[49] (2) Muḥammad ascends into heaven on Gabriel's back, praying two cycles of liturgical prayer with the angels of each heaven, and traversing a five-hundred-year journey between each of the heavens;[50] (3) he encounters wondrous angels in the seventh heaven and beyond, including a polycephalous angel whose number of heads, mouths, tongues, et cetera, are all multiples of seventy thousand,[51] and other angels said to be seen openly weeping for fear of God;[52] (4) Gabriel, presumably because of his being forced to stop at his "*known station*" at the Lote Tree, passes Muḥammad on to other angels, who convey the Prophet into God's presence;[53] and (5) God touches Muḥammad with his "cold hand," before conveying to him the duty of the Muslim community to pray the liturgical prayers fifty times per day.[54] The version conveyed in *Liber Denudationis* is fairly detailed, but the Arabic original it drew from was originally much longer and more complex, as the Christian editor who glosses the narrative freely admits: "The part of the vision which we have not included . . . is longer than that which we have narrated."[55] This confession on behalf of the Christian editor could help to explain why many standard elements of the Ibn ʿAbbās ascension discourse do not appear in the *Liber Denudationis*' version, such as the intimate colloquy scene, or the encounter with the prophets in Jerusalem, to say nothing about the absence of any meeting with prophets in the heavens, with the exception of its portrayal of Moses stationed in the fourth heaven.[56]

In *Liber Denudationis* chapter 12, where the anonymous author recounts the story of Muḥammad's ascension in an extended fashion despite abridging it substantially, the only polemical rebuttal that the author includes is inserted at the chapter's end. Interestingly enough, the author attacks the legitimacy of the Muslim narratives describing the Prophet's journey by drawing on the authority of the Qur'ān itself in order to deny the claim that Muḥammad ever performed any miracles.[57] Therefore, the author asserts, the night journey and ascension story must be nothing but a lie forged by later Muslims in a vain attempt to validate Muḥammad's claim to being a true prophet of God. Somewhat ironically, then, given the author's rejection of the validity of the night journey legend, he nevertheless highlights a detail from the end of the story to serve his polemical purpose: *Liber Denudationis* repeats the trope that one first finds in the Ibn Hishām recension of the Ibn Isḥāq ascension narrative, namely that, on hearing Muḥammad's claim to have traveled to Jerusalem and ascended into the heavens all in a single night, a large number of Muslims immediately abandoned their religion, emulating the action that this Christian author implicitly recommends to those in his audience.[58]

Similar to this polemical conclusion in chapter 12, a previous chapter from *Liber Denudationis*, chapter 4 articulates the author's polemical belief that the majority of those who became Muslim during Muḥammad's lifetime did so out of physical coercion "by the sword."[59] The author alleges that such violence, together with the use of false visions, were the primary tools that the Prophet and his followers used to obtain new converts. He suggests, then, that Muḥammad's ascension narrative serves as an example of one such "false vision." *Liber Denudationis* cites a brief allusion to a scene from Muḥammad's ascension as it attacks the veracity of his prophetic career. Offering more detail here than in chapter 12,[60] when conveying the description of an immense angel who seeks the Prophet's intercession, in this retelling the angel cries literal rivers of tears as it seeks Muḥammad's help to obtain God's forgiveness for the angel's apparent sins. Hearing this angel's plea, the Prophet makes a somewhat ambiguous reply: "Are you you? What could be forthcoming on my account when your Lord created Hellfire?"[61] In this narreme, Muḥammad doubts that he has the power to intercede on behalf of such a powerful and exalted angel, and yet he — or his followers who supposedly fabricated this tale in his name, according to this Christian editor — presumably proceeds to pretend to do so. While the anonymous author never states that Muḥammad accepted the angel's petition for his intercession, this fact must have been understood in the original Arabic narrative that *Liber Denudationis* uses as the base for its polemic. Indeed, in an Ibn ʿAbbās ascension narrative whenever figures ask Muḥammad to intercede with God on their behalf, be they a prophet, an angel, or even his steed Burāq, he agrees to do so. This feature of the base text can also be surmised by the Christian author's vitriolic conclusion to chapter 4 of his work, where he places the blame on Muḥammad and his prideful attempt at deception:

> O unspeakable presumption and unrestrained lies! How could he who was not able to bear the coming of one angel without describing himself as if he were an epileptic . . . take part in so many marvelous things in heaven? O strongest truth by which the falsity of those who try to lie about all things is immediately detected! Are angels spread out in such great bodily magnitude that they are many thousand times greater than the world in circumference? Again, if the angels were good, how did the best [of them] need any pardon? If they were evil, how did they remain in such great loftiness of heaven? In short, they had chosen as a good intercessor the most licentious impostor and pseudo-prophet, whose presumption was so intolerable that he who was not able to give any sure sign of his prophethood to his disciples, boasted that he had interceded on behalf of the highest angels.[62]

The *Liber Denudationis* thus makes the argument that not only is the ascension narrative a manifest forgery that defies both logic and faith in the goodness of angels but also that this lie can be attributed to Muḥammad himself, who attempted to use such a "false vision" to win over gullible converts.

Charles Tieszan argues convincingly that the author of *Liber Denudationis* composed his work not so much to try to sway a Muslim audience to embrace Christianity but rather to convince Mozarab Christians of the superiority of their own beliefs and practices. He argues that, considered together with other anti-Muslim polemics composed in this same period in this same region, the authors of such works "were ultimately concerned for the ways in which their communities upheld the tenets of Christianity in a multi-religious environment. For them, in the context of reconquest and shifting populations, they were eager to sustain and protect what made their faith secure and distinct especially in light of Islam. And it is precisely in their attacks upon Islam that we see these authors saying something about Christian identity."[63] This perceptive insight could also be applied in reverse, to the Muslim authors of anti-Christian polemics and indeed to those learned Muslims who circulated the Islamic ascension narratives to a wide and diverse audience in al-Andalus. As Brooke Olson Vuckovic argues in *Heavenly Journeys, Earthly Concerns*, Islamic ascension narratives first and foremost "reflect the concerns and lives of medieval Muslim scholars,"[64] not only in identifying Muḥammad and his followers as a "distinct confessional community" but also in helping to "construct and reinterpret" distinct gender relations and a distinct moral code within the Islamic community.[65] In other words, similar to the way that *Liber Denudationis* and other related Christian polemical works served to promote a specific vision of Christian communal identity rather than attempting primarily to win over new converts, so too the Islamic ascension narratives that circulated in North Africa and al-Andalus — despite their polemical thrust — were not aimed first and foremost at non-Muslim audiences but instead sought to promote a specific vision of Muslim communal identity.

Beyond such consideration of the context of interreligious polemics in examining the ascension narratives that appear in these historical sources from al-Andalus, another way in which the evidence provided in *Liber Denudationis* is valuable for the present study appears in the way it offers important testimony to the type of Islamic ascension narratives circulating in al-Andalus near the beginning of the sixth/twelfth century. Clearly, a retelling of the Ibn ʿAbbās version of the ascension discourse serves as the main Arabic proof text at the author's disposal. Its fantastic elements, such as the description of the enormous angel mentioned above, serve as grist for the mill for the author's attacks on the story of Muḥammad's ascension and by extension the claim to Muḥammad being a prophet. In light of the fact that the Ibn ʿAbbās version of Muḥammad's ascension in particular serves in this way as a basis for Christian anti-Muslim discourses in al-Andalus beginning with *Liber Denudationis* near the start of the sixth/twelfth century and continuing in the following century with the famous *Liber Scalae Machometi*, this use of the Ibn ʿAbbās versions of Muḥammad's ascension helps to explain the proliferation of Muslim authors in al-Andalus who come to discuss many of the details of this type of approach to Muḥammad's ascension during the same period. Even though the Ibn ʿAbbās narratives may not have satisfied the rigors of hadith criticism that many Muslim adherents of the Mālikī approach to Islamic jurisprudence normally might have valued, as we shall see in the chapter that follows, even prominent Mālikī traditionists and biographers demonstrate their engagement with such widely-circulated versions as they comment on the legend in general, and what the story communicates about Muḥammad's exalted status vis-à-vis other prophets in particular.

CHAPTER THREE.

Emerging Andalūsī Mālikī Traditions

Transmitting Prophetic Reports: The Approach of Qāḍī ʿIyāḍ

In the previous chapter, we already were introduced to the work of Qāḍī ʿIyāḍ (d. 544/1149) in his famous book titled *al-Shifāʾ* (*The Cure*). When speaking of the incident in which Satan allegedly attempted to convince the Prophet that some of the pre-Islamic goddesses were "high-flying cranes whose intercession is to be sought" and false verses were allowed to become intermixed with true verses from the Star chapter (Q 53:19–28), thus providing a pretext for later anti-Muslim polemics attacking Muḥammad and the legitimacy of the qurʾānic revelation, Qāḍī ʿIyāḍ wrote the following: "If the Satanic Verses were true, the Jews would have used [such verses] against the Muslims in the same way that they did with the night journey (*al-isrāʾ*)."[1] Here Qāḍī ʿIyāḍ makes it clear that the qurʾānic account of the night journey and subsequent reports of the story of Muḥammad's miraculous traveling to Jerusalem and the heavens had by his time become the focus of interreligious controversy. Through an examination of Qāḍī ʿIyāḍ's more focused commentary on both some of the full hadith reports on Muḥammad's night journey as well as fragmentary anecdotes that he transmits on the subject at the beginning of the section of his *Shifāʾ* devoted to this specific topic, one gets a sense for what types of stories about the Prophet's journey circulated in official circles in al-Andalus at the time, and how some of its Mālikī Sunnī scholars, such as Qāḍī ʿIyāḍ, treated these reports.

Surveying Qāḍī ʿIyāḍ's chapter on this theme one finds that, as one expects from a mainstream Sunnī traditionist, after citing the relevant qurʾānic passages, Qāḍī ʿIyāḍ begins by transmitting hadith reports on Muḥammad's ascension appearing in the two main Sunnī sound collections (*Ṣaḥīḥ*), that by Muslim b. Ḥajjāj (d. 261/875) and that by Muḥammad b. Ismaʿīl Bukhārī (d. 256/870).[2]

Somewhat surprisingly, however, he follows this introduction by listing a series of more fragmentary additional details about the story that are less authenticated but that he nevertheless considers relevant and "useful to [his] purpose."[3] As we shall see, that purpose includes both elucidating key elements of the journey for a Muslim audience, as well as participating in a broader cultural debate centering around the merits of Muḥammad's prophetic career in comparison with those of Adam, David, Moses, Jesus, and others whom Muslims consider prophets and whom many Jews and Christians also consider as pivotal holy figures.

As mentioned above, the author begins in a fairly conventional way by citing the Night Journey verse (Q 17:1) and the verses from the beginning of the Star chapter (Q 53:1–18). He follows these quotations with an extended citation of the long report from Muslim's collection (number 259, attributed to Anas b. Mālik via Thābit al-Bunānī),[4] which unlike most of the other narratives in the two major canonical hadith collections links Muḥammad's journey to Jerusalem to his heavenly ascent.[5] Qāḍī ʿIyāḍ praises this particular report for being the "most complete,"[6] after earlier making the more general remark, "There is no disagreement among Muslims about the truth of the night journey he was taken on, since it is an explicit text in the Qurʾān, and since many widespread reports recount it in detail, expounding on its wonders and the setting apart of our Prophet Muḥammad, by it."[7] Through assertions such as this one, it becomes plain that Qāḍī ʿIyāḍ draws on the reports of the night journey and ascension primarily to serve his wider agenda, namely to promote the love, respect, and honor of Muḥammad among Muslims and non-Muslims of the Iberian Peninsula, and to elevate the status of the Prophet Muḥammad vis-à-vis other Abrahamic prophets.

Although Qāḍī ʿIyāḍ claims that Muslims do not disagree about the night journey and ascension as an article of faith, that does not mean that he ignores the variations and differences between the different hadith reports. In fact, the very title of this section of his work — "On [God's] Giving of Benefit by what is Included in the Blessings of the Night Journey: The Intimate Colloquy, the Vision [of God], the Serving as *Imām* of the Prophets." — highlights details not found anywhere in the canonical Sunnī ascension accounts from sound hadith collections.[8] Although not present in these collections, all of these details mentioned in the heading do appear in Qāḍī ʿIyāḍ's discussion that follows, but he cites them in a more fragmentary fashion than the sound reports, as the author supplements the former with additional anecdotes and scenes that are not included in the one long report of Anas as transmitted via Thābit and collated by Muslim, the one that he deems the "most complete" (as well as the most trustworthy) and thus cites in full.

Instead of also citing the variant reports in full, Qāḍī ʿIyāḍ merely includes brief allusions to phrases from these other reports that differ from the Thābit account. For example, he presents the beginning of the Abu Dharr report from Bukhārī's collection, which offers the fascinating detail about the roof of Muḥammad's house being split open directly before Gabriel descends and washes the interior of the Prophet's chest.[9] Next, he provides the following observation about the version of the Anas b. Mālik narrative transmitted by Mālik b. Ṣaʿṣaʿa, comparing it with the long sound report transmitted by Thābit: "Qatāda related something similar from Anas from Mālik b. Ṣaʿṣaʿa, which contains advancement and delay [of some details], addition and subtraction [of elements], and difference in the arrangement of the prophets in the heavens. The report of Thābit from Anas [i.e., Muslim, number 259] is more sound and more excellent."[10] This remark openly points out the disparities between these two reports on the level of detail, even though both came to be accepted as sound hadith by later Sunnī tradition. As he had asserted at the outset, Qāḍī ʿIyāḍ acknowledges these differences, and maintains that the account transmitted by Thābit from Muslim's collection is superior to the others, such as this particular report from Mālik b. Ṣaʿṣaʿa recorded by Bukhārī, not only because he finds the former the most complete but also because he considers it the most accurate.

Despite his insistence on the superiority of Muslim's first long ascension report, he proceeds to provide a whole series of additional details (*ziyādāt*) that he draws from a range of other reports that he deems as containing "useful points" (*nuqaṭ mufīda*) that advance his purpose,[11] and in this he does not limit himself to sound Sunnī reports transmitted in the Muslim and Bukhārī collections of hadith. In fact, in the section that follows, he describes several lengthy excerpts from a noncanonical report ascribed to the companion Abu Hurayra that appears in Ṭabarī's Qurʾān commentary and Bayhaqī's later work *Dalāʾil al-nubuwwa* (*Indications of Prophecy*).[12] In accord with the author's purpose to extol the merits of the Pure One (*al-Muṣṭafā*, i.e., the Prophet Muḥammad), he focuses special attention on two scenes that provide additional "useful points" from this Abu Hurayra narrative, both of which involve recognizing the high status of Muḥammad vis-à-vis the other prophets. The first of these scenes takes place in Jerusalem, just after the Prophet prays with all the angels gathered there, where he then meets the rest of his prophetic cohort for the first time:

> He met the spirits of the prophets, who praised their lord. And [Abu Hurayra] recounted the speech of each one of them, Abraham Moses, Jesus, David, and Solomon [who praised the lord while recalling how each had been favored by God]. Then he mentioned the speech of the

> Prophet: "As for Muḥammad, he praised his lord, great and mighty, saying: 'Each of you praised your lord, and so I will praise my lord! Praise be to God who sent me as a *mercy to the worlds* (Q 21:107), sent to *all the people as a bringer of good news and as a warner* (Q 34:28). He sent down upon me the *Divider* [i.e., the Qur'ān] (Q 25:1), in which is the elucidation of each and every thing. He made my community the *best of communities* (Q 3:110) and a *middle community* (Q 2:143), who will be the first and the last. He *opened* my *chest* for me *and removed my burden* (Q 94:1–2). *He raised my mention* (Q 94:4). He made me the Opener and the [Final] Seal.'" Abraham responded, "By this he favored you, Muḥammad, [over all the rest of us]." Then he recounted the way he was made to ascend from the first heaven, up from heaven to heaven, similar to what has preceded.[13]

This scene describes Muḥammad meeting with the spirits of the other prophets in Jerusalem as described in the extended report ascribed to Abu Hurayra, not found in the major Sunnī hadith collections but prominent in Ṭabarī's Qur'ān commentary and other major collections. One may surmise that "spirits" (*arwāḥ*) of the prophets are specified here given that these prophets had died to their worldly existence long before Muḥammad lived, and yet the bodily resurrection on the final "day of arising" (*yawm al-qiyāma*) has not yet taken place. It also might serve to address the problem confronting Muslim commentators to explain why, after meeting the other prophets in Jerusalem, Muḥammad later on the ascension portion of his journey asks Gabriel to identify the prophets whom he subsequently encounters in the various levels of the heavens.

In any case, at the heart of this narreme is a contrast between the way God has sent down favor on a certain subset of previous prophets (with an emphasis on some of those particularly dear to Jews and Christians) and the blessings God bestows on Muḥammad, many of which are drawn directly from qur'ānic citations, with Abraham at the end affirming Muḥammad's high status. While it is not possible at this stage in our understanding to reconstruct the context in which reports such as this first may have circulated, for our author Qāḍī ʿIyāḍ, the report serves an unmistakable contemporary polemical purpose, since in this report the patriarch Abraham, revered by Jews, Christians, and Muslims alike, boldly proclaims that Muḥammad's blessings and merits place him in a category above the rest of his prophetic peers. This exaltation of Muḥammad position vis-à-vis the other prophets becomes a familiar refrain in the night journey section of Qāḍī ʿIyāḍ's *Shifāʾ*, which makes perfect sense since the goal of this work as a whole is to discuss the duties that Muslims and non-Muslims owe to the Prophet because of his blessed status.

The Abu Hurayra report supplies a very similar message in a second narreme that Qāḍī ʿIyāḍ cites at length shortly after the completion of the first, its context being Muḥammad's colloquy with God in the vicinity of the Lote Tree in the highest heavens, with bits of the dialogue between Muḥammad and his lord being drawn directly from the Qurʾān. God invites the Prophet to make a request, that is, to ask for a boon at this high station; in response, Muḥammad introduces what I have called the "favor of the prophets" narreme:

> It *was covered* by light, and by angels, which is [the meaning of God's saying]: "*When the Lote Tree was covered by what covered.*" (Q 53:16).
>
> [God], blessed and exalted, said: "Ask!"
>
> [Muḥammad] replied: You took *Abraham as an intimate friend* (Q 4:125) and gave him a great kingdom; you *spoke to Moses directly* (Q 4:164); you gave David a great kingdom, worked iron for him, and enchanted the mountains for him; you gave Solomon a great kingdom, and enchanted for him jinn, men, devils, and the winds, and *gave him a kingdom such that befits no one after him* (Q 38:35); you taught Jesus the Torah and the Evangel (Q 3:48), you made him heal the blind and the leper (3:49), and you protected him and his mother from the accursed Satan (Q 3:36), who never found any path to them. [What blessing is there particular to me?] His Lord answered him: [Though I took Abraham as an intimate friend,] I took you as both an intimate friend and a beloved, as it is written in the Torah [119], "*Muḥammad, beloved of the Most Merciful.*" I sent you *to all the people* (Q 34:38). I made your community to be the first and the last. I made for your community that a sermon would not be permitted until they bear witness that you are my servant and my messenger. I made you the first of the prophets created, and the last of them sent. I gave you the *seven rhymed verses* (Q 15:87) that I had not given to a prophet before you. I gave you the seals of the Cow chapter (Q 2:285–286)[14] from a treasury beneath my throne, which I had not given to any prophet before you. I made you as the opener and the sealer.[15]

While the eulogy contest in the first quotation cited above from Abu Hurayra's version of the ascension tale focuses on the way Muḥammad and the rest of the prophets compare and contrast the way God favors each of them, here in this second instance instead we find Muḥammad himself recalling the merits of the other prophets before God, asking whether or not he will be similarly or differently favored by the divinity. One could imagine, hypothetically, that God could have told him that some other prophet was more highly favored than he, at least in some particular quality or ability. Instead, as expected from Qāḍī ʿIyāḍ's polemical framework, as well as the conventions of this trope from most ascension narratives in which it appears, in this second narreme God informs Muḥammad about the ways in which the favors he has been given meet if not surpass those granted to any other prophet.

For example, as we saw at the outset, if Abraham has been given the designation *khalīl* (intimate friend of God), Muḥammad here is told by God that he has been given that title and an even better one: "I took you as both *khalīl* (intimate friend) and *ḥabīb* (beloved)."[16] Presumably in response to the great kingdoms granted to the previous prophets Abraham, David, and Solomon, God tells Muḥammad that he has been sent to "all people,"[17] with the implication being that the entire world will eventually serve as his dominion. Although God does not promise Muḥammad that he will rule as king over the world in his lifetime, he does inform him in a variety of ways that his particular community (*umma*) will be the very best of all communities (e.g., see Q 3:110). Moreover, among the group of prophets, Muḥammad enjoys the designation of being the "first of the prophets created, and the last of them sent"[18] as well as "the opener and the sealer."[19] These designations seem to provide a direct rejoinder to Christian claims about Jesus, for instance the references in the Book of Revelation to the figure on the throne (representing Jesus and/or God) as "the *alpha* and the *omega*," as well as references in both Revelation and Christian interpretations of the book of Isaiah in which the Lord God (which Christians see as including Jesus as part of the Trinity) is said to be the "first and the last."[20] Muḥammad's title of "sealer" undoubtedly refers to his designation as "seal of the prophets," another way of stating that according to Muslim belief, he remains "the last of [the prophets] sent." The notion that Muḥammad's revelation was not only the last and final revelation but is in addition the most complete, containing elements not found in those of previous prophets, gets raised explicitly in this scene in which God informs Muḥammad that the "seven rhymed verses" (Q 15:87; often understood as an allusion to Q 1) and the "Seals of the Cow chapter" (Q 2:285–286) were not given to any other prophet before him.[21] In another version of this same scene circulating in the same cultural context, these particular parts of the Qurʾān were mentioned by God as favors that balanced and even exceeded the favor of the vast kingdom that God had previously granted to the prophet Solomon.[22]

While parts of Abu Hurayra's version of the trope of the favor of the prophets seem to be in direct dialogue with Christian conceptions of Jesus, the way this version declares Muḥammad's status as elevated above Moses, David, and Solomon could be seen as also directed at Jews and their claims about these figures.

Abu Hurayra's report does not place in the voice of God any direct rejoinder to Moses's designation as the one to whom God "spoke . . . directly" (Q 4:164; Arabic: *kalim Allah*). Other versions of this same narreme, however, such as the one appearing in the Madrid MS Real Academia Codera 241 fragmentary version from approximately the same historical context, do include this specific rejoinder: "And if I spoke to Moses directly, I did that on Mount Sinai, and I have spoken to you, O Muḥammad, above the seven heavens."[23] Although Qāḍī ʿIyāḍ does not include that particular detail in his *Shifāʾ*, here or elsewhere, he does recount two different anecdotes in which Moses recognizes Muḥammad's superiority when Muḥammad literally surpasses him, ascending to a higher level in the heavens. The first version comes in Mālik b. Ṣaʿṣaʿa's ascension report from Bukhārī's sound collection in which Moses weeps on Muḥammad's ascending higher than he and leading more of his community to Paradise, which remains, in fact, the only detail that Qāḍī ʿIyāḍ sees fit to mention from this particular version of the tale during his wide-ranging discussion of the Prophet's ascent.[24] The second version appears in a brief narreme that comes shortly after Qāḍī ʿIyāḍ's citation of Abu Hurayra's favor of the Prophet narreme: "In the narration of Sharik: He saw Moses in the seventh [heaven], he said, out of [Moses'] favor of speaking with God. Then [Muḥammad] was raised high above that to what only God knows, [as a response to which] Moses said: 'I did not imagine that anyone would be raised over me.'"[25] Unlike in the first instance, in this second instance Moses does not cry, he simply acknowledges that though God allows him the honor of abiding in the seventh heaven (presumably higher than any other prophet, before Muḥammad's arrival) on account of his favor of speaking with God directly, yet nevertheless God grants Muḥammad the blessing of ascending even higher still, something that Moses himself did not expect.

As we see in these types of references, Qāḍī ʿIyāḍ's analysis of the story of Muḥammad's night journey and heavenly ascension is largely characterized not by the citation of full reports of ascension hadith but rather by episodic and fragmentary references to particular scenes and specific details. The fact that Qāḍī ʿIyāḍ explicitly tells the reader that he will include a mention of those "points" that are particularly "useful to [his] purpose" raises the broader question of what that particular purpose may be. For instance, in this latest example, why should he record in particular the way that Muḥammad rises above Moses, and the expression of Moses's dismay and/or surprise at that fact? As suggested above, the answer undoubtedly arises when one considers that the work as a whole, whose title could be rendered in English as *The Cure in Coming to Know the Truths of the Pure [Prophet Muḥammad]*, aims to instill in the reader a sense of Muḥammad's high status and his superiority in comparison to the rest of the prophets, including those revered by Jews and Christians.

While Qāḍī ʿIyāḍ uses references from the ascension reports to emphasize Muḥammad's superiority to the rest of the prophets, he also includes a few references that suggest that Muḥammad's high status was recognized even by the angels, and further, that it even exceeded the level of some or all of God's angels. At the beginning of the Abu Hurayra report, Gabriel guides Muḥammad to Jerusalem, where they pray there together with "the angels," and on learning of his identity, the angels excitedly reply, "May God grant him long life as a brother and a viceregent! Most blessed of brothers, most blessed of viceregents!"[26] One could interpret these phrases simply to mean that the angels recognize Muḥammad's superiority over other humans. The fact that they call him "brother," however, suggests that they consider him a kindred servant of God, and perhaps the most blessed among them.

Whether Muḥammad's status exceeds that of his guide, the angel Gabriel, remains an open issue for Qāḍī ʿIyāḍ, for he cites two reports in close succession that suggest different answers to this question. In the report about Gabriel and Muḥammad ascending to heaven in a pair of vehicles resembling birds' nests, Muḥammad glances at Gabriel and the latter's strength in cleaving to the heavens, by which he "knew the favor of [Gabriel's] knowledge of God over [his]."[27] Despite Gabriel's superior knowledge, the veil subsequently drops for Muḥammad, and then God "revealed to him what he revealed" (Q 53:10) at that stage, in the midst of his vision of a blinding light. In the report from Muḥammad's cousin and son-in-law, ʿAlī b. Abī Ṭālib, that Qāḍī ʿIyāḍ cites immediately after this one, in contrast, the narrative also describes Muḥammad ascending higher than Gabriel is able to go, all the way up to the level of the veil. At the very final highest stages of his ascent, one of God's highest angels — one whom Gabriel had never seen prior to that day — facilitates the process by which Muḥammad learns the phrases of the call to prayer. After this lesson, "according to the report, the angel took [Muḥammad] by the hand and advanced him, and [Muḥammad] served as the imam for the people of the heaven, among whom were Adam and Noah."[28] The idea that Muḥammad's leading of liturgical prayer in the heavens involved not only human prophets but also all the angels more broadly is suggested by the comment made by ʿAlī's great-grandson and father of the pivotal scholar Jaʿfar al-Ṣādiq, Muḥammad b. ʿAlī b. Ḥusayn b. ʿAlī b. Abī Ṭālib, at the end of this report: "God [thus] completed for Muḥammad the honor [of being] over the people of the heavens and the earth (*ahl al-samawāt wa ʾl-arḍ*)."[29] Seen in that light, Muḥammad could thus be conceived as the prayer leader for, and the superior of, all of God's creatures, even the very highest of God's angels.

To this point we have been focusing attention on those ascension-related hadith reports that Qāḍī ʿIyāḍ refers to in his section of *al-Shifāʾ* devoted to the night journey, but it is important to recognize that the author also alludes to narremes from different night journey reports throughout his work. For instance, in the introduction to the very first chapter of the first section of *al-Shifāʾ*, he quotes an anecdote that he does not discuss in the night journey section but that he cites several times elsewhere in his work, the idea that Burāq shied when it first encountered the Prophet Muḥammad on the night that he conveyed him on his journey: "Anas said that *Burāq* was brought bridled and saddled to the Prophet on the evening of his night journey. It shied away from the Prophet, so Gabriel said to it, 'Do you do this to Muḥammad? No one more honored by God than he has ever ridden you." Anas related that upon this, *Burāq* broke out into a sweat."[30] This narreme is placed near the opening of two different chapters of the first part of Qāḍī ʿIyāḍ's book, namely chapter 1, "God's Praise and Great Esteem of [Muḥammad]," and chapter 3, "The Sound and Well-Known Reports Related about the Immense Value Placed on [the Prophet] by His Lord, His Exalted Position, and His Nobility in this World and the Next."[31] Despite its overt connection to the events of the night journey, Qāḍī ʿIyāḍ chooses to relate this anecdote in other sections of his work (aside from the night journey section) in order to illustrate Muḥammad's high stature through a brief anecdote about the Prophet and Burāq's first meeting. Through Qāḍī ʿIyāḍ's placement of this short narreme, it becomes clear that our author is less interested in compiling an exhaustive inventory of reports about Muḥammad's miraculous experience on the night journey and more interested in emphasizing certain key details from these reports, those "useful points" (*nuqaṭ mufīda*) that advance his apologetic purpose of defending and exalting the Prophet beyond all polemical attacks, and raising his fame in the region among Muslims and non-Muslims alike.

Interpretation of Prophetic Biography: al-Suhaylī

A commonality of ideas and discourse does not necessitate a commonality in genre, as one witnesses when exploring the commentary of the *Sirat Rasūl Allah* (*Biography of the Messenger of God*) composed in al-Andalus by the scholar al-Suhaylī (d. 581/1185) and the connections between this work and the writings of other Muslim exegetes of the period. Suhaylī transmits and interprets the night journey and ascension as a rich and complete tale through the context of presenting his commentary on Ibn Hishām's recension of Ibn Isḥāq's composite ascension discourse recorded in the latter's famous *Sīrat Rasūl Allāh*. As described above, the *Sīra* weaves together disparate strands of narrative to form a more complete tale. Although it cites some of its sources, other details appearing in the *Sīra* remain completely uncited and anonymous. Unlike the hadith reports on which it is largely based, the *Sīra* shows much less concern with chains of transmission of separate narremes. In the section of the biography describing the night journey from Jerusalem to Mecca and back, Ibn Isḥāq simply lists a whole cluster of authority figures at the outset, claiming that he pieced together the tale that follows this "group citation" from each of their different accounts. Despite this lack of precision when citing sources in the original *Sīra*, Suhaylī attempts to bring his edition of the work up to the scholarly standards of his time as he adds to the specificity of source material along with his commentary on the story.

For instance, the description of Burāq's introduction to the Prophet appears three times in the *Sīra*, with the third being an anecdote about Burāq shying away and then sweating before the Prophet (the brief reference that Qāḍī ʿIyāḍ had placed near the very start of his work, as we have seen). In his commentary on this anecdote, Suhaylī attempts to draw on the sources at his disposal to answer the question of why Burāq might have acted in this standoffish and/or nervous fashion when he first came into the Prophet's presence. Did Burāq not have experience being around the prophets or was he not aware of Muḥammad's exalted status? Our commentator offers several possible explanations for Burāq's behavior in an attempt to answer these questions, informing the reader of the specific sources where his anecdotes on this topic originated:

> On the shying of Burāq when the Prophet rode him, and Gabriel said to him: "Aren't you ashamed, Burāq, no servant of God before Muḥammad more noble than he has ridden you!" Here is what Ibn Baṭṭāl said in the *Commentary on al-Jāmiʿ al-Ṣaḥīḥ* [in explanation of Burāq's shying]: "This was after the period of Burāq with the [earlier] prophets, and thus a long period [had passed] between Jesus and Muḥammad."
>
> Another scholar transmitted a different reason [for Burāq shying], saying in the report of the night journey: "Gabriel said to Muḥammad when Burāq shied, 'Perhaps, Muḥammad, you touched the yellow [idol] today,' and the Prophet indicated that he did not touch it, except that he passed by it, saying [as he did so], 'Perish the one who worships you instead of God,' and he did not touch it apart from that." This was from the transmission of Abū Saʿd al-Naysabūrī [= ʿAbd al-Malik al-Khargushī/al-Kharjushī] in *Sharaf al-Muṣṭafā*. And God knows best. In the *Musnad* of al-Bazzār there is mention of the "yel-

> low one" as being an idol, some of it made of gold. The Messenger of God broke it on the day of the conquest [of Mecca].[32]

In this passage, Suhaylī draws on two specific earlier commentaries that present two distinct explanations for why Burāq shied on first encountering the Prophet. He does not attempt to adjudicate between the two possibilities; instead, for him it is sufficient to transmit those interpretations that help to shed light on the meaning of the story as conveyed in this and other works of hadith exegesis.

Just as Suhaylī felt the need to explain the scene in some sound reports (and, of course, Ibn Isḥāq's *Sīra*) that depict the shying of Burāq, so too he seeks to find a reason why a majority of ascension reports depict the angels at the gate to each of the heavens as asking Gabriel whether or not Muḥammad has been "sent." Does this question signal that the angels remain ignorant of Muḥammad's high station? Could it be that they are not aware whether or not the revelation has already come to him? Might this detail be taken as evidence that the journey took place near the beginning of the Prophet's prophetic career? Suhaylī rejects each of these hypothetical positions in his commentary on the *Sira* as he searches for a convincing rationale behind the questions that the angels pose to Gabriel:

> About what was asked about the meaning of the angels of each of the heavens asking Gabriel, "Who is with you?" to which he replied, "Muḥammad." "Was he sent to it?" "Yes." This is the expression of the report in the sound collections. And according to the people of knowledge, their question about his being sent meant, "Has he been sent to the sky?" since they had known from reports that he would ascend to it. Were they to have meant his being sent to creatures previously, they would have said, "Has he been sent?" without adding "to it." It is unlikely that [God] would conceal from the angels his having been sent to creatures, and they not know about it until the eve of the night journey.
>
> In the report that has been given earlier in the book there is also proof, where it mentions the glorifications of the angels of the seven heavens [on the birth of Muḥammad and/or the start of his prophecy], then the glorification of the angels of each heaven, ending with them each asking the other about what they were glorifying, until the question came to the angels of the seventh heaven, who said, "Our Lord commanded it to take place thus." And then the report ended with the first heaven. Consider the report in its entirety. In this we find what

> proves that the angels already knew about the prophetic career of Muḥammad when it began. Rather than [the idea that the angels were ignorant of Muḥammad being sent as a prophet, the angel] says, "Was he sent to it?" or in other words, "Was he sent to it [i.e., the sky] on Burāq?"
>
> What we find in the previous report of Anas when the angels of the first heaven ask, "Was he sent?," just as we find [the expression] in the *Sīra*, i.e.[,] without the "to it," this rather comes in the vision that he saw in his heart, as mentioned before, and that was before he had been inspired [with prophecy] as had come in the report about [the vision of the night journey] with his eye. . . . Indeed the night journey had first been [in dream] visions, then it was a [physical] vision. For that reason, in all the transmissions, we only find this one where they say, "Has he been sent to it?" And God knows best.[33]

For Suhaylī, the night journey and ascension took place on more than one occasion, first in one or more dream visions and only later as a physical journey that includes the "vision of the eye." This theory about a multiplicity of journeys helps to explain why in some sound versions of the story there is an extra prepositional phrase ("to it") added to the end of the angels' question. Without such an additional preposition, it seems to the author that the question indicates Muḥammad having been sent as a prophet to humanity, relating to his night journey via dream vision (or "vision of the heart") at the very beginning of his prophetic career. In contrast, with the addition of the grammatical preposition "to it," Suhaylī contends that the question refers to Muḥammad's physical night journey and bodily ascension in the middle of his prophetic career, with the question now indicating the Prophet's "being sent to the sky/heavens." In other words, in this latter case, the angels essentially ask Gabriel whether or not this is indeed that very night, foretold to them, that Muḥammad would be fetched from the earth and sent into the skies. The fact that this explanation hinges on the presence or absence of a seemingly insignificant short prepositional phrase (ʿilay-hi) demonstrates the degree to which Suhaylī pays close attention to grammar, revealing his abiding interest in and expertise on the subject. Moreover, his drawing a distinction between two different night journeys helps him to avoid what might otherwise appear to be a contradiction in the hadith reports.

Avoiding contradiction between reports likewise motivates Suhaylī's remarks about the passage from the ascension narrative in which Muḥammad states that all of the angels laughed and smiled when greeting him on his journey, all, that is, except Mālik, the Guardian of the Fire. If such is the case, then, how can this idea be reconciled with a different report, not as frequently collated with the ascension discourse, in which the angel Michael is described as not ever laughing since the day that God created Jahannam (a fiery place, often associated with one of the levels of Hellfire, depicted in the Qur'ān as a place of postmortem punishment)?

> If the two hadith are sound, one is faced with reconciling them: It could be that he did not laugh since God created the Fire until this time [during the ascension] in which he laughed with the Messenger of God. Thus the hadith would be general, but intending specificity. Or it could be that the first hadith took place with the Messenger of God before this last hadith [took place], then there happened afterwards what happened with him, laughing in his presence. . . . And God know best.[34]

Like a true expert in legal reasoning, Suhaylī sees one possible way to resolve the apparent contradiction, by understanding one of the reports as not conveying an absolute negation of Michael laughing since the creation of Jahannam but rather conveying a more narrow and specific meaning, intending that he did not laugh between that time and the time when he encountered Muḥammad (either on the ascension or on a different occasion, described in yet another report). This example demonstrates one way that Suhaylī strives to reconcile apparent contradictions between reports that Sunnī scholars otherwise consider sound, thus seeking to maintain the integrity of even the smaller details of the composite account of the ascension story as told by Ibn Isḥāq in the *Sīra*.

In his commentary on the reports of the ascension as transmitted in the *Sīra* and elsewhere, Suhaylī also shows attention to small details when he discusses why Idrīs/Enoch, who was one of the oldest of the human prophets, nevertheless addresses Muḥammad as "brother" rather than "son," unlike the way Adam and Abraham both address Muḥammad paternally as "son." According to Suhaylī's hypothesis, this difference must indicate that Muḥammad and Enoch are not blood relatives the way Muḥammad and Adam and Abraham are: "Idrīs is not the grandfather of Noah, and not among the ancestors of the Messenger of God (i.e., a direct blood descendent), because he said, 'Welcome to the righteous brother' and did not say 'Welcome to the righteous son' [as Adam and Abraham did]."[35] The discrepancy in address thus can be attributed to a different genealogical relationship among these prophets. Recall that in the Islamic tradition, Idrīs/ Enoch is seen as a unique human being who was taken up into the heavens to abide there until Judgment Day without first suffering physical death. Some Muslims understand such an idea as being behind the qur'ānic expression that says of this prophet that God "*raised him up to a high place*" (Q 19:57), a phrase frequently cited in hadith reports after Muḥammad encounters him in the skies, often, but not always, in the fourth heaven. Suhaylī addresses the issue of how this position of Idrīs in the fourth heaven merits the label "a high place" when in the *Sīra* and sound ascension reports, Muḥammad encounters other prophets in even higher heavens. Since the heavenly station of Enoch/Idrīs is not the highest (assuming the order of the heavens correlates to the heights of the respective heavens), what could the qur'ānic expression mean? Suhaylī draws on one of the "stories of the prophets," present both in works from that specific genre and also in select Qur'ān commentaries, to unpack the phrase: "This — and God knows best — [goes] with what he recalled from Ka'b b. al-Aḥbār, namely that Idrīs is special among all the prophets in that he raised him up before his death to the fourth heaven. An angel who had been his friend raised him up to him, and this was the angel who was responsible for the Sun, according to what he recounted. Idrīs asked [the angel] to show him the Garden, and God gave permission for that."[36] Unlike the explanations for the raising of Idrīs/Enoch that one finds in the extracanonical Jewish and Christian Enoch literature, here God gives Idrīs/Enoch's angelic friend permission to bring him up into the fourth heaven — associated in ancient astronomy with the sphere of the sun — and from there to take him on a tour of the paradisiacal Garden. As if this explanation were not enough, Suhaylī combines it with a short anecdote that shares common features with the stories told about the death of Moses and/or others who seek to evade the angel of death by traveling to a remote location: "When he was in the fourth heaven, the Angel of Death saw [Idrīs/Enoch] there and was astonished, and he said, 'I was commanded to seize the spirit of Idrīs this very hour in the fourth heaven!' So he seized him there, and raised him alive to that high place specific to him from among all the prophets."[37] Since Suhaylī previously stated that Idrīs/Enoch was brought into the fourth heaven before experiencing physical death, this additional anecdote must be understood as being included to assure the reader that Idrīs will, in the future, experience death just as other creatures do, and at that time the Angel of Death will take his soul from the fourth heaven where he resides. Additionally, this extra explanation also suggests that the "high place" from the phrase of Q19:57 might well indicate another location up beyond the fourth heaven, for his station in the fourth heaven is not the same as the "high place" that the Qur'ān indicates for him.

In the *Sīra* account, as with the official order in most sound Sunnī reports, Muḥammad encounters Moses in the sixth heaven, and as in the vast majority of accounts, Moses serves as the figure who encourages Muḥammad to ask for a reduction of the number of required liturgical prayers, since the initial command to observe fifty per day was too heavy a burden for the community of Moses to bear. Suhaylī comments on and explains the care that Moses shows toward the Muslim community with reference to a "famous hadith" in which Moses reads a description of Muḥammad's *umma* on the tablets he receives from God and wishes to be among them, that is, included in the Prophet's community.[38] With this report, Moses shows his love for the Muslim community and his wish to be included as part of Muḥammad's intercession with God. Citing this report in his commentary, Suhaylī contends with the Jews and Christians of his milieu, claiming Moses as a champion of the Muslim umma.

Perhaps the most interesting and intriguing section of Suhaylī's long commentary on the *Sīra*'s account of Muḥammad's ascension comes in a long passage where the author recounts the discussion of earlier scholars from al-Andalus who interpret the position of each of the prophets in the heavens through an allegorical lens more commonly associated with dream interpretation (*taʿbīr*), here serving as a type of prophecy of what was to come later in Muḥammad's life. According to this passage, certain features of the lives of the prophets whom Muḥammad encounters in the heavens can be said to have a direct parallel to events in the life of Muḥammad, and thus could be used to help interpret events of the Prophet's later life typologically:

> Just as the actions of Adam's enemy got him expelled from the Garden, so too the actions of Muḥammad's enemies will get him expelled from Mecca; just as members of the Jewish community sought to bring about the deaths of Jesus and John, so too certain Jews will seek to kill Muḥammad; just as Joseph forgave the brothers who betrayed him, so too Muḥammad will forgive his relatives who fought against him; just as Idrīs/Enoch wrote letters to the kings of the world calling on them to obey God, so too Muḥammad will do the same for the sovereigns of his age; just as Aaron became the beloved of his people, so too will Muḥammad become the beloved of the Quraysh; just as Moses led the conquest into the holy land that God vacated for him, so too will God do the same for the Muslim conquest of not only the holy land but also of Mecca; and just as Abraham was found at the celestial "Frequented House" to which seventy thousand angels regularly come in pilgrimage, so too will Muḥammad lead something like seventy thousand of his followers to the Kaʿba in Mecca for the Farewell Pilgrimage in the last year of his life.[39]

Although Suhaylī serves as transmitter rather than originator of this symbolic way of interpreting events of Muḥammad's life vis-à-vis the position of the prophets in the heavens, a similar type of typological allegorical interpretation resonates with the way others from the region, especially western contemplatives such as Ibn Barrajān, come to view the story of Muḥammad's ascension as revealing esoteric truths for those who can unlock its mysteries.

CHAPTER FOUR.

Intertextual Qurʾān and Prophetic Reports: Ibn Barrajān

As we have seen previously, Qurʾān commentary (*tafsīr*) on key passages from the Star chapter (Q 53:1–18) and the Night Journey verse (Q 17:1) became the touchstone for later Muslims to explore interpretations and examine retellings of Muḥammad's otherworldly journey, and mystical commentaries of the Qurʾān such as one finds with the pair of works composed by the important contemplative scholar from al-Andalus, Ibn Barrajān (d. 536/1141), are no exception. In these two separate works of Qurʾān exegesis, largely directed toward his community of his fellow mystics and those who follow the Masarran technique of symbolically "crossing over" (*iʿtibār*) to contemplation of the divine through creation,[1] Ibn Barrajān's exploratory mapping of narrative "terrains" pertaining to diverse dimensions of the *miʿrāj* story sketches out some intriguing esoteric details building on the framework of outlines provided in the ascension-related reports known from the first centuries of Islamic history. Yet as we shall see, new narremes that had not been seen in the hadith reports circulating in the earliest centuries also began to appear in Ibn Barrajān's commentaries. As a survey of his exegetical discussions of the legend of Muḥammad's otherworldly journeys will make plain, the terrain that Ibn Barrajān explores ranges beyond the level of most Qurʾān or hadith commentary that one typically might have previously associated with the word "mystical."

For instance, given the polemical context of the fifth-/eleventh- and sixth-/twelfth-century al-Andalus described in chapter 2, resulting in debates over Muḥammad's status vis-à-vis other figures in the prophetic tradition, an illustration of Ibn Barrajān's wide-ranging "mystical" horizon composed at least partially in answer to that challenge might be seen in the following summary that he includes in his discussion of the Night Journey verse (Q 17:1) to elucidate some of the signs that the Prophet witnessed that night:

On His saying, "In order to show him some of our signs" (Q 17:1)

[God] intends — and [God] is most knowing — the signs (*al-āyāt*) that he showed him between the two *masjid*s:

[1] On the way, in the [broad] land there was a sweet-smelling wind, then on the narrow land was a rancid-smelling wind. Gabriel told [Muḥammad] regarding the first, "It is the land of the Garden [of Paradise]," and regarding the second, "It is the land of Jahannam";

[2] and what he showed him about the one from the Jews who called him, then the caller from the Christians, then the woman clothed in finery and jewelry who called him to the point that she almost overcame him;

[3] and Gabriel's bringing him the two cups, one with wine and the other with milk; the first cup, of wine, [representing] going astray, the cup of the milk [representing] innate nature (*al-fiṭr*), which is al-Islam;

[4] and his encounter with Moses, standing in his grave, praying liturgical prayer; and Jesus, in a site between the two mosques, [also] praying; and their commissioning him with his community (*umma*);

[5] and his encounter with Abraham beneath a tree, surrounded by more children than he had ever seen before;

[6] and his seeing a man stoking the Fire [of Hellfire], who was Mālik, Keeper of the Fire;

[7] then his encounter with Jesus and Moses and the [other] prophets in the heavens according to their stations;

[8] and other things that God showed him on their path to Jerusalem.[2]

This apocalyptic tour both terrestrial and heavenly is remarkable for the way that it highlights Gabriel conveying knowledge of the unseen to Muḥammad throughout his special journey, not only in the way that communities of Jews and Christians seek to draw Muslims away from the correct path but also how much (but not all) of this knowledge revolves around the holy sites and current activities associated with sacred figures that many Jews and Christians likewise revere, such as Abraham, Moses, and Jesus. That Moses and Jesus appear in this report on the road to Jerusalem praying to God demonstrates that these spiritual forebearers are still active and present (if, in some cases, in their graves), engaged in the worship of God on Earth, just as the Muslim community will be enjoined at the culmination of the Prophet's heavenly journey with the establishment of the duty of worshipping God through the performance of the five daily liturgical prayers. Muḥammad will also go on to encounter these figures in their proper stations in the heavens above.[3] This tour of holy sites and multiple encounters with Abraham, Moses, and Jesus serves multiple functions in this specific narreme: an initiatic revelation of secret knowledge, a confirmation of Muḥammad's legacy as rightful heir to previous prophets (especially in point number four, above), and a polemic against those Jews and Christians who assert the superiority of their claims to these figures (and/or the relative status of these figures) over that of Muslims. Finally, it is worth noting that this report foregrounds the polemical dimension by including instances of propagandists from among the confessional communities of Jews and Christians who attempt to lead Muḥammad away from the proper path, and by extension attempt to lead his entire community astray, as Gabriel's subsequent explanations of these particular events make clear.

A similar report, in which Muḥammad not only encounters what I have elsewhere called "distractors" on the road to Jerusalem but also receives a terrestrial tour of sacred sites of the "holy land" associated with select previous prophets, has been examined by Vuckovic, who attributes the first instance of such a narreme to a much later exegetical work by the western commentator Muḥammad ibn Aḥmad al-Qurṭubī (d. 671/1273).[4] Earlier hadith collections as well as versions of the Ibn ʿAbbās tales, however, demonstrate that these types of "road to Jerusalem" scenes circulated as part of *miʿrāj* discourses much earlier than the time of al-Qurṭubī.[5] Ibn Barrajān's summary of these "signs," above, confirms that it had reached the attention of at least some circles of Iberian scholars by the sixth/twelfth century at the latest, where it unambiguously became part of the western debates over the significance of Muḥammad's journey.

As the above polemical anecdotes illustrate, like his predecessors, Ibn Barrajān's Qurʾān commentaries are undoubtedly informed by the hadith reports and stories that were in circulation in al-Andalus at the time. Nevertheless, Ibn Barrajān also pays special attention to qurʾānic language and the uniqueness of the nature of qurʾānic discourse in a way that is rarely seen in other extant *tafsir*s. Yousef Casewit, a contemporary expert on Ibn Barrajān's work, insists that we see in this technique the exegete's tendency to first and foremost interpret the Qurʾān through the Qurʾān itself via the Qurʾān's "structure" (*naẓm*), an exegetical approach in which proximate verses and chapters of the sacred scripture are interpreted as elucidating one another, even beyond the narrative unit of the sura.[6] Several fascinating examples of this technique appear in Ibn Barrajān's commentary on the key night journey and ascension passages from the Qurʾān, as the following review will illustrate.

Wisdom Deciphered, the Unseen Discovered

Especially in his later commentary titled *al-Īḍāḥ al-ḥikma* (*Wisdom Deciphered, The Unseen Discovered*),[7] Ibn Barrajān helps to explain the glorification of God conveyed at the outset of the Night Journey verse (the word *subḥān*, "glorified be," the very first word of Q 17:1) by contrasting that with references to inglorious sinful individuals and communities cited in verses from the end of the suras that preceded it (namely suras 14–16):

> When he mentioned in what was mentioned previously from Surat al-Naḥl (Q 16) and [Surat] al-Ḥijr (Q 15) and Surat Ibrahim (Q 14), [we find] what he recounted to us about the deniers of the message, their rejection of their messengers, and their debating with them. Also [he mentioned previously, in Q 15:28–44] what took place between Iblis — God curse him — out of scorn and pride, turning from the imitation of Adam, [refusing] the bowing down before [Adam] and [recognizing] him as *imām*, [Iblis] boasting regarding his nature, showing contempt for [Adam's] being created out of clay, through his saying: "*I am not one to bow down before a person whom you created out of dry clay, slime moulded into shape*" (Q 15:33). Great and exalted be he, [God] thus opens this sura with honoring and celebrating him (i.e.[,] the human being, Muḥammad, here acting in a role parallel to that of Adam as possessor of knowledge).[8]

The polemical context still shines through here, for there is an explicit rebuke against those who deny Muḥammad's prophetic role, just as previous prophets had been rejected by both human communities and by the devilish tempter figure Iblis. Ibn Barrajān reaches this conclusion by employing the technique of exploring the Qur'ān's "structure" (*naẓm*) in reading 17:1 in light of passages from the suras that precede it in the written *musḥaf*. Connecting the meaning of the verses from the end of immediately proximate suras with the opening verses of Q 17 is something that one rarely sees in premodern exegesis on the Night Journey verse, perhaps because the sura in general, and this verse in particular, is often treated as an independent unit of analysis. This idea of a broadened understanding of the meaning of the initial "glorified be" at the opening of the Night Journey verse, then, may then be understood as an intriguing contribution by Ibn Barrajān to the exegesis of Q 17:1, an understanding that emerges from the interreligious polemical context in which he lived.[9]

Ibn Barrajān devotes the vast majority of his exegesis of the first eighteen verses of the Qur'ān's Star chapter (Sura 53, *al-Najm*) in his shorter "minor" commentary titled *al-Īḍāḥ* to exploring aspects of the story of the night journey and ascension in something of a narrative chronological order.[10] In proceeding roughly chronologically, our exegete tends not to present entire hadith reports in the manner of Ṭabarī's *tafsīr* from two centuries previous,[11] nor to offer a single composite story in the manner of Ibn Isḥāq's *sīra* (as transmitted in the recension of Ibn Hishām). Instead, Ibn Barrajān provides an exegesis of more discrete narremes from disparate hadith reports, fragments of narrative that he strings together in a logical sequence to form something of an episodic and fragmentary composite tale, whose telling he frequently interrupts to explore some dimension that he wishes to bring to the attention of his audience. In this shorter Qur'ān commentary by Ibn Barrajān, the esoteric dimension of these narrative interruptions appears early in the narrative sequence presented as exegesis to the opening verses of Q 53, shortly after Ibn Barrajān describes how Muḥammad related the story to his companions about his "sleeping that night [of the ascension] at the Ḥijr," at which point the angels arrive to gather him for his remarkable journey. The angels who come to the Prophet identify him as distinguishable from his companions because he is "one of the three, between the [other] two," a detail that Ibn Barrajān explains through three separate levels of "inner interpretation" (*ta'wīl*):

> As for his saying in the other [previous report], "One of the two [angelic] figures said to his companion, 'one of the three, between two men,'" the [first] inner meaning of it — and God knows best — refers to [Muḥammad's] being between two truth-speakers, Abu Bakr and 'Umar, who were also the two long-lived [elders].
>
> [Second,] from another perspective, additionally there is his being — I mean his command (*amr*[a]*-hu*) and its [legal] establishment (*shar'*[a]*-hu*), between two Mahdist (*mahdiyya*) caliphates: First, the rightly-guided caliphate (*al-khilāfa al-rāshida*): the caliphate of all of the companions (*khilāfat al-ṣaḥāba . . . ajma'īn*), about which God said of the one who speaks about it, "*God promises the ones who believe among you, and those who do good deeds, that you will seek their viceregency* [or 'will lead them'] *in the earth*" (Q 24:55).
>
> Then there is the second Mahdist caliphate, which God named in his saying, "O you who believe, the one among you who turns away from his religion, God will bring a folk whom he loves and who will love him" (Q 5:54). The Messenger of God said, "This command (*al-amr*) will still be 'apparent' (*ẓāhir*) . . ." — or he said will remain "standing" (*qā'im*) — "until there follows twelve caliphs, all of them from the Quraysh." Six or five [of

> these righteous caliphs] have preceded [our times], and there remain from them six or seven.
>
> [Third,] from yet another perspective, [this anecdote about the angel saying, "one of the three, between two"] refers to [Muḥammad's] being between the two comings [to Earth] of Jesus son of Mary, the servant of God and his messenger.
>
> Each of these [contains] a truth (*ḥaqq*) of his existence. The being of both of the angels resembled that of Jesus son of Mary, informing [the Prophet] about him. It was the first [of them] who said, [in the words of Jesus,] "*O people of Israel, I am a messenger of God to you, speaking truly about what you possess of the Torah and good news of a messenger who will come after me, whose name is Aḥmad.*" (Q 61:6).[12]

Intriguingly, Ibn Barrajān interprets this seemingly minor detail about the arrival of the angels into Muḥammad's presence on that special night, drawn from select hadith reports about the beginning of the Prophet's otherworldly journey, by elaborating three different esoteric ways, some with obvious political connotations. The first interpretation places Muḥammad among his close companions Abū Bakr and ʿUmar, whose status is elevated in Ibn Barrajān's exegesis by labeling them both as *ṣiddiqīn*, "those who attest to the truth." This formulation expands the honorific often applied to Abū Bakr, *al-ṣiddiq*, to his caliphal successor ʿUmar b. al-Khattāb, thus underscoring Sunnī claims for their rightful leadership of the Muslim community after Muḥammad's death over and against the Shīʿī claims for ʿAlī and his descendants.

Ibn Barrajān's second interpretation of the esoteric meaning of the statement of the angels, "one of the three, between two," claims that Muḥammad symbolically rests between two groups of divinely-guided "Mahdi" figures, the first representing the earliest "rightly guided" caliphs of whom Abū Bakr and ʿUmar led the way, and the second representing a caliphate of Muslim messianic figures yet to come. Intriguingly, with the assertion that "six or five [of these righteous caliphs] have preceded [our times], and there remain from them six or seven," Ibn Barrajān apparently voices a critique of the reigning al-Murābiṭ (Almoravid) Muslims in the West, and potentially even his support for the revivalist claims of those Muslims who oppose them (e.g., leaders of the al-Muwaḥḥid / Almohad movement that was rising from the south). He comes to this intriguing — and dangerously subversive — political position by drawing on two qurʾānic verses and applying them to his contemporary context, arguing that God has sent this new group of leaders to replace the corrupt rule of those who have turned away from Islam (Q 24:55 and 5:54 as excerpted above). As Casewit argues, the numbers six and seven are especially significant for Ibn Barrajān as representing something akin to perfection or the completion of a cycle of time,[13] so one need not read his use of number symbolism here as necessarily drawing on Shīʿī numerology (e.g., whether Fāṭimid Ismāʿīlī, or else Imāmī, in light of Ibn Barrajān's model of there being twelve righteous leaders preceding the eschaton). That being said, his esoteric interpretation of this detail from the story of Muḥammad's night journey does indicate his view about the age in which he lived as representing a pivotal one, led by a righteous messianic "Mahdi" who ushers in the second half of the age (sixth or seventh out of twelve) leading to the approach of the expected end of times.

Ibn Barrajān presents his third and final esoteric interpretation of the narreme of the angels identifying the Prophet as "one of the three, between two," with the idea that it refers to the Prophet Muḥammad being positioned after the first prophetic mission of Jesus on Earth and before Jesus's messianic return on the last day to restore order and justice in the world. The idea that Jesus will return to the world to play a messianic role at the end of times is widely accepted by mainstream Muslims, despite many non-Muslims being unaware of this. What remain less conventional in Ibn Barrajān's third esoteric point, however, are (1) the highlighting of Muḥammad's place as identified by angels from the beginning of his prophetic career as significantly positioned between these two "comings" of Jesus; and (2) the linking of the two comings of Jesus, along with the two companions sleeping near Muḥammad, together with the two angels who arrive to collect Muḥammad for his journey. In this scene, the angels serve symbolically to "embody" and make present Jesus and his enunciation regarding the subsequent mission of Muḥammad by speaking prophetic words attributed to Jesus in the Qurʾān.

According to Ibn Barrajān, each of these esoteric levels of interpreting this brief detail from the start of the night journey narrative represents "a truth" (*ḥaqq*), a pivotal concept in his cosmology, for different ideations of it relate to the ways in which the divinity becomes manifest in creation, and the ways in which creation serves to reveal or point to the divinity, as we shall explore further in what follows.[14] The precise intra- and interreligious dimensions of the above anecdote about the three ways of interpreting the angelic statement about Muḥammad being "one of the three, between two," connected to his situatedness "in the middle" of these two human, prophetic, and/or otherworldly "guides," must remain somewhat conjectural at this point. Given the references to messianic speculations and connecting some Muslim leaders of his contemporary age with the approach of the eschaton, there are undoubtedly political dimensions. Nevertheless, suffice it for us to note at this stage how Ibn Barrajān offers his mystical *ta'wīl* (esoteric commentary) of this single small narrative element from the story of the night journey to develop his ideas about Muḥammad's centrality to this cosmological drama, and the Prophet's relationship to the awaited dawning of a messianic age.

Reminder of Understandings

Another way to get a sense of how Ibn Barrajān approaches the telling of the story of Muḥammad's night journey and ascension is to examine the way that he concisely unpacks the essence of the story in his earlier and lengthier "major" commentary, *Tanbīh al-afhām* (*Reminder of Understandings*):

> In what is sound [hadith] from the Messenger of God, it is said that he "rode Burāq, with Gabriel going with him, to Jerusalem." He said, "I tied al-Burāq with the ring that the prophets used, and then I entered the place of prayer, and I performed two cycles of liturgical prayer . . ." [a report that continues all the way] to his saying, "I was brought [up] via the ladder (*al-mi'rāj*)." And he described it and recalled that he ascended on it to the heavens, one by one, up to what was raised up above that.[15]

In this brief paragraph, Ibn Barrajān summarizes the entire journey in a few sentences, making it clear that the journey to Jerusalem and the ascension up into the heavens and beyond — to a site not specified here but asserted elsewhere in this same commentary as the location where the Prophet heard the "scratching of the pens" — were part of the very same event. That the matter is more complex than one single composite journey, however, Ibn Barrajān goes on to insist in the "caveat" or "reminder" (*tanbīh*)[16] section that immediately follows this opening paragraph, which raises the idea that Muḥammad experienced the combined journey to Jerusalem and ascent up through the heavens on more than one occasion.[17] This idea of multiple ascensions deserves greater scholarly attention, since in the formative period of Islamic history, most Sunnī scholars insist that the combined night journey and ascension must have taken place on the same evening at the exact same time of Muḥammad's prophetic career.

At this point, it is sufficient to note that by way of explanation of the brief paragraph that he offers above, Ibn Barrajān unpacks the idea of the "signs" (*ayāt*) shown to the Prophet on his journey(s) as similarly being multiple, ranging from his encounters with different individuals on the road to Jerusalem[18] to his vision of the different prophets in their stations to his witnessing of several signs in the uppermost heavens: "the Frequented House, the Garden and the Fire, [the river] *al-Kawthar* and what is there, the highest *Malakūt* (celestial "realm of power"), the Lote Tree of the Boundary and what covered it, and what [God] taught him and '*revealed to*' him [there of] '*what he revealed*.'"[19] Having invoked the Prophet's encounter with God in the ultimate climax of his ascent, the author then diverges into a long excursus into the intricate theological discussions regarding whether or not God can be seen, whether Muḥammad in fact saw God on his journey(s), and if so in what fashion, a debate that provoked controversy even in the formative period of Muslim exegesis.

Looking beyond such intellectual debates, however intriguing they might be, let us now turn to a broader examination of select passages from Ibn Barrajān's "major" commentary that illustrate some of his most distinctive and unique interpretations of the meaning of the Prophet's otherworldly journey(s). Recall that the *Tanbīh* is the first of the two extensive mystical Qur'ān commentaries that he composed. While not every verse of the Qur'ān receives Ibn Barrajān's exegetical attention in this commentary, the Night Journey verse (Q 17:1) and the opening verses of the Star chapter (Q 53:1–18) both elicit in-depth exegesis, not only separately but also together. That is, through the technique of understanding the "Qur'ān through the Qur'ān" first and foremost, Ibn Barrajān's discussion of one of these passages inevitably leads to his discussion of elements from the other as well. The commentary on both focuses on some traditional areas of exegetical inquiry: the meaning of key terms from the verses, the important hadith reports that help guide the believer's understanding of the central verses, and the meaning of the passages in relation to their surrounding qur'ānic contexts. In addition to these expected areas of inquiry, Ibn Barrajān takes up some less common themes, such as the esoteric analysis of select key terms and phrases from these central verses, understandings that frequently spring from his more contemplative orientation.

When it comes to the meaning of key terms, one can see how Ibn Barrajān focuses on key words at the start of each of the two passages, words that he considers especially worthy of mystical exegesis. The first term of the Night Journey verse, "glorified be" (*subḥān*, Q 17:1), and also the initial word from the first verse of the Star chapter after which it derives its name, "the star" (*al-najm*, Q 53:1), serve as good examples.[20] In both cases, Ibn Barrajān presents multiple possible interpretations of the respective key term, and he advances a preferred interpretation and understanding that he defends through references to other passages from the Qur'ān, as well as by allusions to pre-Islamic poetry. For instance, with regard to the Arabic term *al-najm*, Ibn Barrajān explains that while it could be taken at face value to mean "the star" or another heavenly body, the word also might refer to a portion of the Qur'ān (as opposed to the work as a whole) sent down at a particular moment, or else "shooting flame" (*shihāb*^un *thāqib*^un) used to repel unwelcome attempts at eavesdropping on heavenly voices, an activity the Qur'ān links to certain rebellious figures ("satans," see Q 37:7–10, also Q 67:5).[21] This secondary meaning that stems from his technique of attempting to read the Qur'ān through the Qur'ān, although not Ibn Barrajān's preferred understanding in this case, helps to underscore the contrast between those rejected from hearing heavenly voices and the great favor that the Prophet receives when hearing the "scratching of the pens" (*ṣarīf al-aqlām*) at the highest stage of his ascension.[22]

Ibn Barrajān makes frequent use of hadith reports as part of his early qur'ānic exegesis in the *Tanbīh*. For example, in unpacking the qur'ānic reference "He revealed to his servant what he revealed" (Q 53:10), he again cites a hadith reference to the "scratching of the pens," and immediately follows it with the idea that is even more common in the ascension reports, namely that at the climax of the journey God imposed on Muḥammad and his community the duty to observe the liturgical prayers fifty times per day.[23] This, then, offers an example of how the exegete draws on details from select hadith reports to help explain the meaning of qur'ānic references. Another example appears somewhat later in the *Tanbīh* where our author unpacks the ambiguous qur'ānic phrase "When the Lote Tree was covered by what covered" (Q 53:16) by citing descriptions of what covers this heavenly tree as portrayed in select hadith reports, ranging from the appearance of sapphire on the tree, or a green *rafraf*, and/or angels on each of its leaves.[24] For Ibn Barrajān, the "vision" granted to the Prophet in the vicinity of this heavenly tree takes on special prominence in his later "minor" exegesis *Īḍāḥ*, perhaps because it serves as a touchstone for his idea of the discovery of signs or manifestations of the divinity through God's creation, which we will examine shortly. Here in the earlier "major" commentary known as *Tanbīh*, the focus rests more on the idea of the tree as a site where Muḥammad draws extremely close to the divinity, and the meaning of such "nearness" becomes the main focus of the exegete's attention.

Illustrating how Ibn Barrajān interprets the night journey and ascension passages from the Qur'ān together to illuminate one another, our contemplative presents in *Tanbīh* an esoteric understanding of the Night Journey verse (Q 17:1) through reading it together with his discussion of two different degrees of proximity, both invoked by the qur'ānic phrase drawn from the Star chapter: "he drew near and descended / and was the distance of two bows or closer" (Q 53:8–9). Perhaps to signal entry into this mystical type of exegesis,[25] Ibn Barrajān invokes the verb "crossing over" (*'abara*) in this context, writing that "the Qur'ān 'crosses over' about [describing Muḥammad's] state in the Truth's saying, '*Then he drew near*' in nearness '*and descended.*'"[26] Giving symbolic meaning to the concept of drawing near, he explains that this passage points to two distinct types of mystical nearness that must be distinguished. The first type of nearness, he asserts, is the "nearness of a creature" (*qurb khalqa*), a physical nearness that nevertheless describes being as close as two physical entities can get: "closer to a being than the spirit of that being [to its body], closer to the eye than the faculty of sight, closer than the spirit to its carrier, or than the life of living creature to the living creature."[27] These comparisons are reminiscent of the qur'ānic phrase ascribed to God when the divinity describes his nearness to the human with the phrase, "We are closer to him than [his] jugular vein" (Q 50:16). Ibn Barrajān does not draw on this particular verse in this context but instead offers a series of metaphysical and philosophical metaphors of extreme and almost incomprehensible nearness. He uses those metaphors to differentiate the first type of nearness, *qurb khalqa*, from a second yet even closer type of spiritual nearness, the "nearness of sainthood" (*qurb wilāya*). This second virtually ineffable state of nearness describes a mystical closeness that can no longer be invoked through concise metaphors but only alluded to more elliptically through a pair of reports that fall into the category of "sacred sayings" (hadith *qudsī*),[28] two sayings that Ibn Barrajān here invokes unconventionally to explain this ultimate nearness:

> The nearness of sainthood outstrips the first type of description of nearness until it crosses over from it/him (ʿabara ʿan-*hu*), through the saying of the Truth: "Indeed I am present, conquering the heart of the servant who remembers me [through *dhikr*] until I become the hearing through which he hears, the sight through which he sees, the hand through which he grasps, and the leg through which he walks." Also [it outstrips the first type of description of nearness] until he says: "Son of Adam, I was ill and you did not visit me, hungry and you did not feed me, thirsty and you did you not give me to drink, naked and you did not clothe me. . . . As for you, had you done that for my servant, you would have done it for me."[29]

The first of the divine sayings cited in the above description is a variant of the "sacred saying" called *ḥadīth al-nawāful* ("the hadith of supererogatory devotions"), for most commonly it opens with the idea that the servant draws near to the deity through such devotions, and as a consequence, the deity becomes "the hearing through which he hears, the seeing through which he sees," et cetera. This first sacred utterance became of favorite of early eastern Sufi descriptions of some of the highest states of mystical experience, but it was not as common for these early Sufis to draw on this report in their understanding of the verse "he drew near and descended / and was the distance of two bows or closer" (Q

53:8–9) the way Ibn Barrajān does here. The second sacred utterance is considered a standard hadith report related to Muḥammad in the Islamic tradition, one that also closely echoes a passage in the Christian New Testament (Matt. 25:35–45) about how the treatment of the least of God's servants on Earth reflects how one treats the divinity as well.[30] In both examples of sacred sayings that Ibn Barrajān cites to explain Q 53:8–9, the nearness between servant and deity becomes so extreme that a mystical "slippage" between the two occurs, with the one entity (servant and/or deity) actually or metaphorically appearing to stand in the place of the other. Ibn Barrajān elaborates further about this second higher mystical state of nearness: "One does not mention place nor extension to it, rather in this [mystical state] is the cutting off of distance."[31] In other words, this more exalted type of proximity is not a function of spatial location (i.e., extreme physical closeness) but rather involves an approach to a type of mystical nearness in which the very idea of location or distance could be said to no longer apply. Although he does not invoke the concept of "union" here, nevertheless, at such a level of sainthood, the boundaries between what had appeared to be discrete entities comes to be realized as perspectival, and the actions carried out by or upon God's servant are said to reflect directly on the divinity. At such a level of nearness, the whole notion of physical distance or proximity becomes virtually meaningless, or at least paradoxical.

Ibn Barrajān elaborates on this idea even further in his commentary, explaining that in describing such an exalted state of mystical nearness, at this point there appears "the recollection of the mounts: namely Burāq, the ladder and the ascent, the opening of the heavens one after the other, the proceeding to the Lote Tree of the Boundary, then advancing to the heights to the appearance, and [finally] the 'place of sitting.'"[32] In other words, when the saint achieves the supreme level of nearness alluded to by Muḥammad's reaching the stage described by the qur'ānic verses "he drew near and descended / and was the distance of two bows or closer" (Q 53:8–9), such an utter nearness forces the recollection of the diverse means that conveyed the Prophet (or the saint, more generally) on the journey leading up to such a state of proximity. What we have here is an overview of the Prophet's mystical ascension itinerary as a whole, broken down into discrete thematic units based on the particular "mounts" that carry the Prophet along on his journey, culminating in the one that brings him to the "place of the sitting" (*mustawā*) at the heavenly tree or throne in the company of the divinity.[33] For Ibn Barrajān, this ultimate "place of sitting" serves as a mystical state that the exalted "nearness of sainthood" (*qurb wilāya*) causes one to recollect. In this very culmination of his ascension, the Prophet alone sits with the divine presence, and hears the voice of God as it addresses him directly without intermediary.

While the above passage demonstrates that such mystical understandings of select details from the Night Journey verse and the opening verses of the Star chapter do appear in *al-Tanbīh*, they come to the fore even more prominently in Ibn Barrajān's later and shorter ("minor") Qur'ān commentary known as *Īḍāḥ al-ḥikma*. Casewit's claim that the *Īḍāḥ* was likely composed for a specialized audience of Ibn Barrajān's contemplative followers in al-Andalus[34] gains support from even a casual glance at his exegesis of the Night Journey verse in this "minor" commentary. After citing the majority of Q 17:1, "Glory to the one who caused his servant to journey by night from the sacred place of prayer to the furthest place of prayer whose precincts we have blessed in order to show him some of our signs," Ibn Barrajān begins his exegesis in *Īḍāḥ* with an exploration of the first word in the verse, "glorified," which evokes for him the entire Neoplatonic cycle of emanation/descent followed by return/ascent:

> God, great be his greatness and exalted his highness and his subject, glorifies himself (*sabbaḥa . . . nafsa-hu*) when he mentions his servant through his night journey with him, out of wonder at his exalted subject:
>
> How he created him from clay, then a drop of "*despicable water*" (Q 77:20) then "*shaped him*" (Q 32:9), and prepared him with a spirit from him, until he enabled him for this immensity, "*the angels descending*" with "*the spirit*" (Q 97:4) upon him from his "*command*" (*amr*) in order to warn and to proclaim good news about him, great be his greatness. He conveyed to him his command and prohibition (*amr-hu wa nahī-hi*), and "*caused him to journey by night*" to "*the furthest place of prayer*" (Q 17:1).
>
> Next, he caused him to ascend to the highest heaven, then on to "*the Lote Tree of the Boundary*" (*sidrat al-muntahā*) (Q 53:14), and caused him to enter "*the Garden of the Refuge*" (Q 53:15). [He continued to] raise him up, exalting him up to the [highest] "place of the sitting" (*aʿlā bi-hi ilā al-mustawā*), and [there] "*he revealed to*" him, "*his servant, what he revealed*" (Q 53:10). So glorified (*subḥāna-hu*) and exalted be he, "to him is the praise in the after world/End (*al-ākhira*)" (Q 34:1) and at the first. To him is the fullness of wise sayings (*al-ḥikam*), at both the beginning as well as at the final limit (*al-muntahā*).[35]

The specifics of this myth of creation via emanation and return, and the esoteric technical vocabulary it employs, have already been surveyed by Casewit.[36]

While it is beyond the scope of this chapter to revisit the specific Neoplatonic outlines here, it remains crucial for our understanding of Ibn Barrajān's exegesis of Muḥammad's ascension to call attention to three key aspects of the above passage.

First, we see in the above selection that Ibn Barrajān draws on a variety of different verses to help explain this single word (*subḥān*) from a single verse of the Qur'ān (Q 17:1), illustrating again the concept of qur'ānic "hegemony" and giving preference to exegesis of "the Qur'ān via the Qur'ān." Second, an important theme that Ibn Barrajān draws out in this passage is the glorification of the human servant of God,[37] a concept he then uses to elaborate on the remarkable structuring (*naẓm*) of the Qur'ān and how the doubters who reject the veracity of Muḥammad's night journey could be seen as aligning themselves with the doubting of Adam on behalf of the satanic Iblis (e.g., in Q 15:33), and the doubters of the Prophet's wife 'Ā'isha when the latter was accused of infidelity (e.g., Q 24:16–18).[38] Third and most importantly, as we shall see shortly, Ibn Barrajān highlights the role of the divine command (*amr*) in the above Neoplatonic passage. Here and elsewhere the divine command (*amr*) has a pivotal function both in the creation of everything apart from God at the very beginning of time (a sending downward), as well as in the return of the ascending hero as a foreshadowing of the last days (a sending upward). In nonmystical exegesis of the Night Journey verse, it is rare to encounter an exegete offering such wide-ranging qur'ānic references, brought together in service of explaining this single touchstone verse in such an incredible depth of meaning, a fact that offers further evidence for the thesis that the *Īḍāḥ* was composed for an exclusive audience of Ibn Barrajān's advanced mystical pupils, likely delivered in the course of his private oral teaching sessions.[39]

The Esoteric Meaning of Muslim Prayer

The bulk of the commentary in the *Īḍāḥ* regarding the meaning of the opening verses of the Star chapter (Q 53:1–18) is comprised of a series of paragraphs commenting on different fragments of *mi'rāj*-related hadith reports, and one of the noteworthy themes that Ibn Barrajān explores in these passages is the connection between Muḥammad's ascension and the liturgical prayer of believers.[40] Of course, many Muslim exegetes make such a connection between the *mi'rāj* and *ṣalāt* on a surface level, since most reports describe the Prophet at the highest point of the ascension receiving the duty for the community to observe the five daily prayers (originally assigned as fifty). As recounted by Abu al-Ḥasan Hujwiri (d. ca. 465/1072), however, some Nishapuri Sufis had argued for a more intimate connection between ascension and prayer, sometimes under the general rubric of an alleged prophetic hadith, "Each liturgical prayer (*namāz*) is an ascension for me," or the broader idea that "prayer is the ascension of the believers," that is, that through praying *ṣalāt* a regular Muslim symbolically rises into the presence of God just as Muḥammad ascended to God during the *mi ʿrāj*.[41] Ibn Barrajān builds on this early mystical idea and takes it a step further, offering a series of exegetical observations on the symbolic dimensions of the different steps not only during but also preceding *ṣalāt*, as well as the deep direct correspondences between the *mi ʿrāj* and *ṣalāt* that the mystic may perceive in the interior reality of the ritual.

With Ibn Barrajān's nuanced elucidation of the prayer ritual as a symbolic link to connect the experience of the common Muslim and the mystical Muslim alike with the otherworldly journey of the Prophet (when the ritual is understood properly), it should not come as a surprise that he "bookends" the start and finish of a long section of commentary on this theme by presenting two different versions of the report in which Gabriel teaches Muḥammad the call to prayer (*adhān*).[42] In the hadith report from which this discussion springs, the divine voice responds to nearly every phrase of the formulaic phrases that ring out in most Muslim-majority countries five times per day. Ibn Barrajān's inclusion of this fascinating report about the origins of the *adhān*, which also happens to appear near the end of the discussion of the *mi ʿrāj* in Qāḍī ʿIyāḍ's *Shifā ʾ*, gives further support for the idea that this narreme, which would come to be rejected later by other Sunnī Muslim traditionists as what they consider to be an unreliable "forged" report, was generally accepted by these western fifth-/eleventh-century Sunnī scholars as being fairly reliable. Indeed, Ibn Barrajān never questions the validity of this or the other hadith reports he cites in service of interpreting the mystical meaning of Muḥammad's journey, nor does he pay more than the scantest attention to chains of hadith transmission (the authenticating *isnad* chains that precede the text of each report). As with his contemporary Qāḍī ʿIyāḍ, Ibn Barrajān seems to suggest that the above report merits inclusion in a discussion of the story of Muḥammad's ascension because it serves a specific purpose. For Ibn Barrajān, there is no doubt that each of the elements of liturgical prayer, from the call to prayer and pre-*ṣalāt* ablutions to the different bodily postures in each phase of the prayer ritual (*rak ʿa*), work together to make the *ṣalāt* one of the key lenses through which our exegete views esoteric meanings in the story of Muḥammad's night journey and ascension.

For example, Ibn Barrajān compares the opening of Muḥammad's heart near the start of the night journey to the ritual cleansing that every Muslim makes as part of *ṣalāt* preparations, leading to a state of ritual purity (*tahāra*) that is a precondition for properly performed liturgical prayers:

> The opening of [the Prophet's] chest and the cleansing of the heart is equivalent to the commanded purity [*tahāra,* i.e., prior to liturgical prayer], in his saying, "When you arise for liturgical prayer, wash your faces . . ." to his saying [at the end of the same verse], "God does not wish to make a difficulty for you, but to make you [ritually] pure, in order that you might receive his blessing, and perhaps that you will be thankful." (Q 5:6). In jurisprudence (*al-fiqh*) it is said that the purpose for us in [entering a state of] purity for liturgical prayer is [for the sake of achieving] a purity of the 'inner' (*al-bāṭin*). The opening of the chest renews repentance, and the directing of the intention.[43]

In a fairly straightforward fashion, Ibn Barrajān draws on the process that his Muslim audience would find familiar, the ritual washing of minor ablutions before each *ṣalāt* session in order to approach prayers in a state of inner as well as outer ritual purity, and uses that embodied experience of his followers to explain the reason why the angels opened Muḥammad's chest and washed his heart before taking him on his miraculous journey. Moreover, he claims that this initial process of repentance and the setting of one's intentions (*nīya*) are common to both. In other words, Ibn Barrajān's exegesis makes literal the idea that Muḥammad's ascension and a believer's prayers follow the very same familiar ritual pattern.

In another passage, Ibn Barrajān goes on to address the ritual ablutions before prayer, known as *wuḍū'*, even more specifically: "The ascending to the highest heavens [itself] is a metaphor for the saying of the Messenger of God: 'The one who cleans oneself in ablution . . .' — and it says in another [transmission], 'the one who makes himself ritually pure.'"[44] In what follows in this section of his minor commentary, Ibn Barrajān emphasizes that the performance of liturgical prayer bears a direct connection to Muḥammad's night journey: "When he was made ritually pure, Burāq was brought to him; he rushed to the [furthest] place of prayer and prayed two cycles in it."[45] In this context, our exegete implies that part of the purpose of the speed with which Burāq "rushes" the Prophet to Jerusalem — often depicted in the hadith reports as traveling at the speed of sight — has to do with preserving the Prophet's state of ritual purity for the sake of his liturgical prayers at that distant place of prayer (*masjid al-aqṣā*).

Clearly for Ibn Barrajān, then, not only is there no question about whether or not Muḥammad stopped in Jerusalem during his journey, as one sometimes finds in other exegetes, but beyond this idea, there is also no doubt that he prayed liturgical prayers there, a detail that Ibn Barrajān draws special significance from given the way he comes to understand *ṣalāt* as the symbolic center of the Prophet's otherworldly journey. Here, as one finds in a limited number of hadith reports, Muḥammad prays alone in Jerusalem, not leading the other prophets in liturgical prayer as appears in other reports, and as comes to be widely accepted in most later composite versions of the tale. For Ibn Barrajān, Muḥammad may have prayed by himself in Jerusalem, but he led the prophets in prayer near the culmination of the ascension, at the Lote Tree of the Boundary. Our exegete here symbolically links this gathering for liturgical prayer at the Lote Tree with the apocalyptic gathering that will take place with the second coming of Jesus.[46] As we shall see in what follows, the Lote Tree and the events that transpire there receive a great deal of exegetical attention in Ibn Barrajān's commentaries, and this may have something to do with the concept shared among many of the Muʿtabirūn mystics that one's contemplation of the created world points to the divinity. The most crucial point to notice in our examination of passages from the "minor" commentary *Īḍāḥ*, however, is how Ibn Barrajān draws a direct connection between the preparation for and performance of liturgical prayer on the one hand, and the distinct stages of Muḥammad's miraculous journey on the other.

While he focuses on other details when discussing the intermediate stages of Muḥammad's journey after Jerusalem and during his passage through the seven heavens, he highlights the theme of liturgical prayer again when discussing the Prophet's experience at the apex of his heavenly ascent:

> The [highest] "place of sitting" (*al-mustawā*) — and God knows best — is like the position of liturgical prayer, in terms of what is there. The creature "sits" in what is there, uniting in what it is upon its expanses among the favorer and favored, the one who arrived and the one to whom one arrives, the high [and] the highest, regarding whom "*there is none like unto him*" (Q 42:11). In this way [should we understand] the one praying in God's presence, in what is required of him in that condition. As [God] says, "*Undertake the liturgical prayer . . .*" (Q 27:3). He seeks to hear, through the hearing of his heart, the praising of the speech of his lord upon the recitation of the Qurʾān, and [also to hear] his remembrance of him [that likewise follows] his remembrance of him — he, his lord, as he stands in his presence — just as he loves his lord and seeks to please him. It is from hearing the scratching of the pens and what [took place] there that the liturgical prayers were required, and the inspiration inspired (Q 53:10).[47]

Here Ibn Barrajān makes an explicit link between the cycle of positions an ordinary believer goes through as s/he performs liturgical prayer and the exalted position of "sitting" that Muḥammad found himself in when arriving in the divine presence. At such a high station, the Prophet received the duty for the Muslim community to pray fifty times per day, a duty that God subsequently reduced to five (whose performance nevertheless merits the reward of fifty). The fact that this duty was revealed in this climax of the *mi ʿrāj* provides Ibn Barrajān with sufficient evidence to make the connection between the Prophet's ascension and the liturgical prayers of the rest of the Muslim community. In what immediately follows, he goes on to explain the symbolic connection between the key verses from the Star chapter of the Qur'ān and a number of the bodily postures a person assumes as part of liturgical prayer:

> The worshipper is standing in the presence of his lord in his prayer, just as was said previously, and that is his "*sitting*" (Q 53:6). Then "*he drew near*" (*danā*) (Q 53:8), this is the state of his bowing (*rukū ʿ*), and thus "*he descended*" (Q 53:8), which is his state of touching his head down (*sujūd*), "*and he was two bows or closer*" (Q 53:9), [meaning] the approach of the touching of the head down to the screen (the heavenly *hijāb*), and "*so draw near*" (Q 96:19), i.e.[,] drawing as close as the servant [Muḥammad] was to his lord in the touching down of the head.[48]

At the level of this highest "place of sitting" (*mustawā*), the Prophet hears the "scratching of the pens," presumably the writing out of God's commands (e.g., for the Muslims to perform their daily liturgical prayers) on the heavenly tablet, a phrase that appears at the climax of the ascension in a famous hadith report from Bukhārī's collection.[49] Ibn Barrajān connects this "hearing" at the highest stage of the ascension to Muḥammad receiving the duty for his community to observe the daily *ṣalāt* prayers on the one hand, and on the other, he connects it to the ordinary believer listening to the Qur'ān recitation during *ṣalāt* and seeking to hear God's voice: "He seeks to hear, through the hearing of his heart, the praising of the speech of his lord upon the recitation of the Qur'ān."[50] The interior effect of listening to the recitation of God's words in both situations, according to this mystical commentary, is particularly striking. One could argue that Ibn Barrajān's exegesis here takes the idea of the mystical saying that circulated in Khurasan and further east, that "liturgical prayer is the ascension of the believers," to its logical conclusion by connecting a series of details from the *ṣalāt* ritual with the exalted events that the Prophet experienced at the climax of his ascension.

Beyond simply connecting the body postures of the Muslim *ṣalāt* ritual to the Prophet's heavenly journey, Ibn Barrajān delves more deeply into the specifics of the *miʿrāj* story at this stage to elaborate on more hidden knowledge about the details of the heavenly liturgy, the classes of the highest of angels, and the writing down of the God's decree (*al-amr*) to perform the liturgical prayers. As mentioned previously, however, when Ibn Barrajān makes explicit reference to the actions of the divine command (*al-amr*), he also has its cosmic role in mind as this command participates in the boundary moments[51] of Neoplatonic creation: the sending down of the heavenly spirit that results in the creation of the cosmos, along with and the sending down of God's word through revelation; the upward return of God's creatures, including perhaps first and foremost the ascension of the Prophet, who represents the conduit of God's final and most complete revelation to the world; and the uniting of all being at the end of times, imagined as a day of reunion and reunification between the divine and the creation. Given the richness of this passage, I offer a translation of it here at some length:

> The Messenger of God used to say in his touching his head down (*sujūd*) [in liturgical prayer], and also perhaps during his bowing (*rukūʿ*): "Holy, glorified be the lord of the angels and the spirit (*al-rūḥ*)." What is above the Lote Tree of the Boundary is especially for the command (*al-amr*) and the spirit (*al-rūḥ*).[52] The command descends together with the angels, while the spirit [descends] to each angel. What is below the Lote Tree of the Boundary is the domain of the angels, the spirit, and the command for the present, until God comes together with his command, and what is below the heavens will [then] be the place for all creatures, angels, the spirit, and the command. "*The angels descend with the spirit, from his command, on whom he pleases of his servants*" (Q 16:2).
>
> The revelation through the spirit breathes out (*nafatha*) in the mind, discourse, and similar things,[53] while the revelation through the angel comes through the companionship of the spirit: "*The angels descend, the spirit upon them* [i.e., the angels], *by the permission of their lord* [*from every command*]" (Q 97:4);[54] "*Say: The spirit is from the command of my lord*" (Q 17:85), in other words, [it is] a subject of my lord. The angels are the elect (*khāṣṣa*) of God, while the spirit and the command are the elect of the elect. So as for the saying of the Messenger of God, "Holy, glorified . . . ," that refers to God, the highest of the high. He is the lord of the angels and the spirit, and moreover of all beings, since the creation was in the midst of the command and the spirit. The angels are "*the ones ar-*

> *rayed in rows*" (Q 37:165). They do not know [anything] except by his permission." (cf. Q 37:168–169). They are "*the ones who proclaim* [God's] *glory*" (Q 37:166). The Messenger of God said, "When we came to the Lote Tree of the Boundary, Gabriel said to me, 'At this spot stops the leader of the angels.'" (cf. Q 37:164)
>
> [Muḥammad] continued, "I was brought up [even higher in my ascension] until I appeared at the level in which I heard the scratching of the pens . . . ."[55] The sound of the scratching from the pens reflects the state (*al-ḥāl*) of their being used for writing. In that place, it is an allusion for the scratching of the command (*al-amr*) as it scratches. He scratches out a command and speaks it, confirming good deeds (*al-ḥasanāt*) and substituting them for evil ones, just as it was [established] previously in the Mother of the Book. That is the scratching of the pens, the state of their being written down. It is the speech of prophecies (*al-inbā*ʾ), [all] pointing toward an immense prophecy.[56]

After invoking a report in which the Prophet praises and worships God through the phrase "Holy and glorified be the lord" (and we will have more to say on this phrase shortly), in the above selection Ibn Barrajān draws on several different qurʾānic passages in order to explore the relationship between distinct heavenly powers: the spirit, the command, and the angels. The spirit and the command he identifies with the highest of the celestial beings that serve God (the "elect of the elect"). He states that they were present with God at the time of the creation, not equivalent to but resonating with both Christian conceptions of the Trinity and certain Neoplatonic ideas of the highest intellects that "spilled over" from highest to lowest at the beginning of time and thus reflect the descending "outflowing" movement of emanation in the creation of the universe. Ibn Barrajān insists that God remains lord and supreme over all, however, including the spirit and the command, which he insists are not themselves divine but rather some of the highest and most exalted of God's subjects. While both the spirit and the command originate in the highest realm beyond the Lote Tree, they descend from those heights together with the angels (on which he cites Q 97:4 and 17:85 as proof texts) to the realms below the Lote Tree, comprised of the lower heavens and earths that are inhabited by the rest of God's creation.

At this point, Ibn Barrajān intertextually draws on a series of verses about angels from a different part of the Qurʾān, the sura titled "Those Arranged in Rows" (Q 37), explaining how the angels, no matter how lofty, remain unambiguously subordinate to God. Angels, he says, each have their specific and known station (Q 37:164), illustrated here by the narreme common from the Ibn ʿAbbās ascension reports in which Gabriel informs Muḥammad that he cannot ascend any farther beyond the station of the Lote Tree.[57] Moreover, the angels are the ones said to be "arranged in rows" in order to worship God and "proclaim his glory" (Q 37:165–166). Furthermore, the text asserts that the angels themselves are ignorant of the divine decrees, and indeed ignorant of any other kinds of divine knowledge, possessing knowledge only of that which God allows them to know (a specific understanding of Q 37:168-–169).

Since the Prophet's heavenly journey involves his encounter with numerous groups of angels and celestial hierarchies, this discussion of the place of angels as being wholly subordinate to God is not completely unexpected. That being said, one wonders why Ibn Barrajān feels it so important to clarify to his audience of advanced students that the Prophet, when calling out "Holy and glorified be the lord" in the midst of his prayers, was praising God alone and no other being. That is, his specifying the divinity as the recipient of this adoration makes it seem as if, without this specification, there might be some danger that some of his students might misinterpret the intended recipient of the Prophet's expression of praise. Could there be some question of whether Muḥammad might have come to express such praise for one of the angels at the Lote Tree, erroneously interpreting the situation of seeing some of the highest of the angelic powers there and mistaking one of them for the divinity? In other words, might he have fallen victim to thinking there were "two powers in heaven," as was the sin ascribed to Rabbi ʾAḥer in 3 Enoch 16?[58] To avoid any idolatrous "association" (*shirk*) such as that, Ibn Barrajān proclaims, "So as for the saying of the Messenger of God, 'Holy, glorified . . . ,' that refers to God, the highest of the high."[59] My allusion here to the Jewish apocalyptic text of 3 Enoch as a potential subtext for Ibn Barrajān's statement is not accidental, since Muḥammad's expression of praise for God in this passage and elsewhere in *Īḍāḥ* is reminiscent of the hymn of praise that the angels sing in God's presence as recorded in *Isaiah* 6:3, "Holy, holy, holy." This famous phrase, known in Hebrew as the *qedushah*, often appears in the Jewish Hekhalot texts as part of the heavenly liturgy when the angels are depicted as worshipping God in the vicinity of the divine throne.[60] Given the intertextual language of ascent to the divine realms that he and other western authors shared during this period, I would contend that Ibn Barrajān might well be drawing on this type of Jewish (and Christian) trope from 3 Enoch or other similar Hekhalot texts, along with his intertextual allusions to verses from Q 37, to describe how Muḥammad worships together with the angels and highest of the heavenly host. Not guilty of the "two powers in heaven" error, Muḥammad is shown praising God together with all the rest of the heavenly powers precisely at this boundary moment at the Lote Tree, followed only by his reaching the level at which he hears the "scratching of the pens," which Ibn Barrajān seems to represent in this report as the climax of the Prophet's heavenly ascent.[61]

Let us briefly turn to a different but related passage, from another teaching session recorded elsewhere in his minor commentary, where Ibn Barrajān more explicitly connects Muḥammad's worshipful expression of glory to God together with the liturgy of the angels. He makes the following interpretive move through an exegesis of the central part of the opening verses from the Star chapter (Q 53:1–18), which in some other reports was the pretext for describing Muḥammad's journey not only up to but also beyond the limit of the Lote Tree:

> Or [in a different version], it is as [Muḥammad] said (in a hadith report): "Then he himself [i.e., Gabriel] took him to what 'crossed over' it, [referred to] in [God's] saying, "*Then he drew close and descended / and was a distance of two bows or closer*" (Q 53:8–9) together with his saying, "*taught to him by one of great power*" (Q 53:5). He taught him every language. Or perhaps among what he himself taught him was what to say or do [on each stage of the journey, the stages being]: [1] when he journeyed by night with him on Burāq, [2] when he ascended with him the steps of the ladders (*al-ma ʿārij*), [3] when he went with him to the Lote Tree of the Boundary, [4] [when] he proceeded further with him, ascending to the world of the spirit, then the [highest] "place of sitting" (*al-mustawā*), then to the closest approach (Q 53:8). . . . [Throughout] all of this was the glorification of the angels, "Glory, holy, lord of the angels and the spirit!" Perhaps this is an additional meaning of [God's] aforementioned saying, "*taught by one of great power and strength who sat* (*istawā*)." (Q 53:5–6).[62]

The worshipful song of the angels resembles but is not exactly equivalent to the *qedushah* here and in the other passages from *Īḍāḥ* cited above, and Ibn Barrajān offers it in this particular passage as one possible interpretation of the knowledge taught to the Prophet "by one of great power" (Q 53:5) during his heavenly journey. The identity of the one doing the teaching here is usually the angel Gabriel in most mainstream commentaries, but since the previous report argues that the latter was forced to stop at the Lote Tree, this passage initially leaves open the question of whether this allusion from Q 53:5 could refer to the divinity instead. Such an option is foreclosed in what immediately follows, however, where Ibn Barrajān makes clear that the knowledge conveyed to Muḥammad that night cannot be limited to the angelic liturgy alone:

> The Prophet elaborated [on the meaning of this verse in a hadith report]: "Gabriel '*taught him,*' then '*he sat* . . .' (Q 53:5–6) in knowledge, wisdom, prophecy, and in what he intended for him in what he desired from him in that. '*He* [Muḥammad] *sat* (*istawā*)' at the place of sitting (*al-mustawā*) where he was made to hear the scratching of the pens." The saying of the [divine] Truth indicates this: "*while he was on the highest horizon . . . he revealed to his servant what he revealed*" (Q 53:7, 10). In other words, everything that he revealed to him until he took him [i.e., until the day Muḥammad died], he revealed to him that very night in a compact (*muḥkam*) manner. Then gradually he apportioned it out in portions, just as he did with the Qur'ān.[63]

In this passage, Ibn Barrajān suggests that Muḥammad received the entirety of the knowledge that he would receive in his lifetime, the sum total not only of prophetic knowledge but also of hidden esoteric contemplative and/or mystical knowledge,[64] all in this single moment at the climax of his heavenly journey, even though its full and less condensed expression would continue to unfold for the rest of his life. This fullness of knowledge, which may relate to the knowledge of all that will transpire during the Prophet's lifetime, and even a greater scope of knowledge extending to all things in the universe,[65] might well be what Ibn Barrajān means at the end of the long passage quoted above when he refers to "the immense prophecy" that the Prophet receives in the highest of heavens through hearing the sound of the "scratching of the pens."[66] While Ibn Barrajān does not directly invoke in this passage the broader idea that Muḥammad was granted comprehensive knowledge of all things at the climax of his ascent, nor does he allude to the idea that Enoch received the totality of divine knowledge when transformed into the angel Metatron,[67] the context and subtext of his remarks suggests that he was well aware of such stories, and his understanding of the degree of "hidden" knowledge conveyed to Muḥammad on that evening was that it was truly capacious.

The Inner Journey

While there are many other mystical lenses that Ibn Barrajān employs in his commentary on Muḥammad's Night Journey and heavenly ascent, let us content ourselves with examining just one more as we move toward this chapter's conclusion, for the different ways he discusses the details surrounding the Lote Tree of the Boundary nicely illustrate the method of allegorical substitution that lies at the heart of his interpretive technique of mystical "crossing over" (*ta'bīr*).

We have already seen how for Ibn Barrajān the Lote Tree serves as the site of Muḥammad leading the other prophets and angels in liturgical prayer, but it also becomes for him a pivotal symbol that connects the outer journey of the ascending hero to God (the physical travel from the earth to the uppermost spheres of the heavenly realms) to the inner journey of the ascension to God that takes place within the body, and the return to a state of original oneness through both inner and outer journeys. Ibn Barrajān begins making a case for the connection between the Lote Tree on the one hand and a person's body on the other by arguing for a mystical linkage between the Arabic words for "lote tree" (*al-sidra*) and "chest" (*al-ṣadr*), even while recognizing that these two words begin with two different sibilant letters of the Arabic alphabet, *sīn* in the first case and *ṣod* in the second: "The word 'lote tree' (*al-sidra*) comes from [the word] 'chest' (*al-ṣadr*), for in our exposition of spiritual meaning, the difference between the letters *sīn* and *ṣad* do not concern us. Also, the nearness of the expression [of Lote Tree] crosses over [in mystical meaning] to that [other word], I mean 'the chest' (*al-ṣadr*), and the existence of what is found therein."[68] When articulating this same mystical association a second time in his exposition, he goes on to explain how the rivers at the base of the Lote Tree of the Boundary both flow upward and downward, not only implicitly drawing a parallel between those heavenly rivers and the flowing of blood from the chest upward and downward through the body but also making a connection to the Neoplatonic idea of the "flowing out" that brought about the creation of the universe itself, which will be followed by the "flowing in" as all of creation returns to the One:

> From it proceeds [both] what descends from above, and what ascends from below: two rivers diverging from it [in each direction]. Among [these rivers] are the two apparent (*al-ẓāhirān*) to the people of the world, the Nile and the Euphrates. . . . The light of the two was made to cease until they return to what is there [at the Lote Tree], "*on a day that the earth will be changed for other than earth and the heavens* . . ." (Q 14:48) just as [God] did with Adam, and with the earth, returning all to its first [state].[69]

This passage deals with the mystical exegesis of the first two of four rivers flowing under the heavenly Lote Tree, those that are visible and apparent, just as the circulation of blood in the body can be observed. The luminous nature of these "apparent" and observable rivers, however, remains hidden until the eschatological final day, evoked by Ibn Barrajān by his allusion to the "day of arising" in Q 14:48.[70]

These two outer and apparent rivers are juxtaposed and mirrored by two inner, hidden rivers, which our author likewise interprets on several different levels:

> The two hidden (*al-bāṭin*) ones are the river of al-Kawthar and the river [al-Salsabīl].[71] One washes in al-Kawthar an apparent [layer] of that [hidden state]. Like this, the Qur'ān, Sunna, consensus (*al-ijmā'*), and the teachings of the good people[72] [serve to wash], thus his previous and future sins become forgiven for him. Like this is al-Salsabīl, his spring of righteousness, and the straight path of God. [Muḥammad] said, "Follow it, since it reaches to the Garden," or in another [version], "Journey along it, just as the one who follows the Qur'ān and the Sunna arrives through that means to the Garden." His saying "since it reaches the Garden," [means] since it leads one directly [to it]. It is thus for the believing servant who serves God and trusts in him, as he commands him. When he dies, God's command brings him immediately to the Garden: "*It is said, 'Enter the Garden,' and he said, 'If only my people were to know*'" (Q 36:26). "[Regard] *the good, who, upon their passing away, the angels say, 'Peace be upon you, enter into the Garden of which you know*'" (Q 16:32).[73]

Here Ibn Barrajān presents a discussion of the two hidden rivers that flow under the Lote Tree that lead the righteous on their return journey to God, and these hidden rivers have the power to wipe away one's misdeeds. The cleansing power of heavenly rivers is a trope that appears in select narremes from noncanonical reports about Muḥammad's ascension, such as the Abu Hurayra report as preserved in Ibn Jarīr al-Ṭabarī's commentary,[74] or select later versions of the ascension reports ascribed to Ibn 'Abbās. Beyond merely playing this role in purifying the faithful and preparing the servant for God's forgiveness, however, Ibn Barrajān also describes these hidden rivers as guides that one may follow to enter Paradise, just as our exegete claims about the four sources of Mālikī jurisprudence (Qur'ān, Sunna, consensus (*al-ijmā'*), and the teachings of the good people, i.e., the people of Medina), and following the straight path of God (*ṣirāṭ Allāh al-mustaqīm*). Ibn Barrajān's discussion of the hidden rivers, then, demonstrates how he understands these aspects of the heavenly landscape to serve as symbols for and guides to the servant of God's eschatological return to the Paradise of the divine presence.

Ibn Barrajān's exploration of the symbol of the Lote Tree of the Boundary does not stop there, however, for he also takes great interest in delving into the hidden meaning of the qur'ānic mention of the Lote Tree being covered by something that the Qur'ān does not describe directly, employing a circumlocution instead in the verse in question: "when the Lote Tree was covered by what covered [it]" (Q 53:16). After first discussing how each leaf of the tree was covered by an angel, one of the more common explanations offered by premodern exegetes (after the idea that it was covered by countless "golden butterflies"),[75] Ibn Barrajān then delves into the idea, found as a minority opinion in the earliest of Qur'ān commentaries, that God manifested himself to the tree together with his angels.[76] For our exegete, this theophany at the Lote Tree bears direct comparison to the way the divinity revealed himself on Earth to Mount Sinai at the request of Moses:

> The Messenger of God said, "Then I returned to the Lote Tree of the Boundary, and it was '*covered*' by the command (*al-amr*) of God '*by what covered*' (Q 53:16). On each of its leaves landed an angel, and God supported it by his support, such that no one could describe it because of its beauty."[77] This — and God knows best — is because God manifested himself (*tajallī*) to the Lote Tree, and he supported it so that it would be able to bear the revelation of the most high. Had he not supported it with support from him, he would have leveled it, just as was done to the mountain [when God revealed himself at Sinai]. This is a sign about how God supports his worshippers in the Garden, on the day that he manifests himself (*tajallī*) to them, and raises for them the veil. Do not ask about the beauty and splendor, for he exceeds them in [being able to describe] that, just as was done with the Lote Tree. This is one of the states (*ḥāl min aḥwāl*) of their inclining to that which "no eye has seen, no ear has heard, nor has it occurred to the heart of humanity."[78] That is because they see in what is there what no eye has seen, and they hear in the speech of the most high what no ear has heard, and they witness what has not occurred to the heart of humanity, namely witnessing what the Messenger of God saw by sight when he was at the Lote Tree of the Boundary (Q 53:13–15), a sign.
>
> Regarding that, and [its] likeness, [God] glorified be he, and to him is the praise, struck for him [a sign], and "*manifested . . . to the mountain*," and it became "*leveled*" from his majesty, "*and Moses fell down thunderstruck*" (Q 7:143). That was because he supported with his support neither the mountain nor Moses. The mountain, in inner [mystical] interpretation, is Muḥammad. A substitution was made for him, from the mountain to the Lote Tree of the Boundary (Q 53:14), the blessed tree to which

> he manifested himself. One who [goes] to it stops, for there is no place to aim beyond it/him, and all knowledge comes to an end at it/him.[79]

This passage offers a discussion of the manifestation (*tajallī*) of God to the Lote Tree on behalf of Muḥammad, an experience offered as a special favor to the Prophet, which here Ibn Barrajān favorably contrasts with the manifestation of God to the mountain on behalf of Moses, something that neither Moses nor the mountain could bear (Q 7:143). On another level, this experience represents the beatific vision of God that the blessed believer will enjoy in Paradise, and on an even deeper mystical level, it alludes to God appearing directly to Muḥammad at this highest stage, since "the mountain" and "the Lote Tree" are mere symbols for the Prophet himself. In all of these cases, our exegete explains, the vision lies beyond description and is made possible only by divine support (*taʾyīd*) that is offered to God's true worshippers, to Muḥammad, and to the heavenly tree. Ibn Barrajān esoterically interprets the mountain (*al-jabal*) as a reference to the Prophet himself, obliterated in the first manifestation at the time of Moses but able to bear the manifestation during the ascension, when God provides the necessary support so that the Lote Tree / Mountain / Prophet Muḥammad could bear God's appearance. The idea that the Lote Tree serves as the absolute limit for those who ascend to it is underscored by the interpretation of the tree/the Prophet as the site of the divine theophany, and thus Ibn Barrajān insists that "there is no place to aim beyond it."

The trope of vaunting the superiority of Muḥammad over Moses, due to the different sites of their encounters with God and/or their differing abilities to bear the vision of God, appears in some of the earliest mystical sayings about the Prophet's ascension.[80] Competition between Muḥammad and Moses on the night of the ascension forms another theme, side by side with Moses coming to Muḥammad's assistance in his bargaining with God, in many broader ascension narratives.[81] Ibn Barrajān builds on that same polemical theme in exalting Muḥammad over Moses here by contrasting their experiences of a divine theophany. Nevertheless, the way Ibn Barrajān draws a mystical association between Muḥammad and the mountain, and by extension Muḥammad, Mount Sinai, and the Lote Tree — all of which reflect the manifestation of God in creation through the favor of his divine support — distinguishes this mystical exegesis from those of mystics of previous generations.

According to Casewit, Ibn Barrajān's foremost project in the teaching sessions that come to be recorded in his minor Qurān commentary known as *Īḍāḥ al-ḥikma* "is to instruct his disciples on how to behold the unseen (*ghayb*), or as he puts it repeatedly, to 'cross over from the visible into the invisible' (*al-ʿibra min al-shāhid ilā al-ghāʾib*)."[82] From what we have seen of his exegesis on the narrative of Muḥammad's ascension, and its enumeration of a series of hidden associations between things in creation (Sinai, the heart, the body postures of liturgical prayer) and divine realities (the Lote Tree as seat of the divine encounter, the heavenly rivers that flow underneath that tree, the stages of the mystic's return journey), Casewit's description of this technique for "crossing over" as a touchstone of Ibn Barrajān's exegesis in general helps to illuminate this specific case from his mystical *tafsīr* as well. Since such teachings aim to collapse the distinctions between this world and the next, to see heavenly realities present in mundane actions and manifestations, Ibn Barrajān underscores his Neoplatonic understanding of the process of creation and return, seeing this wider drama as the backdrop for the events of the Prophet's journeying upward through the heavens (preceded by God's sending down of the creation and sending down of the Qurʾān).

Furthermore, we have seen how Ibn Barrajān draws into his teachings elements of the common set of symbols and associations that must have also been shared by many Jewish and Christian writers with whose ideas he and his Andalusian contemporaries were in dialogue, such as the role of the spirit in the moment of creation, or the exalted mystic on arriving at the heights participating in the heavenly liturgy of the angels, or the danger of the ascending hero mistaking one of the heavenly powers for the divinity, or the ascending hero becoming mystically subsumed upon the manifestation of the divinity.[83] Both of Ibn Barrajān's commentaries demonstrate an eclectic, unique approach to finding mystical meaning in the story of Muḥammad's heavenly journey. They represent a mystical approach grounded in the Masarran concept of "crossing over" (*ʿitibār*) applied to an understanding of unseen realities through the contemplation of God's signs in the world, but also one grounded in the even wider context of Jewish-Muslim-Christian debates in al-Andalus, seeing Muḥammad's journey to and encounter with God as a sign that depicts a climax in the broader story of creation, Abrahamic prophecy, ascension/return, and ultimately, an approach to union.

CHAPTER FIVE.

Contemplation of the Visionary Experience: Ibn Qaṣī

This chapter explores how symbols and scenes from the narratives of the highest stages of Muḥammad's Night Journey get taken up in the work of Ibn Barrajān's contemporary, Ibn Qaṣī (d. 546/1151). This enigmatic figure outlived Ibn Barrajān for more than a decade, and while his insights on the ascension appear not to show direct knowledge of Ibn Barrajān's work, nevertheless, as we shall see, they both wrestle in a parallel fashion with some of the very same issues. Ibn Qaṣī and Ibn Barrajān were living in the same period and reacting to similar political, social, and religious movements in the region.[1] They both took up an examination of Muḥammad's otherworldly journey as part of their mystical teachings to their respective contemplative followers, yet a comparison between their works suggests that the two were working and teaching independently and not in direct conversation with one another's ideas surrounding Muḥammad's ascension. To a higher degree than Ibn Barrajān, however, Ibn Qaṣī's approach to the Prophet's divine vision seems to have been directly in conversation with esoteric and perhaps Ismāʿīlī-valenced ideas that were in circulation in the eleventh-century Mediterranean.

Before exploring the issue of Ibn Qaṣī's creative use of esoteric ideas and formulation of new and distinctive interpretations of Muḥammad's ascension, we should bear in mind that the study of Ibn Qaṣī's work among western academics is relatively recent, and aside from those of Josef Dreher and Michael Ebstein, have generally focused mainly on Ibn Qaṣī as a renegade political leader who led a brief revolt against the waning rule of the Murābiṭūn (Almoravid) dynasty from several fortified locations in the far west of Iberia in what is today the nation of Portugal.[2] We might explain the generally unfavorable depiction of the biographical notices on this rebel given that earlier studies had to rely on references in secondary works often hostile to him and his ideas. David Goodrich's

Columbia University dissertation in the field of political science (1978) was the first to present the entire Arabic text of Ibn Qaṣī's main work, *Khalʿ al-naʿlayn wa-qtibās al-nūr min mawḍiʿ al-qadamayn* (*The Removing of the Sandals and the Taking of the Light from the Place of the Two Feet*), based on Goodrich's study of the only manuscript that was known to him, one accompanied by a commentary from his much more famous successor of the next generation of Iberian mystics, Ibn ʿArabī (d. 638/1240).[3] Advancing our knowledge of the text even further, the other major western study focused solely on Ibn Qaṣī's work was a dissertation by Josef Dreher for the philosophy faculty of the Rheinischen Friedrich-Wilhelm University (1985), which offers a series of extensive excerpts in Arabic as well as German translation, some detailed commentary, and analysis of *Khalʿ al-naʿlayn* based on two manuscripts of the text.[4] Both Goodrich and Dreher explore the claim that Ibn Qaṣī assumed the title not only of Imām but also of Mahdi (awaited messianic leader), distancing himself from such pretensions only when seeking aid from the rising al-Muwaḥḥidūn (Almohad) North African forces whose leaders had different ideas about to whom such titles should be applied. While the tragic fate of his political career may be intriguing to many, for the present consideration of western mystical interpretations of the Prophet's ascension, it will be more pertinent to consider Ibn Qaṣī's use and development of esoteric symbolic systems, especially those related to the highest heavenly realms.

For instance, we have seen that the concept of the "place of sitting" (*al-mustawā*) is one that Ibn Barrajān makes use of in his commentary,[5] and thus it is especially interesting, as Dreher notes, how in the opening lines of *Khalʿ al-naʿlayn*, after the formulaic praises to God and to the Prophet, Ibn Qaṣī sees fit to include a similar lofty greeting addressed to "al-mustawā al-aʿlā" (the "highest place of sitting") as if it, too, represents a living being that also deserves praise.[6] As Dreher suggests, the answer lies in recognizing *al-mustawā* as connected to the "sphere of life" (*al-ḥayy*) and the first emanation in creation that is linked to the "comprehensive" aspect of the divine throne.[7] The Neoplatonic resonance of this idea is clear enough, but its significance with regard to Ibn Qaṣī's interpretation of Muḥammad's night journey deserves further exploration. Further suggestive details can be found by examining the cosmology of esoteric treatises in circulation, such as those associated with the Ikhwān al-Ṣafāʾ (Brethren of Purity). An important historical source containing a notice on Ibn Qaṣī by the author Ibn al-Khaṭīb presents evidence that Ibn Qaṣī was familiar with these esoteric treatises, and Goodrich briefly examines a few parallels between concepts described in *The Removing of the Sandals* and the writings of the Brethren.[8]

The idea that Ibn Qaṣī was familiar with and likely in places drew directly from the well of symbols that nourished Ismāʿīlī-valenced esotericism, perhaps through the mediation of treatises by the group known as the Brethren of Purity, has been explored in more depth by Michael Ebstein.[9] Acknowledging Ibn Qaṣī's rhetorical eloquence, Ebstein asserts that "his writing is intentionally esoteric: [he] attempted to cloak the mystical knowledge contained in his work in encrypted language that could only be deciphered and understood by a select few," especially when writing about eschatological issues, messianism, and the status of "God's friends."[10] As is evident in his discussion of the vision of God that forms the heart of Ibn Qaṣī's discourse on Muḥammad's ascension and serves as the main focus of the treatise "Removing of the Removing" that we shall analyze in some depth in this chapter, the author contends that the multiple and apparently mutually exclusive ways of describing the vision of God in diverse hadith reports could all be shown to be correct from a certain vantage point. He argues that each perspective reflects different levels of understanding of the knowledge that emanates from the light of the creator and flows outward into lower and lower levels of creation. This Neoplatonic framework was not exclusive to Ismāʿīlī-valenced esotericists, of course, for esoteric thinkers of different stripes in the western Mediterranean did tend to share this cosmology, but the apparently relativistic epistemology that Ibn Qaṣī advances with regard to our subject is worthy of note and further consideration.

Ebstein argues that while the Neoplatonic model was widely shared between the Iberian mystics examined in our study, nevertheless "contrary to other Andalusī mystics who were influenced by Neoplatonic philosophy . . . Ibn Qaṣī did not employ the familiar scheme of the universal intellect and universal soul, but rather developed an idiosyncratic cosmological system . . . [which was] nonetheless inspired by Neoplatonic thought."[11] As Ebstein goes on to explain, and as Dreher before him had described,[12] in this system Ibn Qaṣī depicts an outward flow emanating from the divine essence (*dhāt*) and descending through six spheres, from highest to lowest:

> (1) the sphere of life, *falak al-ḥayāt* (= encompassing/comprehensive throne, *al-ʿarsh al-muḥīt*);
> (2) the sphere of mercy, *falak al-raḥma* (= the noble throne, *al-ʿarsh al-karīm*);
> (3) the mighty footstool, *al-kursī al-ʿazīz* (= the great throne, *al-ʿarsh al-ʿaẓīm*);
> (4) the glorious throne, *al-ʿarsh al-majīd*;
> (5) the heaven's sphere (*falak al-samāʾ*);
> (6) the earth's sphere (*falak al-arḍ*).[13]

The divine throne (*al-ʿarsh*) appears in different aspects and at different levels in the four uppermost portions of this schema, which may be especially significant given Ibn Masarra's alleged emphasis on the highest of all esoteric knowledge being revealed at and/or from God's throne, a concept perhaps stemming from the thought of Sahl al-Tustarī.[14] Still, even more important for our present study is the fact that Ibn Qaṣī locates the sphere of life (*falak al-ḥayāt*), and by extension the highest place of sitting (*al-mustawā al-aʿlā*), at the very uppermost level of creation, for that explains the numerous references to this realm throughout his discussion of Muḥammad's ascension later in his key work titled *Khalʿ al-naʿlayn*. This sphere of life represents the highest realm of being, the site where Muḥammad's mystical vision during his night journey could ultimately be located.

Removing of the Removing

In a relatively short section of his larger work *Khalʿ al-naʿlayn*, which bears the clever title "Khalʿ al-khalʿ" ("The Removing of the Removing"), Ibn Qaṣī turns to the above cosmological framework in order to explain how, during his ascension, Muḥammad perceives the divinity as a light that descends on the Lote Tree, the same light that according to our author connects all things in existence. The section explores Muḥammad's night journey vision in the wider context of examining competing truth claims about the Prophet's vision of Gabriel after the first revelation of the Qurʾān and his subsequent vision of God on the "highest horizon" (Q 53:7) during his ascension. Ibn Qaṣī's approach to this subject in *Khalʿ al-naʿlayn* (the title itself a reference to Moses's experience of standing in the divine presence at the burning bush)[15] does not take the form of a traditional qurʾānic exegesis but rather reads much more like an oral discourse, what Walid Saleh might define as a scholastic or teaching exegesis.[16] As we have seen with Ibn Barrajān's "lesser" commentary titled *al-Idāḥ*, individual sections of *Khalʿ al-naʿlayn* were likely delivered orally to a specialist audience of Ibn Qaṣī's fellow contemplatives, with each session dedicated to the explication of some particular qurʾānic passage or problem. In other words, while certainly nothing like a comprehensive verse by verse Qurʾān commentary, we might be justified in classifying *Khalʿ al-naʿlayn* as a specialized mystical *tafsīr* that focuses on select themes in each of its short portions.

"The Removing of the Removing"[17] ("Khalʿ al-khalʿ") and the section that immediately follows it and is sometimes included within it, at times given the independent title "The Criterion and the Making-Plain" ("al-Furqān wa ʾl-bayān"),[18] may well have circulated together as an independent treatise, at least for a couple of decades after Ibn Qaṣī's death, as will be discussed at the conclusion of this chapter. Both of these sections begin and end with references to particular passages in the Qur'ān that allude to various upper horizons, suggesting that Ibn Qaṣī's proof text in this portion of his wider *Khalʿ al-naʿlayn* was to explain to his followers some of the mystical dimensions of those qur'ānic "horizons," a topic which in turn leads him to discuss Muḥammad's otherworldly journey and the possibility of the vision of God.

The touchstone passage with which "The Removing of the Removing" opens focuses on a single ambiguous qur'ānic verse, Q 81:23, one preceded and followed by verses that insist on the Prophet's veracity and forthrightness: "Your friend has not gone mad / he saw him on the clear horizon / he does not hoard for himself the unseen" (Q 81:22–24). For Ibn Qaṣī and others like him, the allusion to the Prophet's vision on the "clear horizon" (*al-ufuq al-mubīn*) naturally intertextually evokes the passage near the beginning of the Star chapter of the Qur'ān in which another prophetic vision is described through similarly elliptical language as taking place on "the highest horizon" (*al-ufuq al-aʿlā*) (Q 53:7). As we have discussed previously, the latter verse opens with a masculine pronoun "he," the active agent of the seeing, most frequently understood by Muslim commentators as referring to the Prophet Muḥammad. The verse's second masculine pronoun, standing for the direct object of the vision, remains more open to exegetical debate, and is most often described as either Gabriel or God.[19] Establishing the respective meaning of the qur'ānic phrase "the highest horizon" (Q 53:7) and the similar-sounding qur'ānic phrase "the clear horizon" (Q 81:23), and explaining the relationship between these two qur'ānic references, thus becomes the central issue that Ibn Qaṣī explores in the brief section "The Removing of the Removing."

Two Horizons

The first thing that strikes one about Ibn Qaṣī's approach to the discussion of the mystical issues arising through the exegesis of the above qur'ānic references to "horizons," and indeed his approach to other issues surrounding the prophetic heavenly visions, is how he strives to maintain the truth and validity of all the multifarious interpretations that Muslims subsequently advance about these experiences, both in hadith reports and in subsequent Qur'ān commentaries. As we have seen, a number of these interpretations sharply diverge from one another, and, in fact, they appear at times to outline mutually exclusive positions on the question of who saw whom, how, where, and when. Given the degree to which these different interpretations appear on the surface to contradict each other, how would it be possible for each of them simultaneously to remain valid? On the one hand, after enumerating a list of figures who were said to transmit reports of Muhammad's ascension and/or vision of God,[20] Ibn Qaṣī advances the idea that each scholar transmitted the interpretation that was within their capacity to understand.[21] On the other hand, Ibn Qaṣī points to a deeper mystical insight that sheds light on the Neoplatonic model that he embraces, namely that each of the different interpretations of Muḥammad's visions reflects a certain truth (*ḥaqq*) that corresponds to a particular stage of divine emanation or disclosure. He develops these twin ideas over the course of "The Removing of the Removing," but he first introduces the idea of such a plurality of truths near its very outset:

> Sects of the knowers (*firaq min al-ʿārifīn*) talked about the meaning of "*the highest horizon*" (Q 53:7) and "*the clear horizon*" (Q 81:23) and each went on his way. . . . The companions [of the Prophet] separated into paths that [distinct] sects followed and embraced. Each disbursed to a way, taking a position, speaking with integrity, not anything excessive. . . . There were those who said, "He saw God," and what they said was the truth. Then there were those who said, "[He saw] Gabriel twice," and what they said was the truth. [Then there were those who said, "He saw a light," and what they said was the truth.][22] There were those who said, "He saw with his heart," and what they said was the truth. Then there were those who said, "He saw with his two eyes," and what they said was the truth. Then there was the one who said, "Whoever claims that Muḥammad saw his lord with the two eyes of his head has lied, for God proclaims, '*Sight does not comprehend him*'" (Q 6:103), and what he said was the truth. [The Prophet] only gave them to drink from the remainder of his cup on the carpet of his intimacy, and only measured for each one of them a pebble's-weight of his understanding on the scale of his perception.[23]

In answer to the question of how one can maintain the validity of what appear to be mutually exclusive positions, such as the idea that the statement "Muḥammad saw his lord with the two eyes of his head" can simultaneously have the status of a falsehood and a truth, Ibn Qaṣī insists that each of these claims contains a small jewel of truth from the larger treasury of the wider Truth, the understanding of which transcends any one of these particular assertions.

Delving into the depths of Ibn Qaṣī's interpretation of the two proof text references from the Qurʾān to "horizons," unlike some others who consider them synonymous and interchangeable, our mystical author here associates "the clear horizon" (Q 81:23) with Muḥammad's vision of Gabriel in his towering form (what elsewhere will be called his "true created form") blocking the horizon of the earth from the Prophet's sight shortly after the initial revelation of the Qur᾽ān to him on the mountain outside of Mecca, as detailed in the *Sīra* literature such as that of Ibn Hishām's recension of Ibn Isḥāq's biography of the Messenger of God (*Sīrat Rasūl Allāh*).[24] This "clear horizon" must be distinguished from "the highest horizon" (Q 53:7), which Ibn Qaṣī interprets as a reference to Muḥammad's vision during his heavenly ascent from the "station of the spirit of holiness / the Holy Spirit"[25] (*maqām rūḥ al-quds*) up to the highest place of sitting (*mustawā al-a'lā*), where the Prophet reported that he heard "the scratching of the pens" (*ṣarīf al-aqlām*).[26] Yet the object of the vision at this uppermost station remains ambiguous. For Ibn Qaṣī, following the Neoplatonic model of emanation, the flowing out (here understood as referring to the "sending down" or "descent") from the original One subsequently engenders a process of flowing back (in this case "ascent"). The manifestations (*tajallīyāt*) of this return depend at each level on the next-highest one:

> The [very] highest manifests to the [first] highest, which is below that highest. Then that highest manifests to that nearer[27] highest that is below that one, and so on, vessel (*mil᾽*) to vessel to vessel of the heaven. The faithful spirit did not manifest on "*the clear horizon*" (Q 81:23) until the highest pen was manifest to him on his most resplendent addition. The highest pen did not manifest from that resplendent addition until the spirit of sanctity manifested to it on "*the highest horizon*" (Q 53:7). The spirit of sanctity did not manifest on "*the highest horizon*" until the greatest cover (*al-'aṭiyya al-kubrā*) in the most life-giving and most sacred veil (*al-ḥijāb al-aqdas al-aḥyā*) was manifest to him. . . . All of this represents surrounding veils, exteriors to the enormity of the essence, and the lights of the naming names and the exalted qualities.[28]

This passage describes stage after stage of ascent that is contingent on the earlier stages of Neoplatonic descent,[29] with each requiring the next-highest sphere or being to reveal or manifest (*tajallī*) itself in order for the process to continue, step by step, in an obvious parallel to the stages of Muḥammad's ascension that proceeded heaven by heaven, finally traversing the upperworldly realms beyond all the levels of outer veils.

Throughout the stages of return, it simultaneously remains true for Ibn Qaṣī that all of existence remains one, which has a unified essence (*al-dhāt*) in its innermost dimension (*al-bāṭin*), an essence that progressive levels of veils on the outer dimensions (*al-ẓāhir*) cover over. These covering veils range from the outward forms of the angelic heavenly host (*al-malā al-aʿlā*) all the way down to the created form of Adam (*ṣūrat* Ādam).[30] Just as Gabriel appears to Muḥammad in the human form of the latter's handsome companion Dihya al-Kalbī, according to a famous transmitted report, so too, according to Ibn Qaṣī, God is also able to assume this "Dihyan" form when he so desires. The divine essence hidden underneath the veil of the human form becomes one way, then, that Ibn Qaṣī validates the idea presented in some reports that Muḥammad saw God in a created form, explaining how this vision could have occurred without it impinging on what for mainstream Muslims becomes the sin of associationism (*shirk*) in imagining that God ever manifests in creation in the form of a human being:

> In this most beautiful shape and resplendent relation, [God] the almighty (majestic be his majesty and blessed be his names) manifested for the possessor of the dear vision that he (i.e.[,] the Prophet) mentioned. It is a veil from among the veils of the names and attributes over the enormity of the essence, just as the shape which the faithful spirit Gabriel used to take [when appearing] to the chosen one [Muḥammad] is a veil over the enormity of the encompassing through which he manifested the manifestation, blocking "*the highest horizon*" (Q 53:7)[31] from the levels of the nearest [first] heaven.[32]

He develops this same analogy between Gabriel's assuming a human form and God's capability of assuming a human form later in the chapter, as he comes to discuss the divine self-disclosure to the Prophet at the Lote Tree of the Boundary as one of the meanings of the qurʾānic verse "he saw some of the greatest signs of his lord" (Q 53:18):

> The lord "*descended and approached*," (Q 53:8) and he manifested in the shining nearest veil out of beneficent favor through the close revelation and the generous sitting (*al-mustawā*), responding to speech. He descended on the veil of brilliance and might to the veil of kindness and mercy. He manifested in a veiled beneficent shape and a contented essence to the completion of the favor and blessing, just as the faithful spirit descended to the representational Dihyan human form. [In the latter form, Gabriel] did not show him greater than the shape which he knew, and he did not see the blocking of the horizons, nor was he different [from his familiar shape]. Rather, he saw in a Muḥammadan vision a Muḥammadan shape, an eternal veiling, the light of its glorification, the veil of its essence.[33]

This passage further develops the idea of how and for what reasons God might assume a familiar human form for the sake of Muḥammad: firstly, because it was a form known and thus calming to him; and secondly, because in premodern theories of how the process of vision takes place, the faculty of sight entails an outward projection of light from the viewer.[34] It stands to reason, then, that a "Muḥammadan vision" would take a "Muḥammadan shape," an anthropomorphic form that was nothing but another veil covering over the otherwise overwhelming and incomprehensible divine essence.[35]

A similar logic allows Ibn Qaṣī to insist that those who claim that on the night of the ascension Muḥammad saw some sort of light, or saw only Gabriel, not God, are also correct. The Dihyan form that Muḥammad perceived was an angelic veil, not the divine essence itself: "So when he manifested [himself to Muḥammad] to approach and make stable, it was the faithful spirit [Gabriel] and no other. Thus, the one who says of the Dihyan-form of veiling that it was the faithful spirit, he speaks truly."[36] Moreover, this "representational veil" is "the light of the most high and the spirit of Life,"[37] the latter alluding to the highest sphere of creation. In each case, the object of perception involves the projection of light from the seer, "from the lowest to the highest, [and from] the resplendent light of the manifestation to the sanctity of the beautiful names of God,"[38] a process that reflects and reverses the outward flow of light out of which the universe was formed. As Goodrich comments, "According to this theory [advanced by Ibn Qaṣī in *The Removing of the Sandals*], one only sees in proportion to the strength of one's own light."[39] Just as in the previous passage that asserts the validity of different interpretations of Muḥammad's vision according to the understanding of the exegete, so too in this passage the degree to which one's light ascends to the heights depends on the strength of one's faculties, with Muḥammad's vision shining the way for others to follow.

Near the beginning of Ibn Qaṣī's larger work, the author describes the highest "truths" (*ḥaqāʾiq*) as the means by which, after the time of the Prophet, the elect could also ascend, following his lead. "As for *al-ḥaqāʾiq*, they are the mounts of the highest [levels] (*dawāʾib al-ʿulā*), the most spiritual of the spirits of Life (*al-ḥayāt*), the degrees of the seekers, the ascensions of the knowers (*al-maʿārij al-ʿārifīn*) to the heights (*al-ʿilliyīn*). So, the one who steps on their carpets sits level (*istāwā*), and the one who rides their Burāq reaches the Lote Tree of the boundary."[40] Here we find the one place in Ibn Qaṣī's work where he suggests that the heavenly journey in which Muḥammad ascends to the highest level serves to blaze the trail of the Neoplatonic return, a path potentially available to all the "seekers" (*al-sālikīn*) and "knowers" (*al-ʿārifīn*) who may subsequently ride "their Burāq" all the way to the Lote Tree following his lead.

Beyond the fascination of this Neoplatonic theory of emanation and its bearing on Ibn Qaṣī's understanding of the process of perception, the short treatise titled "The Removing of the Removing" can be understood further as outlining what the author understands as the events at the highest levels of the night journey after the Prophet has proceeded through the levels of the upper realm (*al-Malakūt*), which incidentally is the basis for the name of part 1 of the work *The Removing of the Sandals* as a whole, "[Things Pertaining to] the Upper/ Angelic Realm" (*al-Malakūtiyya*), the same section in the midst of which this particular short treatise "Removing of the Removing" has been placed in its present configuration.[41] Ibn Qaṣī begins to narrate the events of the climax of the ascension midway through the section, drawing liberally from the opening verses of the Star chapter of the Qur'ān for textual support of his wider narrative framework:

> When he was on this happy night journey, then, and the miracle of the making dear and making noble was due, he caused him to ascend to "*the highest horizon*" (Q 53:7) in the most luminous sanctity, and caused him to hear the exalted "scratching of the pens" and make sanctified the spirits of Life.[42] When the veil of secrets was raised for him from the source of the lights and from the radiance of the meadow of the presence of the dignified one (*al-waqār*), thus "*he drew near and descended / and was a distance of two bows or nearer*" (Q 53:8–9). [This was] a station of praise and lauding and eulogizing, indicating to him the right of welcome and nearness and contentment, swearing an oath and fidelity. Then he raised for him the dear veil of the manifestation (*ḥijāb al-tajallī al-ʿazīz*) from the intimate discourse of salvation (*munājāt al-najāt*) and the salvation of nearness and Life (*najāt al-qurb wa* 'l-ḥayāt). He traced back to purity and magnified contentment while the high essence descended in the sacred veil. The viewer was sanctified, and the vision was made transcendent (*tanazzaha al-marāʾī*). The sending down / revelation was in the sending down / revelation (*al-tanzīl fī* 'l-tanzīl), and the nearest manifestation was in the manifestation. He was made to see with the eyes, and he spoke face to face, and he learned and was raised up in the vision. Therefore, "*vision was not excessive nor exceed bounds*" (Q 53:17) and "*the heart did not lie in what it saw*" (Q 53:11); "*indeed he saw him another time / at the Lote Tree of the Boundary*" (Q 53:13–14).[43]

In other words, despite the reference to the riding of al-Burāq in earlier portions of the text, here Ibn Qaṣī skips all the initial phases of the journey for his present discussion of the significance of the Prophet's *miʿrāj*, cutting directly to its very highest stages, where Muḥammad heard the "scratching of the pens" (usually associated with the seventh heaven or beyond), and where the veils were raised and the divine colloquy (*munājāt*) and vision of God then takes place. For our author, these experiences serve as preliminaries to a yet further ascension to the revelation of even higher knowledge, including the gnosis of the divine essence: "He ascended beyond it to the comprehension of lights of the attributes (*anwār min al-ṣifāt*), secrets from the revelations (*asrār min al-tanazzulāt*), the sensations of the wishes (*iḥsāsāt al-irādiyyāt*), the gnosis of the essence (*ma'rifat al-dhāt*), and the decree of the covenant (*taqdīr al-'aqd*) in both the encompassing and non-encompassing veiling."[44] In Ibn Qaṣī's perspective, therefore, the night of the ascension involved not only the Prophet enjoying an audience with God but also the revelation of the secrets of existence and the mysteries of the divinity. For this mystic, Muḥammad's heavenly ascent includes an experience of the highest level of intimacy with the divine short of mystical union.

A Vision of Divinity?

Notice that previously, as quoted above, Ibn Qaṣī describes this intimate audience with the divinity as a "face to face" interaction — parallel to Moses's discourse with God — and in this case involving the "vision of the eyes" (the physical eyes of his head). For those who insist that such physical faculties cannot possibly be adequate to allow for a vision of God, with strong proof texts in the Qur'ān and elsewhere to support that position, Ibn Qaṣī affirms in what follows the truth of that idea and the dangers of imagining a purely physical vision of God with the eyes:

> Others said, [Muḥammad merely claimed,] "I saw with my heart," confirming the saying of the Real, "*The heart did not lie in what it saw*" (Q 53:11) and again [the Prophet's saying], "*Indeed there is nothing like the Real, surrounding all things.*" The veiling light of the Real surrounds all things, and this is not comprehended in the one surrounded, except a particular knowledge that imagining something not encompassed [by the divinity] is mere fantasy. Were he to manifest the enormity and the veilingness of the levels to the state of surroundedness, it would completely crush it, completely overtake the senses, completely make thunderstruck the worlds and the stations. No eye would remain to open, nor [would there remain] acknowledgement of traces, nor [the asking of] how. Thus, he saw this immensity with the eye of his heart. He did not comprehend it with the eye of his head, nor did he want that. His pure wife ['Ā'isha] also affirms this.[45]

Moses at Mount Sinai found that he was not able to see God or even to be present when God revealed himself to the mountain, without Moses collapsing thunderstruck (Q 7:143); similarly here, the text insists that such was Muḥammad's experience also since the divine Real (*al-ḥaqq*) cannot be grasped or encompassed by physical sight. In a particularly picturesque hadith report, alluded to at the end of the above quotation and appearing in some of the earliest sources, such as Ibn Isḥāq's *Sīra*, the Prophet's wife, ʿĀʾisha, was said to have pulled out her hair in frustration and anger upon hearing about those who claimed that Muḥammad saw God on the night of the ascension.

Rather than elaborate on this report attributed to ʿĀʾisha, however, Ibn Qaṣī uses the reference to her anger as described in the report as a pretext to discuss an apparently separate issue, divine anger and the withdrawal of divine mercy from those who are tormented in Hellfire.[46] This discussion leads to an extended tangential exploration into the question of whether minerals, plants, and nonhuman animals have any sense of consciousness or understanding of divine wisdom. At first glance, the topic, addressed again elsewhere in *Khalʿ al-naʿlayn*, appears to be little more than a confusing non sequitur, perhaps drawing on the religious-scientific teachings that Ibn Qaṣī could have drawn from the philosophical treatises of the Brethren of Purity.[47] Yet in view of the chapter as a whole, one can see how such topics fit neatly with the author's wider thesis that nothing exists apart from God, and in fact that something of the divinity rests upon everything in creation.

This idea relates to what precedes and what follows this discussion in the text on the basis that, for Ibn Qaṣī, the Garden and the Fire are merely apparent realities, nothing but two further veils that serve as different sides of the same coin, all being ultimately a part of the divine oneness.[48] Given this insight, and the fact that this whole section of Ibn Qaṣī's work falls under a section devoted to otherworldly realms (*al-Malakūtiyya*), it does not come as a surprise that the discussion of animals and minerals gives way abruptly to a discussion of Paradise, revolving on the prophetic report that states how in the Garden human beings will be able to visit a "market" in which they will have the chance to select whatever bodily shape (*ṣūra*) pleases them.[49] Ibn Qaṣī concludes his elaboration of that tradition with a statement relating it back to the discussion of the divine essence inhering in all things:

> Everything that you witnessed of the lights of life are nothing but shapes in the markets of desire, except that they are from the lights of your degrees and the resplendences of your life. You will forever manifest in your light, veiled in the spirit of your life, and the [divine] essence will be

> upon this. God said, "[*In the earth are signs for the firm in faith*], *and in their selves. Do you not see*?" (Q 51:21). Since you had this capacity, then how about the lord of capacity, God of the first and the last? "*So by the lord of the heaven and the earth, indeed he is a truth like what you articulated*" (Q 51:23).[50]

Returning to the Neoplatonic idea of all things being created out of the emanation of the divine light, and all things ultimately returning to that light, here Ibn Qaṣī insists that all outer forms and shapes consist of this same light, merely in a form veiled from the hidden divine reality that rests within and upon them. If one accepts this basic premise, then all the apparently contradictory reports about what Muḥammad saw at the highest stages of his journey become equally valid, and the distinction between them equally nonsensical: "Since the matter is thus, how could [the Prophet] not say, 'A light is what I saw' if he wished, and say 'I saw in my heart' if he wished, and say 'I saw my lord' if he wished?"[51] This sentiment brings full circle the discussion of the manner of the Prophet's vision on the night of the ascension, supporting the contention that Ibn Qaṣī expressed near the beginning of "The Removing of the Removing," that each of these apparently contradictory exegetical positions itself reflects a truth (*ḥaqq*), even if not the entirety of the divine Truth (*al-ḥaqq*).

Just as in other Muslim ascension narratives from al-Andalus in which the Prophet's tour of the Fire and the Garden are not placed at the end of the story but in fact precede the highest divine audience, so too in Ibn Qaṣī's chapter "The Removing of the Removing," the culmination of the discourse comes not with his elaboration of the nature of Paradise or Hellfire but instead with the Prophet receiving revelation directly from God (here evoked by the qur'ānic synonym al-Furqān, "the Criterion," an Arabic word that exegetes understand with regard to the entire revelation itself, and part of the title of the short section that follows this one[52]). This reference evokes in the mind of Ibn Qaṣī a type of final judgment, the weighing not only people's actions but also their memories, the latter connected to the idea that each of the transmitters conveyed what they were able to bear or carry of the reports they received from God's Messenger to the best of their abilities.[53] For Ibn Qaṣī, ultimately God raises all created beings who follow the Prophet: "He raised us through his way (*sunna*), and he gathered us on the day of judgment with his purity (*ṣafwati-hi*)."[54] The service that the author performs for his audience through his commentary and interpretation of select elements of the story of Muḥammad's otherworldly journey, then, seems to be akin to that of a shamanic spirit guide, revealing the mystery behind the Prophet's visions and experiences while simultaneously illuminating the final journey for his entire audience as manifest in the "awakening"[55] of creation, and its returning to the divine essence.

The Criterion / Making Plain

The section that follows, and which concludes the short "Removing of the Removing" treatise,[56] offers a distinct interpretation of the Prophet's night journey vision as described in qurʾānic proof text from the Star chapter, Q 53:13–18. The discussion of the Prophet's vision in this concise passage follows more closely both the Ibn ʿAbbās ascension narrative as well as the symbolism of Jewish Hekhalot reports that raise the trope of how frightening the heavenly journey can be, especially at its highest stages. This passage opens by describing the intense fear that Muḥammad experienced while seeing the various splendors appearing before him at the Lote Tree:

> When the Lote Tree of the Boundary was raised for him, and he saw what it had of long trunk, levels, and leaves, leveling and branching out both to the heights and depths, and when he saw the stars as sources of the horizons, and the spirit-angels (*al-malāʾ al-rūḥānī*) from the highest of the heavenly heights (*al-ʿilliyūn*) whose size outstripped the branches — they kneeled and prostrated, glorified and magnified [God], longing and seeking ecstasy, "*They glorified night and day, unstopping*" (Q 21:20) — what he saw struck him with terror.
>
> The "*great sign*" (Q 53:18) filled him with awe until he encountered what he heard, and passed from what had gathered, his liver remaining there even while he perceived the burning of livers. Then he was confirmed through the making of intimacy and safety, supplied with Life from the faithful spirit [Gabriel]. He sought his intimacy for safety, and was made tranquil in the sounding of melodious words. He heard the recitation of the Qurʾān, and on [hearing] that, the covers of majesty were unveiled for him, and the curtains of the dear King were raised for him in a multitude[57] of signs. [These were some of the] graces in what the Prophet saw of visions [on his night journey].[58]

Ibn Qaṣī's description here bears significant resemblance to a scene in the Ibn ʿAbbās family of *miʿrāj* narratives, such as the fragmentary version in Madrid Real Academia de Historia MS Olim CCXLI / Codera 241.[59] In the latter, as

Muḥammad is ushered into the near vicinity of the divine presence and witnesses the worshipping of the highest of angels, he experiences a similar wave of fear:

> I heard a caller say, "Angels of the veils, raise the veils that are between me and my beloved (*ḥabībī*) Muḥammad." I looked at the angels who were the guardians of the veils, [and] they raised them, then they trembled suddenly from the amount of light that covered them. I advanced forward and found myself amidst twenty thousand rows of angels standing — they will not kneel or prostrate until Judgment Day — then I advanced forward through twenty thousand rows of angels kneeling and prostrating — [7v] they will not raise their heads until Judgment Day while they are prostrating to God, the exalted. So, I advanced forward and I [thought] everything — all of it — had died, due to its silence from the immensity of the lord, majestic be his majesty. A caller from before God cried out, "Do not be afraid, Muḥammad, nor let fear come upon you." On that, my terror was silenced. A caller cried, "Approach, Muḥammad, for I am your lord!" I continued walking, [but] I knew not how I should greet my lord. My lord inspired me when I said, "Salutations from God, purities are for God, goodnesses and prayers are to God." God responded, "Peace be upon you, O Prophet, and the mercy and blessings of God, the Master, Lord, Peace, Faithful, Protector, Powerful, Conqueror."[60]

In both texts, the Prophet becomes terrified by the things he encounters at the highest stages of his ascension, including the rise of overwhelming fires and the heavenly worship of the angelic multitudes. In each case, the presence of accompanying angels helps to calm the Prophet, providing him with the reassurance that helps him to overcome the petrifying terror that threatens to overwhelm him. What differentiates the two passages is that here Ibn Qaṣī invokes the trope in order to insist that at the Lote Tree itself, Muḥammad did not witness the divine manifestation but rather was able instead to perceive a vision of Gabriel:

> So, it was not what the Prophet saw in [the state of] his humanness. As [God] the exalted says: "*When the Lote Tree was covered by what covered, the sight was not excessive nor exceeding bounds*" (Q 53:16–17). Were it not for the crowding of the light and the multitude of inclinations of the forms, if indeed the covering of the leaves were [instead] a wrap (*ghiṭāʾ*) of lotus fruits, the truth-telling [divine] Real would not have needed to make known that the Lote Tree was a lote tree, nor that the fruit was a fruit. He described the levels of the leaves, and detailed

> the qualities of the fruits, and the words of your lord were complete (*timmat*), establishing the "making clear" of the truth-telling. [In fact] this was the vision of Gabriel, the "other vision" on which all the companions agreed: "*Indeed he saw*" Gabriel "*another time at the Lote Tree of the Boundary*" (Q 53:13–14).[61]

This passage, and its specification that the object of Muḥammad's vision at the Lote Tree must be none other than Gabriel, may seem striking given what Ibn Qaṣī had argued earlier about each of the reports of Muḥammad's divine vision, in all their variations (some of which were mutually exclusive), namely that they each conveyed "a truth" (*ḥaqq*ᵃⁿ). In response, I would argue first that this interpretation does not exclude the others, for it merely reflects what Ibn Qaṣī says about the Prophet's vision at the Lote Tree, not the object of his ultimate vision during the journey as a whole. Further, I would point out that while each of the other interpretations offers "a truth," here at the end of this thematic section, one might expect that Ibn Qaṣī presents his own preferred interpretation of the vision at the Lote Tree (or one that a subsequent follower wished to present as the master's preferred interpretation), understanding the qur'ānic reference to be clear and complete when understood in this way, even while symbolically pointing to deeper dimensions of the entire journey when unpacked in an esoteric fashion.

Ibn Qaṣī then concludes this discussion of Muḥammad's vision by bringing us back to a consideration of the verses that had opened the discussion in the first place, an explanation of the mysteries of the different "horizons" that the Qur'ān invokes in diverse passages. The key, he seems to insist, rests on the fact that what appears to be a "boundary" set by the Lote Tree is in fact no real boundary at all:

> Know that, speaking about "*the Lote Tree of the Boundary*" (Q 53:14), the "Clear Horizon" (Q 81:23), the "Highest Horizon" (Q 53:7),[62] and the "other vision," the first does not [actually] have "a boundary" (*muntahā*). Instead, this is [like] a drop approaching some flowing seas (*biḥār mufīḍa*), or the setting down of a candle when lit by extended rays [of the sun] and the all-encompassing [celestial] lights, in order that a clever one could breathe and a mind could feel, yet the remainder is clear, made clear by a faithful speaker (*nāṭiq amīn*), who speaks eloquently. The Lord, glorified be he, illuminates the paths (*sunan*), and grants blessings and gifts, being the most kind, most true, most beneficent, most faithful. There is no Lord other than he.[63]

The twin metaphors — the drop that loses its individuality in the wider seas and the candlelight that loses its individuated brightness when surrounded by the intensity of rays from the sun or other "all-encompassing lights" — together serve to explain how this "delimited" vision at a place that is described by "a limit" (*muntahā*) is in fact just "a truth" that pales in comparison to "the Truth" (*al-ḥaqq*) that transcends and encompasses all of reality. From the perspective of Neoplatonic cosmology, then, even this sublime vision of Gabriel in his true form, taking place in the vicinity of the very highest sphere, falls short of the divine essence itself yet reflects the subtle way that God eloquently points in the direction of these uppermost stages of the soul's ultimate return.

Other Esoteric Interpretations

Referring to this specific section of the work that we examined above, "The Removing of the Removing," Michael Ebstein argues that Ibn Qaṣī's work owes a substantial debt to the esoteric cosmology and philosophical ideas of the Brethren of Purity in particular and Ismāʿīlī thought more broadly, even though Ibn Qaṣī himself remained a devout Sunnī and those other groups come to be associated in the minds of many with Shīʿism. Yet as Ebstein points out, for Ibn Qaṣī, "The cosmic veils and the angelic beings that populate them are what enable prophetic revelation and mystical unveiling. Viewing the cosmic hypostases as veils that both separate God from creation and function as the only means whereby one may gain access to or knowledge of the Divine realm is a common theme in Ismāʿīlī literature."[64] If one grants Ebstein's claim that Ibn Qaṣī's approach shares elements that are also "a common theme in Ismāʿīlī literature," still that does not necessitate that our author uses these elements because he was influenced by Ismāʿīlī thought, directly or indirectly. For instance, he may share common earlier sources with diverse Ismāʿīlī writers.[65] Nevertheless, even if no definitive connection is established, it remains worthwhile to explore further how Ibn Qaṣī's interpretation of the divine theophany that was a part of the climax of Muḥammad's ascension could be said to be in dialogue with select Ismāʿīlī esoteric concepts, as Ebstein suggests.

Ibn Qaṣī's work did not enjoy wide circulation in his lifetime or after, and indeed the "Removing of the Removing" might have been lost to posterity had the author's son not decided to share this chapter with the figure from al-Andalus whose destiny was to become one of the most famous of Muslim mystics of all time, Muḥyiddīn Ibn ʿArabī (d. 638/1240). One of the surviving manuscripts of *Khalʿ al-naʿlayn* appears together with Ibn ʿArabī's *Sharḥ* or exegetical gloss, apparently originally copied in the presence of the famous "grand shaykh" himself, and published approximately one decade ago by Muḥammad Amrānī.[66] In it, Ibn ʿArabī tells the story of how he received the text *Khalʿ al-naʿlayn* from Ibn Qaṣī's son, finding that it included a chapter, "The Removing of the Removing" (the one discussed at some length above), that was not in the original. He also criticized Ibn Qaṣī for having merely copied the ideas of one of his teachers rather than coming up with new interpretations himself. These charges are beyond the scope of this work to investigate, but suffice it to say that Ibn ʿArabī's skeptical remarks about the "Removing of the Removing" raise the idea that while the treatise may well reflect the thought of Ibn Qaṣī (and/or his contemporaries), it may also nevertheless represent a later composition that is theoretically separable from the rest of the work.

Returning to the historical context in which the authors from this and the previous chapter were writing on and thinking about Muḥammad's ascension, Ibn Qaṣī and his contemporary Ibn Barrajān shared a common oppositional stance against the rise of the North African al-Muwaḥḥidūn (Almohad) movement that unseated and supplanted the prevailing al-Murābiṭūn (Almoravid) line of regional rulers, yet how they expressed their opposition was quite distinct. Ibn Barrajān retreated to the isolation of the small community of contemplatives that he led outside of Ishbiliya/Seville. In contrast, Ibn Qaṣī took a more activist political stance, assuming the leadership over several fortified towns not far from the southwest coast of the Iberian Peninsula in the Algarve region (in what is now the south of modern Portugal), forging alliances with neighboring communities both Muslim and Christian, and apparently making extravagant claims about his high position in the cosmic hierarchy. Despite these differences, Ibn Barrajān and Ibn Qaṣī share a common interest in contemplative esotericism, and they both apply Neoplatonic frameworks to their understanding of cosmological structures and symbols at the heart of their elaborations of key passages that describe the climax of Muḥammad's otherworldly journey. This type of approach paved the way for new approaches to the contemplative ascension that subsequently emerged in the Islamic West after the deaths of Ibn Barrajān and Ibn Qaṣī, including their most famous and outstanding representative in the figure of Ibn ʿArabī.

Conclusion

This study attempts to open a window onto diverse debates and discussions of Muḥammad's ascension by both Muslims and non-Muslims in the eleventh- and twelfth-century Islamic West (al-Maghrib), with a particular emphasis on the works of Muslim scholars writing while the region was largely ruled over by al-Murābiṭūn (Almoravid) and al-Muwaḥḥidūn (Almohad) Amazigh leaders who originated from what is today Morocco. Engagement with official Sunnī reports of Muḥammad's ascension from the standard collections of "sound" hadith was noted in these works, as was to be expected given the Sunna-based emphasis of the Mālikī legal method that predominated throughout al-Maghrib and that experienced something of a resurgence of attention under the aforementioned Amazigh dynasties. A result of this study that may be less expected, however, was the broad engagement of both Muslim and non-Muslim sources with less official and more detailed versions of the story of Muḥammad's ascension, often attributed to the Prophet's cousin Ibn ʿAbbās, that flourished in this cultural context. From Christian and Jewish polemicists to Sufi teachers and political leaders to Qurʾān exegetes and Sīra scholars, apparently many of those who engaged in discussion of Muḥammad's ascension were at least familiar with some variation on this fantastic narrative. Therefore, I would argue that this evidence strongly suggests that such an emphasis in tenth- through eleventh-century Maghrib played a significant role in encouraging the flourishing of such Ibn ʿAbbās ascension narratives not only in this region and period but also beyond, especially in the central and eastern regions of Islamdom.

While the reasons behind the flourishing of the Ibn ʿAbbās ascension narratives in the period under consideration remain somewhat obscure, several possible explanations merit further attention. First, this longer and more fleshed-out account of Muḥammad's otherworldly journey may have spread widely because it met the needs of a broad audience of Muslims, including recent converts, answering questions and filling in gaps about this miraculous event in the Prophet's life. Second, perhaps because of that wide distribution and usage as a "teaching tale," one could understand the way inter- and intrareligious debates in the region would come to hinge on specific details of this particular version of the story, even in those scholarly works that were not composed with polemical intent. Third, the rise of Mālikī traditionalism in the al-Murābiṭ and al-Muwāḥḥid eras brought greater attention to the study of Sunnī hadith, which in the case of the subject of Muḥammad's ascension included the widely circulated

Ibn ʿAbbās reports, despite their not being included in the standard official collections of sound reports. Fourth, claims of the Amazigh leaders in al-Maghrib to lofty titles such as *mahdi* or *imām* may have affected the way scholarly discussions of ascension narratives also included narremes in which the status of eschatological leaders was revealed during Muḥammad's tour of the heavenly realms. Fifth, Iberian Muslim exegetes such as Ibn Barrajān and Ibn Qasī explored some of the esoteric potential of the Ibn ʿAbbās reports as part of their didactic discourses aimed at cultivating a new generation of engaged contemplatives. Sixth and finally, Ismāʿīlī missionary work from propagandists active in the region, whether from Fāṭimī circles or otherwise, could have played a role in encouraging esoteric speculations on the meaning of Muḥammad's ascension, further building on interpretations of depictions of the Prophet's experiences at the very highest levels of his journey that the Ibn ʿAbbās reports describe much more than any other versions do. Even though this study has suggested that there is not sufficient evidence to support Ebstein's theory that much of the esoteric speculation among the Maghribī contemplatives directly owes a debt to Ismāʿīlī "influence,"[1] nevertheless throughout this study we have noted evidence of the gradual rise in esoteric contemplative interpretations more generally, whatever their source.

The wider context of political events in the Mediterranean region also deserves some consideration. It is certainly the case that the Maghrib experienced a great deal of turmoil during the period in question, and it is certainly possible that Fāṭimid activists circulated even in primarily Sunnī scholarly circles before the conquering of the Fāṭimid dynasty in 567/1171 by Salāḥ al-Dīn al-Ayyūbī. But the burden of proof for the Ismāʿīlī thesis must rest on those who postulate the centrality of Ismāʿīlī "influence," and that proof remains elusive. It is just as likely that the propaganda of western Muslims in general in looking toward the resistance against and/or expulsion of Christian Crusader forces from the territories they conquered in the eastern Mediterranean during the period in question (Jerusalem was taken by the Crusaders in 492/1099) sparked the imagination of Muslims to speculate on the meaning, esoteric or otherwise, of Muḥammad's miraculous night journey to Jerusalem and beyond. This possibility, though it should not be overstated, since the eastern Mediterranean did not loom as large in the Muslim imagination as it did in western Christian conceptions of "the Holy Land," certainly deserves further exploration in future studies, especially in light of Ibn Barrajān's famous prediction of the date of the "reconquest" of Jerusalem (583/1187) that he never lived to see, decades before the actual event.[2] It was not long after the Ayyūbī conquests, which took place during the reigns of al-Muwaḥḥid leaders Abū Yaʿqūb Yūsuf I (r. beginning circa 558/1163) and Abū Yūsuf Ya'qūb al-Manṣūr (r. beginning circa 580/1184) that one of the most famous Muslim scholars of Maghribī origin, Muḥyiddin Ibn 'Arabī (d. 638/1240), left on a journey from the Iberian Peninsula eastward, eventually ending up in Damascus, beginning a prolific career as a writer and esoteric specialist that profoundly affected the development of western Muslim esoteric thought.

Ibn 'Arabī's oeuvre spans a vast and deep ocean of esoteric and technical waters, and it is beyond the scope of this work to attempt a comprehensive discussion of how this "grand master" appropriates and interprets the story of the night journey and ascension into his many distinct treatments of the theme across his long scholarly career. A few scholarly works have contributed to our understanding of select pieces of this story of Ibn 'Arabī's engagement with the theme of ascension, but a more comprehensive critical study of his approach to the *mi'rāj* remains a desideratum.[3] Indeed, one of the goals of the present study is to prepare the way for a broader analysis of the way Ibn 'Arabī discusses the ascension, for example in the context of his masterwork *The Meccan Revelations* (*Futuḥāt al-makkiyya*), a theme that deserves to be understood in the context of this monumental work as a whole.[4] In the context of our focus on the theme of ascension in the western Islamic lands up through the sixth/twelfth century, however, we must content ourselves here to note that Ibn 'Arabī composed his treatise titled *Kitāb al-Isrā' ilā al-maqām al-asnā* (*The Book of the Night Journey to the Most Brilliant Station*) early in his career while still in the Maghrib.[5] It describes the quest of a heroic saintly individual, represented by the symbolically named "traveler" (*al-sālik*, usually understood as an allusion to Ibn 'Arabī himself), who first imitates the Prophet's miraculous night journey to Jerusalem accompanied by an angelic guide before being taken up through the heavens. The author explains that he crafts and delivers the work in this form to aid in its memorization as a teaching tool, reminding us of the pedagogical contexts in which Ibn Barrajān's *tafsīr* and Ibn Qasī's treatise likely originated.[6] With Ibn 'Arabī's *Book of the Night Journey to the Most Resplendent Station* we have reached one logical extension to the mystical approach to the exegesis of Muḥammad's ascension in the western Islamic lands that began more modestly with the transmission and interpretation of select hadith reports and specific qur'ānic verses that Muslims came to associate with the Prophet's otherworldly journey, namely the creative appropriation of the framework of the prophetic journey as a basis for an allegorical retelling of the story as applied to journey of the unnamed traveler.[7]

Given Michael Ebstein's thesis of the Ismā'īlī influences on Ibn 'Arabī's thought through the Neoplatonic esoteric form of theosophy that he suggests may have come to the grand master through his reading the treatises of the Brethren of Purity (*al-Ikhwān al-Ṣafā*), unlike in the case of Ibn Barrajān's Qur'ān commentaries that we have examined above, Ibn 'Arabī's *Kitāb al-isrā'* provides ambivalent evidence that such Ismā'īlī ideas might have directly affected his mystical thinking at this early stage of his career. Although the question deserves further consideration, I would contend that it is unlikely that at this early period of Ibn 'Arabī's thought in general, and his ideas about the night journey and ascension in particular, that they draw substantially from the treatises of the Brethren of Purity or are otherwise in dialogue with Fāṭimid Ismā'īlī ascension discourses, as Ebstein argues. More likely, what we find in Ibn 'Arabī's writings is an engagement with the Maghribī traditions of ascension-related exegesis and hadith commentary from the previous century, which he transforms and adapts as part of his project of exploring what in his time can properly be called western Sufi mystical internalizations and explorations of the theme of ascension as part of a first-person spiritual or visionary appropriation of the Prophet's miraculous journey.

In the decades that followed Ibn 'Arabī's composition of his *Kitāb al-isrā'* treatise early in his life, not only did this great shaykh treat the same theme in a variety of ways in his later works, but in addition several other Maghribī writers took up something of his new Sufi approach to a greater or lesser degree. We see glimmerings of this new orientation in the mystical commentary provided along with the focus on Prophetic ascension-related hadith in the work of Ibn 'Arabī's contemporary of Iberian origin named Ibn Diḥya al-Kalbī (d. 633/1235), who apparently did most of his scholarly writing in Egypt.[8] So, too, was the destination of the Cordoba-born Qur'ān commentator Abū Muḥammad al-Qurṭubī (d. 671/1273), who cites Ibn 'Arabī's work in places, and who passes on some familiar ascension-related anecdotes in his exegesis of the relevant passages from the Qur'ān. Of course, interreligious polemic continued unabated in the thirteenth century as well, an outstanding example of which is found in the *Liber Scalae Machometi* (*Book of Muḥammad's Ladder*), which was compiled and translated from multiple Arabic sources into a composite text rendered into several European languages at the court of the Christian ruler Alfonso X of Castille (r. 1252–1284).[9] The work clearly was produced not only to transmit the story of Muḥammad's ascension to a Christian audience but also to highlight its discrepancies and to serve as the basis for attacking its alleged fantastic excesses. Mention should be made of the Qur'ān commentary frequently attributed Ibn 'Arabī but widely understood by scholars to be the work of one of his followers named 'Abd al-Razzāq al-Qashānī (d. ca. 730/1329), which develops some of Ibn 'Arabī's mystical ideas regarding Muḥammad's ascension even further.[10]

Finally, the visionary ascension approach that one finds in Ibn ʿArabī's short *Kitāb al-isrāʾ* receives a creative elaboration in a dream manual that circulated with the multivolume abridgment of *Ṣaḥīḥ Bukhārī* composed by the Maghribī scholar Ibn Abī Jamra (d. ca. 699/1300).[11] With Ibn Abī Jamra's engagement with ascension visions at the end of the seventh/thirteenth century, western esoteric engagement with the story of Muḥammad's ascension can truly be described as having reached a new stage of development in tandem with the engagement of select eastern Sufis of that century,[12] joined later by other western Sufis who explore the theme vis-à-vis the growing importance of noetic dreams and visions of the Prophet.[13] I would contend that this new Maghribī "turn" stems not only from the arrival of eastern Sufi ideas in the Islamic West but also from the profound impact of the writings of earlier Maghribī contemplatives described in this study, as well as the creative vision of the great shaykh Ibn ʿArabī. While a detailed investigation into this new turn in western ascension discourses from the time of Ibn ʿArabī and after will have to await future studies, the present monograph demonstrates the diverse and profound engagements with the theme of Muḥammad's otherworldly journeys composed by generations of western scholars, both Muslim and non-Muslim, in the centuries preceding Ibn ʿArabī's illustrious career.

Appendix

Translation of Real Academia de la Historia MS Codera 241[1]

[1r] [I saw an angel sitting on a throne, with] the entire world between his knees[2] and [the fate of every creature] between his [eyes].[3] He was angry-faced. I asked, "Who is this, Gabriel?" He replied, "This is the Angel of Death, Azra'il. Approach, Muḥammad and greet him." So I approached him and greeted him, and he returned the greeting, saying, "Welcome, Muḥammad!" without smiling at me the way all the other angels had. Gabriel then said to me [by way of explanation], "Muḥammad, neither this Angel of Death nor the Guardian of [the Fire of] Jahannam laugh on any day, nor will they laugh until resurrection day." I approached to the right of the Angel of Death, and I saw an enormous tablet that he looked upon for a long time and did not neglect for a single hour. I said: "Gabriel, what is that enormous tablet that is on the right, between his hands?" He replied, "[On it] are written the names of [all] the [people] [1v] [. . . .][4] [He knows the time of the death of a servant draws near from] his name on the tablet, and the Angel of Death seizes his spirit (*rūḥ*). Since the time God created the angels in the heavens and on the earth, and the jinn, and every person, all of them have been [constantly] under the gaze of the patient Azra'il, Angel of Death, and all of them are under his guardianship."

Then we went a little ways, and suddenly I found myself with a man, handsome of face, sitting on a throne of light. I said, "Gabriel, who is this?" He answered, "Your brother, Idris [=Enoch] the prophet. Go forward, Muḥammad, and greet him." So I went forward and greeted him, and he replied in greeting, saying, "Welcome to you, righteous brother, prophet most favored by God!" Then Gabriel made the call to prayer, and I advanced and I led the angels of the fourth heaven and Idris the prophet in two cycles of ritual prayer.

Gabriel rose [with me] up to the fifth heaven, a distance of five hundred years, and its width was similar to that. Gabriel advanced . . .[5]

[. . . (one or more folios missing here, for the account of the fifth heaven is lost) . . .]

[2r] Gabriel rose [with me] up to the sixth heaven, a distance of five hundred years, and its width was similar to that. Gabriel advanced to the gate. He was asked, "Who is at the gate?" He answered, "Gabriel, and with me is the best of God's creation, Muḥammad son of ʿAbdullāh." The door was opened and we entered in. Suddenly I was with innumerable angels — only God knows their

number — and I found myself with an angel named Dardaya'il sitting on a throne of light. He had seventy thousand wings, and seventy thousand heads, in each of the heads were seventy thousand faces and seventy thousand mouths, each mouth with seventy thousand tongues, each tongue glorifying God in seventy thousand languages, one not resembling the other. I greeted him, and he answered the greeting, "Welcome to you, Muḥammad, rejoice, for you are the most favored of God's creatures!" Then I went a little ways and suddenly found myself with a man, handsome of face, sitting on a throne of light. I asked, "Who is this, Gabriel?" [2v] He replied, "He is your brother Aaron, the prophet (upon him be peace). Approach and greet him." So I approached and greeted him, and he returned the greeting saying, "Welcome to you, Muḥammad, and rejoice, for you are the most favored of God's creatures!" Then Gabriel made the call to prayer, and I advanced and led the angels of the sixth heaven and my brother Aaron in two cycles of ritual prayer.

Then Gabriel rose up [with me] to the seventh heaven, a distance of five hundred years, and its width was something similar to that. Gabriel advanced to the gate, and a voice said, "Who is at the gate?" He answered, "I am Gabriel, and with me is Muḥammad, the best of God's creation." The gate was opened for us, and suddenly we were with an angel sitting on a throne of light. We had not seen an angel more handsome of face than he, nor more eloquent of speech. I greeted him, and he returned the greeting saying, "O Muḥammad, rejoice, for you are the most favored of God's creatures! Do you know, Muḥammad, how long [3r] I have been in this place [waiting for you, in my praise] for you? A thousand years before our father Adam was created." Then that angel snatched me away and swam into a sea of light. Were one of you to be on [its] shore, you would not cross this sea in a hundred years, yet this angel crossed this sea faster than the blink of an eye, and stood me on a second sea, of water. I became terrified because of the immensity of its waves. I saw angels in it, from one ear of [each angel] to its other ear was a distance of five hundred years. Gabriel went and left me, so I was very afraid at the number of the waves of that sea. Gabriel said to me, "Do not fear, and do not be sad."

Next, he crossed with me over that lake until we came to the Lote Tree of the Boundary. I saw that it was a tree, the sweetness of it [3v] was richer, even richer than figs. [It was so immense that] were one to assemble all that God created of angels in the heavens and earth, and all the people and jinn, they could all find shade under just one of its branches. Gabriel stood me next to the tree and said to me, "Muḥammad, this is my station. *There is none among us that does not have a known station* [Q 37:164]. Advance, Muḥammad, and in front of you, you will find one who will direct you to your lord."

I advanced, continuing on, not knowing what I was doing, when all of a sudden there was a voice that called out from before God saying, "Muḥammad, step quickly into the light." So I stood in it, and suddenly a green *rafraf* [Q 55:76] had come out of the sea with a whirl. I sat on it, and it carried me like an arrow shot out of a bow until it threw me onto another sea of green light. I found myself with angels that, had God allowed, one of them could have swallowed the heavens and the earth entirely in a mouthful, [4r] through the power of God. They were glorifying God, the exalted. Then it carried me to a second sea of yellow light. I was suddenly with angels that, had one of them stretched out its palm to the world, it would darken it entirely with a single palm, through the enormity of its size. They were glorifying God, the exalted. Then it carried me to a third sea of black light. When I gazed on it, fell down in petition to God, prostrating on the *rafraf*, calling out, "Do not [forsake] me, my intimate, my devotion." A voice from before God called out, "Muḥammad, do not fear, for indeed I am with you, I hear and see, and I have power over all things."

Then it carried me to a sea of water, in which I saw an enormous angel measuring the water with a measure, and weighing it in a scale. I greeted him, and he returned the greeting saying, "Welcome to you, Muḥammad, and rejoice, for you are the most favored of God's creatures!" I asked him, "Which of the angels are you?" and he replied, "I am Michael (*Mīkāʾīl*)." I asked, "By God almighty, tell me, why you were named Michael? [4v] And why was Gabriel named Gabriel?" He answered, "Muḥammad, is it not enough that you are in this greatest of states, yet you ask me about this [particular] state (*ḥāl*)?" I replied to him, "God helped me to this place. When I descend to the earth, if someone from my community asks me, I will inform him, with God's permission (*bi-idhnillāh*)." He said, "Muḥammad, I was named Michael because I am the one responsible for measuring (*ukayyal*) the drops [of water] and the plants. I measure the water with a measure (*mikyāl*), and I weigh it with a scale, then I send it wherever God wishes. As for Gabriel, he was named Gabriel because no other angel is more intensely powerful than he. He is the one responsible for the drowning and sinking into the ground [of disobedient communities and their cities, on the divine order]. Every community of angels falls under the two hands of Gabriel."

Next [the *rafraf*] carried me to a station in which I saw Isrāfīl. The throne was on his shoulders, the trumpet was in his mouth, and the tablet was hanging between his eyes. I cried out, "Peace be with you, Isrāfīl! What is the reason I see you in this state (*ḥāl*)?" He replied to me, "I listen to the speech of the lord of the worlds." I asked, "So what do you hear him saying?" "He says, 'Be (*kun*),' and the 'k' does not precede the 'n' [5r] before what he wills exists, through his will together with his power." I further enquired, "Isrāfīl, where am I?" He answered me, saying, "Lift up your head, Muḥammad!" So I lifted my head, and suddenly I saw that I was at the [divine] throne of white pearl. It had seventy thousand pillars, filled with angels, each angel glorifying God, the exalted. I saw below the throne an enormous angel in the shape of a rooster, its eyes of emerald, its neck of white silver, and its lower half encrusted with pearls and sapphires. It was glorifying God, the exalted, saying at the end of its crowing, "Remember God, O you who are neglectful!" As the roosters of the earth heard him, they would cry out in response to his cries, and would grow silent with his silences. I greeted him, and he replied to me, "Welcome to you, Muḥammad! Rejoice, for you are the most favored of all of God's creatures!"

I glanced under the throne, and then I found I was with an immense snake that had wrapped itself around the throne seventy times, and its head had grasped its tail. I saw that it had a head the size of the world [5v] seven times over, and to the right of its head were a thousand [more] heads, and the same with the left of its head. In each head were a thousand faces, in each face a thousand mouths, in each mouth a thousand tongues, each tongue glorifying God in a thousand languages. They were saying, "Glorified be God, the great, the greatest of all! Glorified be [the might] that he compels in his realm of power (*Jabarūt*) over all its inhabitants! No eye sees him, even as it glorifies greatly!" [Regarding the description of the heavenly snake:] Its tail to its head was of pearl and emerald, each pearl the length of the world. It had a hundred thousand horns, the width and height of each being a thousand years, all of the horns made of silk, gleaming light, shining white. Its head was of yellow sapphire, and its back of emerald, its right of green sapphire, and the rest of its belly of hidden pearl, beaming to the ends of the heavens and the seven earths, more than seventy times stronger than the light of the sun and moon upon the earth. Between one of its ears to its other was a journey of a thousand years. When it opened up its eyes, were God to allow [6r] it, it could swallow the seven heavens and all in them, [along with] the seven earths and all in them, in a single bite, and that would not be more in its belly than a [tiny] charm in a [wide] field. When it spread its wings, the heavens and the earth resounded with glorification and sanctification, and one heard from its belly the rumble like the rumble of thunder. On each feather of its wings was an angel, in the hands of each of the angels a spear of light, glorifying God in a thousand languages, and sanctifying him. It had two chains of pearls and emeralds and coral, and it had five thousand necklaces, on each necklace was seventy angels, in the hands of each angel a lance of light, glorifying God the exalted, and prostrating to him, and sanctifying him. The eyelashes of its eyes were a distance of a five-hundred-year journey [apart]. I said, "Isrāfīl, what is the story of this snake?" He answered, "When God created the throne, it wondered at its [own] immensity. [6v] And the wonderment was comprehended in God's knowledge, i.e.[,] that this was coming from the throne, so God created that snake and wrapped it around [the throne] seventy times. When the throne became conscious of that snake, it understood fear and fretting. This is one of his wonders, Muḥammad. Approach and greet it." So I approached and greeted it, and it returned the greeting with a voice like the crash of thunder, saying, "Rejoice, Muḥammad, for you are the most favored of God's creatures!"

Then I suddenly found myself with one of the angels of the veils, which had turned to me and greeted me, and it took me by the hand and brought me to the veil of light (*al-nūr*), a veil that was the distance of five hundred years, and its width something similar to that. It brought me across that veil to a veil called the veil of the state (*al-hāl*), a distance of five hundred years and its width similar to that. It brought me across that veil to a third veil called the veil of immensity (*al-*ʿuẓma), a distance of five hundred years and its width something similar to that. It brought me across that [7r] veil to a fourth veil called the veil of power (*al-quwwa*), a distance of five hundred years and its width something similar to that. It brought me across that veil to a fifth veil called the veil of might (*al-*ʿizza), a distance of five hundred years and its width something similar to that. It brought me across that veil to a sixth veil called the veil of immensity (*al-kibriyya*), a distance of five hundred years and its width something similar to that. It brought me across that veil to a seventh veil called the veil of unicity (*al-waḥdāniyya*). I heard a caller say, "Angels of the veils, raise the veils that are between me and my beloved (*ḥabībī*) Muḥammad." I looked at the angels who were the guardians of the veils, [and obeying the command] they raised them. Then they trembled from the amount of light that suddenly covered them. I advanced forward and found myself amidst twenty thousand rows of angels standing — they will not kneel or prostrate until Judgment Day — then I advanced forward through twenty thousand rows of angels kneeling and prostrating — [7v] they will not raise their heads until Judgment Day while they are prostrating to God, the exalted.

So I proceeded forward and I [thought] everything — all of it — had died, due to its silence from the immensity of the lord, majestic be his majesty. [And I became terrified]. A caller from before God cried out, "Do not be afraid, Muḥammad, nor let fear come upon you." On that, my terror was silenced. A caller cried, "Approach, Muḥammad, for I am your lord!" I continued walking, [but] I knew not how I should greet my lord. My lord inspired me [to speak] when I said, "Salutations from God, purities are for God, goodnesses and prayers are to God." God responded, "Peace be upon you, o Prophet, and the mercy and blessings of God, the Master, Lord, Peace, Faithful, Protector, Powerful, Conqueror.[6]

O Muḥammad, [Do you know] what do the heavenly host debate?" [I answered,] "Yes, the 'expiations' (al-*kaffarāt*)." "And what are they, Muḥammad?" My lord inspired me when I replied, "Fulfilling ablutions in hated conditions (i.e.[,] when not required), and walking to the mosques and sitting [8r] in them [for prayer after] prayer." He proclaimed, "You speak the truth, Muḥammad. Ask of me whatever you would like." "My lord, I ask of you for the completion of good deeds (*al-khayrāt*) and the leaving behind of bad things (*al-munkarāt*) and rejection of the forbidden (*al-munākir*). And when you desire strife (*al-fitna*) among people, take me to you not as one of the sowers of strife. And I ask you, my lord, for your love (*ḥubba-ka*), and the love of the one who loves you (*man yuḥibbuka*), [so that] through [the totality] (*bi 'l-kull*) one may incline, and be made to approach you through it." He said: "That is for you, Muḥammad." [God continued, asking me,] "Do you wish to see me with your eyes?" I said to him, "No, my master (*sayyidī*). My eyes have been overwhelmed with light: the light of your majesty (*jalāli-ka*) and the light of your splendor (*bahā 'i-ka*). However, I see you with the eye of my heart (*qalb*)." He said: "Muḥammad, magnified is my subject, and exalted is my place, for I am the Most Mighty (*jabbār* [*al-jabbābīr*]) [of the mighty], the Great of the Greatest (*kabīr al-akābira*), inheritor of the world and the afterworld, Blessed [King][7] without defects that pass away (*fanā*). O Muḥammad, ask of me whatever you would like (*tuḥibbu*)." I noticed [the sword of] strife (*al-fitna*) [hanging][8] from the throne, dripping blood. So I said, "My lord, raise the sword from my community." He replied, "Muḥammad, I sent you with the sword, and most of your community [will not pass away][9] except through the sword."

I said, "My lord, you [8v] [*took*] *Abraham* [*as an intimate friend*],[10] plus you *spoke to Moses* [*directly*].[11] You raised Enoch and Abraham[12] *to a high place*,[13] and you forgave David [his great sins],[14] and you gave his son (Solomon) an *immense kingdom*.[15] So what is there for me, Muḥammad, your Prophet?" God, majestic be his majesty, replied, "O Muḥammad, if I formerly took Abraham as a friend, I have taken you as a friend [and lover]. And if I formerly spoke to Moses directly, I did that on Mount Sinai, and I have spoken to you, O Muḥammad, above the seven heavens. And if I formerly raised up Enoch to a high place, indeed I raised [him only] to the fourth heaven, and you, Muḥammad, [I have raised up] to a site that has not been seen by near angel nor sent [prophet]. And if I formerly forgave David great sins, I have given you, Muḥammad, the river (*al-nahr*) Kawthar, the two rivers [the Nile and Euphrates], and the spring of [life (*al-ḥayāt*)].[16] And if you think I gave Solomon a [great] kingdom, [indeed] I have given you, Muḥammad, the Opening of the Book,[17] [and the seals of the Cow chapter[18]].

Notes

Introduction.

1. Here I am following the argument of Yousef Casewit in *The Mystics of al-Andalus: Ibn Barrajān and Islamic Thought in the Twelfth Century* (Cambridge: Cambridge University Press, 2017) that the term "Sufi" does not properly apply to the Maghribī and Andalūsī figures at the center of this study prior to the time of Ibn ʿArabī (i.e., the very end of the sixth/twelfth century). The term "mystic" and the broader concept of "mysticism" has a long and controversial history in the contemporary study of religion, thus caution must be exercised in the application of this term to data outside of the contexts in which the term originates. It could be argued that "contemplative," the insider term used in this period for a person engaged in the philosophical approach of one who "crosses over" (*muʿtabir*), may serve as a better fit for the period, geography, and genealogical contexts of the main authors whose works will be examined in this study. See the discussion in Casewit, *Mystics of al-Andalus*, 3–5.

2. A selective list of monographs on the subject would include those by Brooke Olson Vuckovic, *Heavenly Journeys, Earthly Concerns* (New York: Routledge, 2005); Frederick Colby, *Narrating Muḥammad's Night Journey* (Albany: State University of New York Press, 2008); R. P. Buckley, *The Night Journey and Ascension in Islam* (London: I. B. Tauris, 2013); and edited volumes by Mohammad Ali Amir-Moezzi, *Le voyage initiatique en terre d'Islam* (Louvain-Paris: Peeters, 1996); and Christiane Gruber and Frederick Colby, *The Prophet's Ascension* (Bloomington: Indiana University Press, 2010). In addition, when it comes to the study of Sufi commentary on Muḥammad's ascension, especially noteworthy are the approaches of Martin Nguyen, "Tracing the Traditions of Exegesis," chapter 6 of *Sufi Master and Qur'an Scholar: Abū'l-Qāsim al-Qushayrī and the 'Laṭā'if al-Ishārāt'* (Oxford: Oxford University Press, 2012); Pieter Coppens, "A Vision at the Utmost Boundary," chapter 7 of *Seeing God in Sufi Qur'an Commentaries: Crossings between This World and the Otherworld* (Edinburgh: Edinburgh University Press, 2018).

3. Especially see Colby, *Narrating Muḥammad's Night Journey*; see also my essay "Ascension Visions of Sufi Masters" in *Words of Experience: Translating Islam with Carl W. Ernst*, ed. Ilyse Morgensein Fuerst and Brannon Wheeler (Sheffield, UK: Equinox, 2021), 94–111.

4. The early story of what is being termed here "eastern Sufism" has been told by a number of scholars, including Ahmet Karamustafa, Alexander Knysh, and, via primary sources, Michael Sells. Coppens, in his otherwise comprehensive tour de force analyzing foundational works of Muslim mystics on the subject of eschatology and the vision of God, excludes consideration of the work of foundational western contemplatives on methodological grounds. See, for instance, his following note: "Excepted

are the *tafsīr* works by Ibn Barrajān (d. 536/1141), which could arguably be labelled as Sufi commentaries as well. . . . The main reason for not including these sources is that they are not genealogically part of the *tafsīr* tradition as it developed in Nishapur and the larger Persia region, and do not refer back to the same authorities" (Coppens, *Seeing God*, 35–36n71).

5. A term I use here as employed by Shahab Ahmed, *What Is Islam? The Importance of Being Islamic* (Princeton, NJ: Princeton University Press, 2015).

6. See Shahab Ahmed, *What Is Islam?*, especially chapters 4 and 5.

7. Ahmed, *What Is Islam?*, 346–347.

8. Ahmed, *What Is Islam?*, 357.

9. This periodization appears to be drawn from the work of historian Marshall Hodgson, *The Venture of Islam*, 3 vols (Chicago, IL: University of Chicago Press, 1974). Using Hodgson's schema, the works most under consideration in the present study, as with the works in the study of Coppens, largely fall in the period that Hodgson labels the "Islamic Earlier Middle Period" (950–1250 CE).

10. It remains beyond the scope of this work to describe the long history of this broad theme in depth and in detail. For accessible surveys, see Ioan Culiano, *Out of This World: Otherworldly Journeys from Gilgamesh to Albert Einstein* (Boston, MA: Shambhala, 1991); Carol and Philip Zaleski, eds., *The Book of Heaven: An Anthology of Writings from Ancient to Modern Times* (Oxford: Oxford University Press, 2000); and John J. Collins and Michael Fishbane, eds., *Death, Ecstasy, and Other Worldly Journeys* (Albany: State University of New York Press, 1995).

11. See Peter Adamson, *The Arabic Plotinus: A Philosophical Study of the Theology of Aristotle* (London: Duckworth, 2002); also see the discussion of this history in Michael Ebstein, *Mysticism and Philosophy in al-Andalus: Ibn Masarra, Ibn al-ʿArabī, and the Ismāʿīlī Tradition* (Leiden: Brill, 2014), 36–38; and essays in *Neoplatonism and Islamic Thought*, ed. Parviz Morewedge (Albany: State University of New York Press, 1992). For a critique of the use and application of the term "Neoplatonism," see Maria Luisa Gatti, "Plotinus: The Platonic Tradition and the Foundations of Neoplatonism," in *The Cambridge Companion to Plotinus*, ed. Lloyd P. Gerson (Cambridge: Cambridge University Press, 1992).

12. In addition to the sources cited in the previous note, see especially Ithmar Gruenwald, *Apocalyptic and Merkavah Mysticism* (Leiden: Brill, 1980); Peter Schäfer, *The Hidden and Manifest God* (Albany: State University of New York Press, 1992); Vita Arbel, *Beholders of Divine Secrets: Mysticism and Myth in the Hekhalot and Merkavah Literature* (Albany: State University of New York Press, 2003); Christopher Rowland and Christopher R. A. Morray-Jones, *The Mystery of God: Early Jewish Mysticim and the New Testament* (Leiden: Brill, 2009); James Davila, *Hekhalot Literature in Translation: Major Texts of Merkavah Mysticism* (Leiden: Brill, 2013); "From Hekhalot Rabbati to the Hekhalot of the Zohar: The Depersonalization of the Mysticism of the Divine Chariot" [in Hebrew], in *Jewish Studies* [*Kavod*] (2017): 143–162; and Joseph Dan, *The Heart and the Fountain: An Anthology of Jewish Mystical Experiences* (Oxford: Oxford University Press, 2002), 49–73.

13. On Ibn Ezra and his engagement with this theme, see Aaron Hughes, *The Texture of the Divine: Imagination in Medieval Islamic and Jewish Thought* (Bloomington:

Indiana University Press, 2004); and Aaron Hughes, "Mi'rāj and the Language of Legitimation in the Medieval Islamic and Jewish Philosophical Traditions: A Case Study of Avicenna and Abraham ibn Ezra," in *The Prophet's Ascension*, ed. Christiane Gruber and Frederick Colby (Bloomington: Indiana University Press, 2010), 72–91.

14. For the *Apocalypse of Paul* and other Christian otherworldly accounts, most of which precede the time period of this study, see Claude Kappler, "L'Apocalypse latine de Paul," in *Apocalypses et voyages dans l'au-delà*, ed. Claude Kappler, et al (Paris: Les Éditions du CERF, 1987), 237–266. See also the accessible translations ed. Eileen Gardiner in *Visions of Heaven and Hell Before Dante* (New York: Italica Press, 1989). Paul's apocalypse appears on pages 13–46 of the latter work. For the passage in Paul's New Testament espistle 2 Cor. 12 and its Jewish mystical contexts, see Alan Segal, "Paul and the Beginning of Jewish Mysticism," in *Death, Ecstasy, and Other Wordly Journeys*, ed. John J. Collins and Michael Fishbane, 95–122 (Albany: State University of New York Press, 1995); finally, see also Martha Himmelfarb, "The Practice of Ascent in the Ancient Mediterranean World," in *Death, Ecstasy, and Other Wordly Journeys*, ed. John J. Collins and Michael Fishbane, 123–154 (Albany: State University of New York Press, 1995).

15. See Uri Rubin, "Muhammad's Night Journey (Isra') to al-Masjid al-Aqsa: Aspects of the Earliest Origins of the Islamic Sanctity of Jerusalem," *Qantara: Revista de estudios árabes* 29, no. 1 (2008): 147–164.

16. Ibn Sa'd, *Tabaqāt al-kubrā* (Beirut: Dār al-Sādir, 1957–1968), 1:213–214; Josef van Ess, "Vision and Ascension: Surat al-Najm and its Relationship with Muḥammad's *mi'rāj*," *Journal of Qur'anic Studies* 1 (1999): 56–57.

17. Although its reliability is uncertain, even one of the very earliest extant Qur'ān commentaries, that ascribed to Muqātil b. Sulaymān (d. 150/767), appears to use the two terms interchangeably, referring to both with a single Arabic word: *isrā'*.

18. Casewit, *Mystics of al-Andalus*, 241–242. According to Casewit's study, most Muslim scholars in al-Andalus did not have a problem working with weakly authenticated reports as long as it was not for juridical purposes (see Casewit, *Mystics of al-Andalus*, 243). While some of the scholars at the center of this study, such as Qāḍī 'Īyāḍ, might sharply disagree with this idea, even he did not consistently provide a detailed chain of transmission for the vast majority of the reports that he cites in his famous work *al-Shifā'* (see chapter 3).

19. See Colby, *Narrating.* That these "unathenticated" reports were also foundational for some of the early eastern Sufi sayings on the Prophet's ascension can be seen from Sulamī's *Subtleties of the Ascension*, trans. Frederick Colby (Louisville, KY: Fons Vitae, 2006); Qushayrī, *Kitāb al-mi'rāj*, ed. Ali Ḥasan 'Abd al-Qādir (Cairo: Dār al-Kutub al-Ḥadītha, 1964), etc.

20. There was no hard-and-fast division between what we in the present day consider "literature" and what we might classify in the category of "religion." Such distinctions do not make much sense when applied to writings from the premodern era.

21. Montgomery Watt, *A History of Islamic Spain* (Edinburgh: Edinburgh University Press, 1965), 92.

22. This is the anonymous fragmentary manuscript analyzed in chapter 1, Madrid Real Academia de Historia, MS Codera 241.

23. For this conception and translation of the term "Murābiṭ," see Maribel Fierro, "Between the Maghreb and al-Andalus," in Maribel Fierro, *The Almohad Revolution Revolution: Politics and Religion in the Islamic West during the Twelfth-Thirteenth Centuries* (Farnham, UK: Ashgate, 2012), 4.

24. In this period one finds the writings of ʿIyāḍ, Ibn Barrajān, Ibn Qasī, whose work will be discussed in detail in the later chapters of this work.

25. Watt, *History of Islamic Spain*, 100.

26. Fierro, "Between the Maghreb and al-Andalus," 4–6 and 12–14.

27. Ebstein goes even further to assert that foundational contemplative writers in Islamic Spain from Ibn Masarra to Ibn ʿArabī were profoundly and directly influenced by Ismāʿīlī thought from both the Fāṭimī missionaries and the epistles of the "Brethren of Purity" (see a summary of this approach especially in his work *Mysticism and Philosophy in al-Andalus*, 2–8 and 28–32).

28. Watt, *History of Islamic Spain*, 101.

29. Fierro, "Between the Maghreb and al-Andalus," 6, where she is speaking specifically about the revolt of Ibn Qasī in southern Portugal.

30. Carl Brockelmann, *Geschichte der Arabischen Litteratur* (Leiden: Brill, 1943–1949), 1:455.

31. M. Talbi, s.v. "ʿIyāḍ b. Mūsā," in *Encyclopaedia of Islam*, 2nd ed. (Leiden: Brill, 1960–).

32. Talbi, *Encyclopaedia of Islam*.

33. See Brockelmann, *Geschichte der Arabischen Litteratur*, 1:455–456.

34. See Casewit, *Mystics of al-Andalus*; a very useful bibliography of recent work on this figure appears in the introduction by Böwering and Casewit to their edition of *Kitāb Īḍāḥ al-ḥikma*.

35. See Casewit, *Mystics of al-Andalus*. According to Casewit, "Andalusīs viewed themselves as involved in a parallel religiopolitical struggle against the forces of the Christian Reconquista. It is perhaps for this reason that Jerusalem occupies such a place of privilege in Ibn Barrajān's religious imagination" (Casewit, *Mystics of al-Andalus*, 295).

36. According to Casewit, Ibn Barrajān's longer or "major" commentary, *Tanbīh al-afhām*, was "composed between the years 515–525 /1120–1130"; his shorter or "lesser" commentary, *Kitāb Īḍāḥ al-ḥikma*, was composed after 525/1130, i.e., in the last decade of his life, "as a supplement to the *Tanbīh*" (Casewit, *Mystics of al-Andalus*, 157, 163).

37. Ibn Barrajān also became known for the idea of what Casewit labels "qurʾānic hegemony," the idea that all things can be explained through the Qurʾān, and thus all sources (such as the Christian New Testament) are open to be interpreted via the Qurʾān. Except with a minor example that will be explored in the next chapter, this hermeneutic principle does not play much of a role in his commentary on the story of Muḥammad's ascension.

38. Casewit, *Mystics of al-Andalus*, 69–70.

39. See the book by Michael Ebstein, *Mysticism and Philosophy in al-Andalus*, although Ebstein does not address the case of Ibn Barrajān directly therein.

40. E.g., Casewit, *Mystics of al-Andalus*, 208.

41. Casewit, *Mystics of al-Andalus*, 268; compare the disparate positions of Daylamī and Baqlī cited in Coppens, *Seeing God*, 240–248.

42. José Bellver, s.v. "Ibn Barrajān," in *Encyclopaedia of Islam*, 3rd ed. (Leiden: Brill, 2007–).

43. Bellver, *Encyclopaedia of Islam.*

44. See David Goodrich, "A Sufi Revolt in Portugal: Ibn Qasī and His *Kitāb Khal' al-na'layn*" (PhD diss., Columbia University, 1978); Josef Dreher, "Das Imamat des islamischen Mystikers Abūlqāsim Aḥmad ibn al-Ḥusain Ibn Qasī (gest. 1151)" (PhD diss., Rhenishen Friedrich-Wilhelm University in Bonn, 1985).

45. Goodrich, "Sufi Revolt in Portugal," 16.

46. Goodrich, "Sufi Revolt in Portugal," 16.

47. On his political activism during the final five years of his life, see Goodrich, "Sufi Revolt in Portugal," 18–27.

48. Wim Raven, s.v. "al-Suhaylī," *Encyclopaedia of Islam*, 2nd ed. (Leiden: Brill, 1960–); Ibn Khallikān, *Wafayāt al-A'yān*, ed. Iḥsān 'Abbās (Beirut: Dār al-Ṣādir, 1977), 3:143–144, who places his birth in Málaga in the year 508/1114.

49. Ibn Khallikān, *Wafayāt al-A'yān*, 3:143.

50. 'Abd al-Raḥmān Wakīl, in the introduction to his edition of Suhaylī's *al-Rawḍ al-unuf* fī sharḥ al-sīra al-nabawiyya (Cairo: Dār al-Kutub al-Ḥadītha, 1967–1970), 1:25.

51. See Maher Jarrar, *Die Prophetenbiographie im islamischen Spanien* (Frankfurt: Peter Lang, 1989), 176–210.

52. 'Abd al-Raḥmān Wakīl, intro to Suhaylī, *al-Rawḍ*, 1:26.

53. See Ibn Barrajān, *A Qur'ān Commentary by Ibn Barrajān of Seville d. 536/1141*: *Īḍāḥ al-ḥikma bi aḥkām al-'ibra*: *Wisdom Deciphered, The Unseen Discovered* [hereafter: *Īḍāḥ*], ed. Gerhard Böwering and Yousef Casewit (Leiden: Brill, 2016), par. 888, p. 636.

54. In his commentary from the following century, the Sufi master Ibn 'Arabī insists that when he first learned the work prior to receiving the present copy from the author's son, this additional chapter had not been included (see chapter 5 below).

Chapter One.

1. See, for instance, Peter Schäfer, *Hidden and Manifest God*, 7–8.

2. Schäfer, *Hidden and Manifest God*, 150–157.

3. See especially J. Horovitz, "Muhammeds Himmelfahrt," *Der Islam* 9 (1919): 159–183. The idea that Muslim ascension narratives were completely derivative from Jewish and Christian apocalyptic works was the position of Ioan Culianu, *Experiences de l'extase: Extase, ascension et recit visionnaire de l'hellenisme au Moyen Age* (Paris: Payot, 1984).

4. B. M. Lewin, *Otzar ha-Geonim*, vol. 4/2 (Ḥagiga), part 1 (Tehuvot), p. 14, cited in Schäfer, *Hidden and Manifest God*, 153–154. See also Gershom Scholem, *Major Trends in Jewish Mysticism* (New York: Schocken, 1946), 49; David Halperin, *The Faces of the Chariot* (Tübingen, Germany: J. C. B. Mohr, 1988), 6, 360, 374; Schäfer, *Hekhalot-Studien* (Tübingen, Germany: J. C. B. Mohr, 1988), 284; Eliot Wolfson,

"Merkavah Traditions in Philosophical Garb: Judah Halevi Reconsidered," in *Proceedings of the American Academy for Jewish Research* 57 (1990–1991): 216.

5. Schäfer, *Hidden and Manifest God*, 161. See also Peter Schäfer, "The Ideal of Piety of the Ashkenazi Hasidim and Its Roots in Jewish Tradition," *Jewish History* 4 (1990): 9–23.

6. For instance, see Peter Schäfer, ed., *Wege mystischer Gotteserfahrung / Mystical Approaches to God* (Munich, Germany: Oldenbourg, 2006); see also references in Wolfson, "Merkavah Traditions in Philosophical Garb," 179–242.

7. See Gerhard Böwering, "The Qurʾān Commentary of al-Sulamī," in *Islamic Studies Presented to Charles J. Adams*, ed. Wael B. Hallaq and Donald P. Little (Leiden: Brill, 1991), 41–56; Nguyen, *Sufi Master and Qurʾān Scholar;* Kristin Z. Sands, "On the Subtleties of Method and Style in the *Laṭāʾif al-ishārāt* of Qushayrī," *Journal of Sufi Studies* 2 (2013): 7–16; Coppens, *Seeing God.*

8. As for his "foundational work," Sulamī's *Ṭabaqāt al-ṣufiyya* (Generations of the Sufis) helped to establish a collection of sayings and brief biographical notices of earlier pious figures, arranging them geographically and by generations in a way that helped provide a basis for Sufi self-definition and history. In this regard, see especially Jean-Jacques Thibon, *L'oeuvre d'Abū ʿAbd al-Raḥmān al-Sulamī (325/937–412/1021) et la formation du soufisme* (Damascus: Institut français du Proche-Orient, 2009).

9. On the foundational work of Qushayrī, first and foremost is his famous *Risāla*, for which see Richard Gramlich, trans., *Das Sendschreiben al-Qusayrīs uber das Sufitum* (Wiesbaden, Germany: Franz Steiner Verlag, 1989); Alexander Knysh, trans., *Al-Qushayrī's Epistle on Sufism: 'Al-Risāla al-Qushayriyya fī ʿilm al-taṣawwuf'* (Reading, UK: Garnet, 2007).

10. See Sulamī, "Bayān laṭāʾif al-miʿrāj," in *Sufi Treatises of Abū ʿAbd al-Raḥmān al-Sulamī (d. 412/1021)*, ed. Gerhard Böwering and Bilal Orfali (Beirut: Dar El-Machreq, 2009), 21–30; Qushayrī, *Kitāb al-miʿrāj*. A significant portion of the material in these treatises is attested elsewhere, including in the Qurʾān commentaries composed by these two early Sufis.

11. In addition to the works mentioned in the previous notes, see also Gerhard Böwering, "From the Word of God to the Vision of God: Muḥammad's Heavenly Journey in Classical Ṣūfī Qurʾān Commentary," in *Le voyage initiatique en terre d'Islam*, ed. Mohammad Ali Amir-Moezzi (Leuven: Peeters, 1996), 205–222; Sulami, *Subtleties of the Ascension.*

12. *Manāḥil al-shifā wa-manāhil al-ṣafā bi-taḥqīq kitab Sharaf al-muṣṭafā taṣnīf . . . Khargūshī* [hereafter *Sharaf al-muṣṭafā*] ed. Abū ʿĀṣim Nabīl b. Hāshim al-Ghamrī, 2:180–190 (Makkah, Saudi Arabia: Dār al-Bashāʾir al-Islamiyya, 2003).

13. Elements of the narremes appearing in Khargūshī's *Sharaf al-muṣṭafā,* 2:171–189 bear extremely close resemblance to the "Primitive Version" of the Ibn ʿAbbās ascension narrative that was recorded as a "forged" report by Ibn Ḥibbān, and later compiled among other "fabricated" hadith by ʿAbd al-Raḥmān Suyūṭī in his *Lāʾālī al-maṣnūʿa fī aḥādīth al-mawḍūʿa* (Beirut: Dār al-Kutub al-ʿIlmiyya, 1996), 1:62–74; on the latter, see the English translation in appendix A of my *Narrating Muḥammad's Night Journey.*

14. Qushayrī, *Kitāb al-miʿrāj*, 43–56.

15. Khargūshī, *Sharaf al-muṣṭafā*, 2:171–179. The editor's title for the chapter suggests that the focus is as much on the names of the prophets in each heaven as on other details, but the accounts that follow show much more interest in angelic names than in the names of the various prophets found in each heavenly realm. For just one example: "From Wahb b. Munabbih from Abū ʿUthmān from Salmān, who said: 'The name of the third heaven is Qaydūn, and the lord said to it, "Be [made of] ruby," so it was.' The name of its guardian is Kawka[b]yālīl. The glorification of its [angelic] people: 'Glorified be the Living who Never Dies!' One who says [that] receives something akin to their merit." (Khargūshī, *Sharaf al-muṣṭafā*, 2:174–175).

16. Khargūshī, *Sharaf al-muṣṭafā*, 2:181–184; compare Qushayrī, *Kitāb al-miʿrāj*, 56–58.

17. Khargūshī, *Sharaf al-muṣṭafā*, 2:190.

18. See "3 (Hebrew Apocalypse of) Enoch," chapter 16, 268, "Rabbi Ishmael said: The Angel Metatron, Prince of the Divine Presence, the glory of highest heaven, said to me: At first I sat upon a great throne at the door of the seventh palace, and I judged all the denizens of the heights on the authority of the Holy One, blessed by he. I assigned greatness, royalty, rank . . . and honor to all the princes of kingdoms, when I sat in the heavenly court. . . . But when ʾAḥer came to behold the vision of the chariot and set eyes upon me, he was afraid and trembled before me. His soul was alarmed to the point of leaving him because of his fear, dread, and terror of me, when he saw me seated upon a throne like a king. . . . Then he opened his mouth and said, 'There are indeed two powers in heaven!' Immediately a divine voice came out from the presence of the Shekinah and said, 'Come back to me, apostate sons — apart from ʾAḥer! Then ʿAnapiʾel YHWH, the honored, glorified, beloved, wonderful, terrible, and dreadful Prince, came at the command of the Holy One, blessed be he, and struck me with sixty lashes of fire and made me stand to my feet"; "3 (Hebrew Apocalypse of) Enoch (5th–6th century AD)," trans. P. Alexander, in *The Old Testament Pseudepigrapha*, ed. James Charlesworth (Garden City, NY: Doubleday, 1983), 268.

19. Qushayrī, *Kitāb al-miʿrāj*, 54.

20. Qushayrī, *Kitāb al-miʿrāj*, 59–60. On these topics as being key indicators of the Ibn ʿAbbās ascension discourse, see my *Narrating Muḥammad's Night Journey*, 32–35 and 136–145.

21. See Colby, *Narrating*; see also Roberto Tottoli, "Muslim Eschatology and the Ascension of the Prophet Muḥammad: Describing Paradise in *Miʿrāj* Traditions and Literature," in *Roads to Paradise*, ed. Sebastian Gunther and Todd Lawson (Leiden: Brill, 2017), 1:858–890.

22. This version was partially translated into English by Rueven Firestone in "Muḥammad's Night Journey and Ascension," in *Windows on the House of Islam*, ed. John Renard (Berkeley: University of California Press, 1998), 336–45. See also Miguel Asín Palacios, *La escatalogía musulmana en la Divina Comedia*, 2nd ed. (Madrid: Consejo Superior de Investigaciones Cientificas, 1943), 440–443; Étienne Renaud, "Le Récit du miʿrāj," in *Apocalypses et Voyages dans l'Au-Delà*, ed. (Paris: Les Éditions du CERF, 1987), 267–290. See the further discussion of this Abū Hurayra report by al-Qāḍī ʿIyāḍ, chapter 3 below.

23. To my knowledge, this version from Ṭabarī has not been translated into English, but it bears a strong connection to parts of the account of the night journey in Ibn Hishām's recension of Ibn Isḥāq's *Sīrat Rasūl Allāh* (where he cites Abū Saʿīd explicitly as well), which has been translated by Alfred Guillaume as *The Life of Muḥammad* (London, Oxford University Press, 1955; Karachi, Pakistan: Oxford University Press, 1967). It also was transmitted in full in the middle period work by al-Bayhaqī (d. 458/1066) titled *Dala'il al-nubuwwa*. Tottoli examines how the Khudrī version of the night journey and ascension was deliberately passed over by many later hadith compilers and other mainstream scholars treating the subject of Muḥammad's otherworldly journey.

24. Colby, *Narrating Muḥammad's Night Journey*, 93–104.

25. A full English translation of this version has now been made available by R. P. Buckley in his work *Night Journey*, 6–18.

26. On this author and his Qur'ān commentary, see Claude Gilliot, "Le commentaire coranique de Hūd B. Muḥakkam/Muḥkim," *Arabica* 44, no. 2 (Apr. 1997): 179–233.

27. Hūd b. Muḥakkam Hawwārī, *Tafsīr Kitāb Allāh al-ʿazīz* (Beirut: Dar al-Gharb al-Islamī, 1990), 2:400.

28. Originally appearing on its own in a fragmentary report, here incorporated into the body of the ascension narrative in a way that we find likewise in the ascension-themed book (*Kitāb al-miʿrāj*) by the pivotal Nishapuri scholar Qushayrī (d. 465/1072), 44 and 102–103. The narreme's inclusion in the telling of the tale of Muḥammad's ascension was to become relatively common in the following centuries.

29. Hawwārī, *Tafsīr Kitāb Allāh al-ʿazīz*, 2:404.

30. Bukhārī, *Ṣaḥīḥ*, ed. Muḥammad Tamīm et al. (Beirut: Sharikat Dār al-Arqam, n.d.), 678–679 (Bad'a al-Khalq #6 on "Remembrance of the Angels"); Bukhārī, *Ṣaḥīḥ*, 812–813 (Manāqib al-Ansār #42 on "The Ascension"). This same scene receives the attention of eastern Sufi authors such as Sulamī and Qushayrī, as well as prominent exegetes from al-Andalus, as will be discussed in subsequent chapters.

31. Hawwārī, *Tafsīr Kitāb Allāh al-ʿazīz*, 2:404–405.

32. Hawwārī never identifies the transmitters of this particular report, offering this vague formulation instead, without any preamble.

33. Hawwārī, *Tafsīr Kitāb Allāh al-ʿazīz*, 2:406; cf. Suhaylī, *al-Rawḍ*, 1:454, which contains a very brief reference to an angel who is likewise forced to stand. The *Kitāb al-miʿrāj* of Qushayrī also contains a report that bears close comparison to this narreme.

34. For an attempt to trace some of these parallels, except with only a partial knowledge of the narratives on the Muslim side of the equation, see David J. Halperin, "Hekhalot and Miʿrāj: Observations on the Heavenly Journey in Judaism and Islam," in *Death, Ecstasy, and Other Worldly Journeys*, ed. John J. Collins and Michael Fishbane (Albany: State University of New York Press, 1995), 269–288; on Metatron narratives, see Steven Wasserstrom, *Between Muslim and Jew: The Problem of Symbiosis under Early Islam* (Princeton, NJ: Princeton University Press, 1995).

35. One exception appears in Suhaylī's work, in a reference from his commentary on the biography of the Prophet that I would argue derives directly from the same

scene in 3 Enoch, with Muḥammad encountering an angel who "stands until the Day." Suhaylī's work will be analyzed below in chapter 3.

36. This broader context of interreligious debate and polemic in the sixth/twelfth century al-Andalus comes as no surprise given the nature of a number of sources that have come down to us from this period, such as Petrus Alfonsi's *Dialogus*, the *Tathlīth al-waḥdāniyya* taken up by one al-Qurṭubī, and the works of Aḥmad al-Khazrajī, including *The Letter of al-Qūṭī*, all of which are briefly summarized and analyzed by Charles L. Tieszan, *Christian Identity amid Islam in Medieval Spain* (Leiden: Brill, 2013), chapter 5, 169–221.

37. See especially the "Favor of the Prophets" section of the fragmentary Real Academia MS Codera 241 discussed below, and compare the portions of the *Liber denudationis* analyzed by Charles L. Tieszen, *Christian Identity amid Islam in Medieval Spain* (Leiden: Brill, 2013), 182–188.

38. What I identify here as the "Primitive Version" has been translated into English in Colby, *Narrating Muḥammad's Night Journey*, appendix A, and analyzed in chapter 2, 29–49.

39. Asín, *La escatalogía musulmana*, 438.

40. Madrid, Real Academia de la Historia MS Codera 241, which in former publications I labeled with the shorthand "Gayangos 241."

41. See the discussion in Colby, *Narrating Muḥammad's Night Journey*, 154–156. The fact that its opening and closing folios — as well as some of those that are intermediate —are missing makes establishing a more precise dating and provenance extremely difficult. My thoughts on this issue have greatly benefitted, however, from personal communications with both Dr. Christiane Gruber and Dr. Cristina Álvarez Millán, as well as my codicological analysis of the physical manuscript in Madrid's Real Academia de la Historia itself.

42. Madrid Real Academia MS Codera 241, fols. 1r–1v.

43. As pointed out by Halperin and other scholars, the idea of a "five-hundred-year" distance separating distinct otherworldly realms is well known from many Jewish Hekhalot texts.

44. The fifth heaven portion of Madrid Real Academia MS Codera 241 is completely missing, as discussed in Colby, *Narrating Muḥammad's Night Journey*, 155, 282n28, and 283n31. On the pattern described here, see my article "Fire in the Upper Heavens," in *Locating Hell in Islamic Traditions*, ed. Christian Lange (Leiden: Brill, 2016), 124–143. Strangely enough, Asín does not pick up on this lacuna from Madrid Real Academia MS Codera 241 in his summary of the text.

45. This trope appears in other later Ibn ʿAbbās ascension narratives, including Istanbul MS Amcazade 95/2 (partially translated in the second appendix to Colby, *NarratingMuḥammad's Night Journey*, 195–234): see the narreme I have labeled "Gabriel Stays Behind" in the translation of fol. 54v, Colby, *Narrating*, 221. Ibn Barrajān discusses this trope in his later (so called "lesser") Qurʾān commentary, *Īḍāḥ*, par. 875 and par. 895.

46. Compare these references to the multiple seas described in the "Primitive Version" of the Ibn ʿAbbās ascension discourse, translated in Colby, *Narrating Muḥammad's Night Journey*, appendix A, 180–184.

47. Compare these scenes to their corresponding narremes in Istanbul MS Amcazade 95/2, fols. 56v–57v, translated in Colby, *Narrating Muḥammad's Night Journey*, appendix A, 223. With regard to God creating a huge snake wrapped around the divine throne to teach the throne a lesson in humility, in light of the importance of the *'arsh* as the first of creation and perhaps the highest divine emanation according to the Iberian contemplative Ibn Masarra and later figures whose ideas we will examine in later chapters, including Ibn Barrajān (see chapter 4) and Ibn Qaṣī (see chapter 5), this particular scene deserves further scholarly consideration. To offer one hypothesis, if some in the Muslim West were thought to venerate the divine throne to a degree that other Muslims deemed excessive, even akin to this veneration coming to constitute *shirk* (associating partners with God), then this scene depicting the enormous snake teaching the throne humility could be understood as akin to similar narremes about a seated angel, potentially mistaken for a divine figure, being forced to stand in order to prevent humans from going gravely astray by misunderstanding its status and in order to teach that angel proper humility.

48. Madrid Real Academia MS Codera 241, fols. 6v–7r; compare Istanbul MS Amcazade 95/2, fols. 58r–58v, translated in Colby, *Narrating Muḥammad's Night Journey*, appendix A, 224; see also the briefer reference to the "*pargod*" (heavenly curtain) from 3 Enoch (*Sefer Hekhalot*), chap. 45.

49. Madrid Real Academia MS Codera 241, fols. 7r–7v; compare two separate attestations of this narreme in Istanbul MS Amcazade 95/2, fols. 47v and 60r (translated in Colby, *Narrating Muḥammad's Night Journey*, appendix A, 226). One might suspect that encountering angels in diverse postures that make up one cycle or *rak'a* in liturgical prayer may help pave the way for the report that circulates in the name of 'Alī that it was on the night of the ascension that Gabriel taught Muḥammad the way to perform the prayers correctly. This report appears near the end of the section specifically devoted to discussing the Prophet's ascension in the *Shifā'* of Qāḍī 'Iyād (d. 544/1149), an Iberian work from the period under consideration that will be examined in chapter 3.

50. See Madrid Real Academia MS Codera 241, fol. 8r.; compare Istanbul MS Amcazade 95/2, fol. 64v., translated in Colby, *Narrating Muḥammad's Night Journey*, appendix A, 230; see also the brief discussion of this scene in Colby, *Narrating Muḥammad's Night Journey*, 143, where a Shī'ī parallel is noted.

51. Madrid Real Academia MS Codera 241, fol. 8r–8v. The manuscript ends abruptly at this point, with its final folio(s) missing. Compare the extensive and distinct version (yet showing numerous points of similarity) transmitted by the later Andalus scholar Qāḍī 'Iyāḍ, *al-Shifā' bi-ta'rīf ḥuqūq al-Muṣṭafā* (Beirut: Dār al-Kutub al-'Ilmiyya, n.d.), 118–119, which draws on and transmits a report attributed to the Prophet and ascribed to his companion and early traditionist, Abu Hurayra: "It was said to me [presumably by Gabriel]: At this Lote Tree will stop everyone from your community who follows your path. It is the Lote Tree of the Boundary, from whose base emerges rivers of uncorrupted water, rivers of milk that never change their taste, rivers of wine refreshing to those who drink, and rivers of pure honey. It is a tree that a rider could go seventy years in its shade. A leaf from it provides shade to all of creation. It *was covered* by light, and by angels, which is [the meaning of God's saying]: '*When the Lote Tree was covered by what covered.*' [God], blessed and exalted, said: 'Ask!'

[Muḥammad] replied: 'You took *Abraham as an intimate friend* and gave him a great kingdom; you *spoke to Moses directly*; you gave David a great kingdom, worked iron for him, and enchanted the mountains for him; you gave Solomon a great kingdom, and enchanted for him jinn, men, devils, and the winds, and *gave him a kingdom such that befits no one after him*; you taught Jesus the Torah and the Evangel, you made him heal the blind and the leper, and you protected him and his mother from the accursed Satan, who never found any path to them. [What blessing is there particular to me?]' His Lord answered him: '[Though I took Abraham as an intimate friend,] I took you as both an intimate friend and a beloved, as it is written in the Torah, "*Muḥammad, beloved of the Most Merciful.*" I sent you *to all the people*. I made your community to be the first and the last. I made for your community that a sermon would not be permitted until they bear witness that you are my servant and my messenger. I made you the first of the prophets created, and the last of them sent. I gave you the *seven rhymed verses* that I had not given to a prophet before you. I gave you the seals of the Cow chapter from a treasury beneath my throne, which I had not given to any prophet before you. I made you as the opener and the sealer.'"

Chapter Two.

1. Maribel Fierro, "Between the Maghreb and al-Andalus," 2.

2. Shlomo Pines, "Shiʿite Terms and Conceptions in Judah Halevi's Kuzari," *Jerusalem Studies in Arabic and Islam* 2 (1980): 165–251; Alfred Ivry, "Ismāʿīlī Theology and Maimonides' Philosophy," in *The Jews of Medieval Islam: Community, Society, and Identity*, ed. Daniel Frank (Leiden: Brill, 1995), 271–300.

3. Ivry, "Ismāʿīlī Theology," 279n31.

4. Pines, "Shiʿite Terms," 218; Ivry, "Ismāʿīlī Theology," 279.

5. See Nader El-Bizri, general editor, forward to *Epistles of the Brethren of Purity* series (Oxford: Oxford University Press and Institute of Ismaili Studies, 2008–). The theory of diffusion of the epistles to the west appears most recently in the intriguing study by Michael Ebstein, *Mysticism and Philosophy in al-Andalus*, who follows Maribel Fierro in arguing that the *Epistles* reached al-Andalus at the hands of Abū al-Qāsim Maslama b. Qāsim al-Qurṭubī (d. 353/964). See Maribel Fierro, "Batinism in al-Andalus," *Studia Islamica* 84 (1996): 87–112; Ebstein, *Mysticism and Philosophy*, 29–30.

6. See, for example, Brethren of Purity, from Epistle 33, trans. Paul E. Walker, *Epistles of the Brethren of Purity: Sciences of the Soul and Intellect,* part 1, *An Arabic Critical Edition and English Translation of Epistles* (Oxford: Oxford University Press and Institute of Ismaili Studies, 2015), 39–52.

7. The texts offer nearly a dozen citations excerpted from the Qurʾān, only two of which have been included here: the first drawn from the end of Q 43:86, and the second from the end of Q 50:16.

8. Brethren of Purity, from Epistle 39 chapter 8, trans. Carmela Baffioni, *Epistles of the Brethren of Purity: Sciences of the Soul and Intellect,* part 3, *An Arabic Critical Edition and English Translation of Epistles* (Oxford: Oxford University Press and Institute of Ismaili Studies, 2017), 161–162; see also *al-Ikhwān al-Ṣafāʾ, Rasāʾil* 3:336–337 (Beirut: Dār al-Ṣādir, 1957).

9. Miguel Asín Palacios, *Abenmassara y su escuela* (1914), subsequently translated as *The Mysticial Philosophy of Ibn Masarra and His Followers*, trans. Elmer H. Douglas and Howard W. Yoder (Leiden: Brill, 1978).

10. S. M. Stern, "Ibn Masarra, follower of Pseudo-Empedocles — an Illusion," in *Actas IV congreso de estudios árabes e islamicos: Coimbra-Lisboa: 1 a 8 Setembro de 1968* (Leiden: Brill, 1971), 325–337; J. Vahid Brown, "Andalusi Mysticism: A Recontextualization," *Journal of Islamic Philosophy* 2 (2006): 69–101; see the more nuanced discussion in Sarah Stroumsa and Sara Sviri, "The Beginnings of Mystical Philosophy in al-Andalus: Ibn Masarra and His *Epistle on Contemplation*," *Jerusalem Studies in Arabic and Islam* 36 (2009): 201–253, especially 209–210.

11. Ebstein, *Mysticism and Philosophy in al-Andalus*, 51.

12. Ebstein, *Mysticism and Philosophy in al-Andalus*, 25–26. Stroumsa and Sviri agree with the rejection of the "Sufi" label, saying "our analysis has identified in Ibn Masarra's works no terms or traits which are unequivocally Sufi" ("Beginnings of Mystical Philosophy," 210). They furthermore agree with the Ismāʿīlī and/or *Ikhwān* connection, concluding that "one sees also the unmistakable traits of Ismāʿīlī-Shīʿī teachings . . . [which] strongly suggest his association with an intellectual-mystical milieu close to that which, later on, produced the *Epistles of the pure brethren*" (Stroumsa and Sviri, "Beginnings of Mystical Philosophy" 214).

13. Stroumsa and Sviri, "Beginnings of Mystical Philosophy," 211.

14. Stroumsa and Sviri, "Beginnings of Mystical Philosophy," 214.

15. Stroumsa and Sviri, "Beginnings of Mystical Philosophy," 213.

16. Translations from Ibn Masarra's *Risālat al-iʿtibār* are those of Stroumsa and Sviri in "Beginnings of Mystical Philosophy," 216–225, unless otherwise noted. That being said, in analyzing this text I likewise consulted both of the following Arabic sources in conjunction with the English translation of Stroumsa and Sviri: Muḥammad Kamāl Ibrahīm Jaʿfar, *Min qaḍāya al-fikr al-islāmī: Dirāsa wa nuṣūṣ* (Cairo: Maktabat Dar al-ʿUlūm, 1978), 346–360; and Pilar Garrido Clemente, "Edición crítica de la *Risālat al-Iʿtibār* de Ibn Masarra de Córdoba," *Miscellanea de estudios árabes y hebraicos, Sección árabe-Islam* 56 (2007): 81–104.

17. See the study by Aaron W. Hughes, *The Texture of the Divine*. Sarah Stroumsa, in her article "Ibn Masarra and the Beginnings of Mystical Thought in al-Andalus," in *Wege mystischer Gotteserfahrung / Mystical Approaches to God*, ed. Peter Schäfer (Munich, Germany: Oldenbourg, 2006), 97–112, concurs that Ibn Masarra's "pointed formulation of this thesis introduces a line of thought which was to gain a particular popularity among Andalusi Aristotelian philosophers, and which is attested in the writings of Ibn al-Sayyid al-Baṭalyawsī and Ibn Ṭufayl, Averroes and Maimonedes. But Ibn Masarra is not an Aristotelian philosopher, just as he is no muʿtazilī theologian" (Stroumsa, "Ibn Masarra," 101).

18. On this subject, see Peter Heath, *Allegory and Philosophy in Avicenna: With a Translation of the Book of the Prophet Muḥammad's Ascent to Heaven (Ibn Sīnā)* (Philadelphia: University of Pennsylvania Press, 1992).

19. Stroumsa and Sviri, "Beginnings of Mystical Philosophy," 217; Jaʿfar, *Min qaḍāya al-fikr al-islāmī*, 346; Garrido Clemente, "Edición crítica," 90.

20. Stroumsa and Sviri, "Beginnings of Mystical Philosophy," 218; Ja'far, *Min qaḍāya al-fikr al-islāmī*, 350; Garrido Clemente, "Edición crítica," 91.

21. Stroumsa and Sviri, "Beginnings of Mystical Philosophy," 218; Ja'far, *Min qaḍāya al-fikr al-islāmī*, 350; Garrido Clemente, "Edición crítica," 92.

22. Stroumsa and Sviri, "Beginnings of Mystical Philosophy," 218; Ja'far, *Min qaḍāya al-fikr al-islāmī*, 351; Garrido Clemente, "Edición crítica," 92.

23. Steven Wasserstrom, "*Sefer Yeẓirah* and Early Islam: A Reappraisal," *Journal of Jewish Thought and Philosophy* 3 (1993): 1–30.

24. Stroumsa, "Ibn Masarra."

25. Stroumsa, "Ibn Masarra," 112.

26. Heath, *Allegory and Philosophy*.

27. Aaron Hughes, "Miraj and the Language of Legitimation in the Medieval Islamic and Jewish Philosophical Traditions: A Case Study of Avicenna and Abraham ibn Ezra." An English translation of the work appears in the appendix to Hughes's study *The Texture of the Divine*.

28. Hughes, *Texture of the Divine*, 199. The biblical allusions are indicated by Hughes in his notes, *Texture of the Divine*, 242–243. With regard to a similar account of Muḥammad's terror at a Sea of Fire, which is assuaged only by the comforting words of Gabriel, see the Primitive Version of the Ibn 'Abbās ascension report as translated in Colby, *Narrating Muḥammad's Night Journey*, 181.

29. Hughes sees in this phrase a reference to and implicit rejection of the "Measure of the Stature" (*Shi'ur Qomah*) theme that forms a part of several of the formative Hekhalot texts such as *Merkavah Rabbah*. See Martin S. Cohen, *The Shi'ur Qomah: Liturgy and Theurgy in Pre-Kabbalistic Jewish Mysticism* (Lanham, MD: University Press of America, 1983); Schäfer, *Hidden and Manifest God*, 99–103.

30. Hughes, *Texture of the Divine*, 205–206 and 244.

31. Colby, *Narrating Muḥammad's Night Journey*, appendix A, 186.

32. See Genesis 28:10–22, evoked by the allusion to verse 17: "He was afraid and said: 'How awesome this place is! This is nothing else but the house of God, the gateway to heaven!'"

33. See Exodus 3:1–4:17, evoked by the allusion to verse 3:5 in which God instructs Moses, "Do not come near! Remove your sandals from your feet, for the place where you stand is holy ground." Note that in the lines that immediately follow, the texts explains the reason for the need to remove the sandals in allegorical terms, the sandals representing the physical body (or "corpse") that holds back the upper soul (*neshamah*) from spiritual progress. Such an allegorical explanation is absent in many later Ibn 'Abbās versions of the Islamic ascension narrative that use the scene as a polemic to argue for the superiority of Muḥammad over and above Moses: the Prophet Muḥammmad is at the point of following Moses's example at the burning bush and removing his sandals when a divine voice commands him not to in order that the vicinity of the divine throne might be honored with the dust from his feet. See, for example, Colby, *Narrating Muḥammad's Night Journey*, appendix B, 226–227.

34. Hughes, *Texture of the Divine*, 207.

35. Hughes, *Texture of the Divine*, 207.

36. Interestingly, this teaching echoes both the Delphic oracle and the parallel saying that Muslims often ascribe to Muḥammad, "He who knows his self (*nafs*) knows his lord."

37. Ehud Krinis, *God's Chosen People: Judah Halevi's "Kuzari" and the Shīʿī Imām Doctrine*, trans. Ann Brener and Tamar Liza Cohen (Turnhourt, Belgium: Brepols, 2014), 3. This same idea was examined by Pines, "Shiʿite Terms," and partially anticipated much earlier by Ignaz Goldziher, "Le ʾAmr ilāhī (ha-ʾinyan ha-ʾelohi) chez Juda Halevi," *Revue des etudes juives* 50 (1905): 32–41.

38. Krinis, *God's Chosen People*, 297. One study that Krinis cites as "pioneering" for tracing this comparative theme is that of David Halperin, "Hekhalot and Miʿrāj," although he correctly notes that the parallels that Halperin traces between Hekhalot texts and the seventeenth-century *Ḥayyat al-qulūb* by al-Majlisī could all be found in much earlier Shīʿī works (Krinis, *God's Chosen People*, 296–297, notes 21 and 22).

39. Krinis, *God's Chosen People*, 297. He also discusses separately another section that he considers "one of the most interesting and important of the treatise," that posits the Rabbi's view of "three sequential stages" of the development of human perfection, the third and highest of which "is one whose description is well-rooted in the world of early Jewish mysticism [i.e., the Hekhalot texts], along with the paramount value it attributes to the active witnessing of the illuminating sights of the upper world." (Krinis, *God's Chosen People*, 297–299).

40. Wolfson, "Merkavah Traditions."

41. Diana Lobel, *Between Mysticism and Philosophy: Sufi Language of Religious Experience in Judah Ha-Levi's* Kuzari (Albany: State University of New York Press, 2000). On *ittiṣāl* and *amr*, see Lobel, *Between Mysticism and Philosophy*, 29–35; on *taʾyīd*, see Lobel, *Between Mysticism and Philosophy*, 120–145; on *mushāhada*, see Lobel, *Between Mysticism and Philosophy*, 103–120 and 139–145.

42. Wolfson, "Merkavah Traditions," 213.

43. David Kaufmann, *Geschichte der Attributenlehre in der judischen Religionsphilosophie von Saadia vis Maimuni* (Gotha, Germany: F. A. Perthes, 1877), 167–168, quoted in Wolfson, "Merkavah Traditions," 213.

44. Lobel, *Between Mysticism and Philosophy*, 139–141. Lobel agrees that "Ha-Levi echoes R. Nissan Gaon here, who argues similarly that there remained among the people some who doubted the prophecy of Moses," perhaps out of concern for the anthropomorphism implied in the Sinai revelation, since "by Ha-Levi's time . . . Biblical anthropomorphism had become a burning issue" (139–140).

45. Qāḍī ʿIyāḍ, *al-Shifāʾ*, cited by Aisha Abdurrahman Bewley in her translation and edition, Qāḍī Abū al-Faḍl ʿIyāḍ, *al-Shifāʾ bi-taʿrīf ḥuqūq al-Muṣṭafā* (*Muḥammad: Messenger of Allah, Ash-Shifāʾ of Qadi Iyad*) (Inverness, UK: Madinah Press, 2011), 302–303.

46. Thomas E. Burman, *Religious Polemic and the Intellectual History of the Mozarabs, c. 1050–1200* (Leiden: Brill, 1994), 53; see further discussion by Tieszen, *Christian Identity*, 172–173.

47. Burman theorizes that Muslims were one of the primary target audiences for the author of *Liber Denudationis* on the basis of the work originally being written in Arabic and even more especially on its occasional use of *isnād* chains as authenticating

devices for hadith reports. His wraps up this argument by asserting, "We can only conclude that, in part at least, these narratives were intended to be convincing to Muslims themselves" (Burman, *Religious Polemic*, 154–155). See further arguments in favor of this idea in Tieszen, *Christian Identity*, 174.

48. Burman, *Religious Polemic*, 152.

49. *Liber Denudationis*, 12.3, from the translation of Burman, *Religious Polemic*, 376–379; compare one Bakrī version of this trope appearing in Istanbul MS Amcazade 95/2, fol. 30r, a version translated in *Narrating Muḥammad's Night Journey*, appendix B, 198.

50. *Liber Denudationis*, 12.4, from Burman, *Religious Polemic*, 378–379. This detail appears at the start of each heaven in the Bakrī version of the Ibn ʿAbbās narrative, as demonstrated in Madrid Real Academia MS Codera 241; for another instance, see Istanbul MS Amcazade 95/2, fol. 39r, translated in *Narrating Muḥammad's Night Journey*, appendix B, 207.

51. For one example, see Istanbul MS Amcazade 95/2, fol. 49v, translated in *Narrating Muḥammad's Night Journey*, appendix B, 217.

52. *Liber Denudationis*, 12.5, from Burman, *Religious Polemic*, 380–381; I do not recall an exact parallel in the Bakrī texts to the single "weeping angel" who approaches Muḥammad on his own and seeks his intercession (as described in *Liber Denudationis*, 4.6). One does find, however, groups of angels who cry out of fear of their lord, for example in Istanbul MS Amcazade 95/2, fol. 48v, translated in *Narrating Muḥammad's Night Journey*, appendix B, 216.

53. *Liber Denudationis*, 12.6, from Burman, *Religious Polemic*, 380–381; compare Istanbul MS Amcazade 95/2, fols. 54v–55v, translated in Colby, *Narrating Muḥammad's Night Journey*, appendix B, 221–222.

54. Colby, *Narrating Muḥammad's Night Journey*, appendix B, 221–222. I have elsewhere labeled the former trope the "cold hand" narreme, and have discussed its collation into the ascension narratives from its original source in a dream vision from a sound hadith transmitted by Tirmidhī (see *Narrating Muḥammad's Night Journey*, 90–91). The trope does not appear in Madrid Real Academia MS Codera 241 (although it might have appeared in the original full version, since the extant text is fragmentary, and ends in the middle of the colloquy), nor in Istanbul MS Amcazade 95/2, but it does appear in numerous other Ibn ʿAbbās ascension narratives, including the "Primitive Version" translated in *Narrating Muḥammad's Night Journey*, appendix A, 186.

55. *Liber Denudationis*, 12.7, from Burman, *Religious Polemic*, 382–383.

56. Moses also can be found in the fourth heaven in Istanbul MS Amcazade 95/2, fols. 43r–44v, translated in *Narrating Muḥammad's Night Journey*, appendix B, 217, but more usually appears in the sixth (and rarely seventh) heaven. As I note in *Narrating Muḥammad's Night Journey*, 41–42, one of the common characteristics of the oral transmission of the Ibn ʿAbbās ascension narratives is the "malleability" of the location of the prophets in the heavens, the order of their appearance often going against what by this time could be called an "official order" in most ascension-related hadith reports that the majority of Sunnī Muslim scholars consider sound: Adam in the first, Jesus and John in the second, Joseph in the third, Idrīs/Enoch in the fourth, Aaron in the

fifth, Moses in the sixth, and Abraham in the seventh heaven. See the widely disparate order found in chart 1, *Narrating Muḥammad's Night Journey*, 138–140.

57. *Liber Denudationis*, 12.8–12.9, from Burman, *Religious Polemic*, 382–383.

58. *Liber Denudationis*, 12.7, from Burman, *Religious Polemic*, 382–383, where the narrative specifies the number of apostate Muslims at sixty thousand.

59. *Liber Denudationis*, 4.1–3, from Burman, *Religious Polemic*, 260–263, a chapter titled "That He Gathered People by Means of the Sword and False Visions." As will be discussed briefly in what follows, the references to the account of Muḥammad's ascension in this chapter come in 4.6–7, translated in Burman, *Religious Polemic*, 266–269. On the coercion trope, compare 12.8, from Burman, *Religious Polemic*, 382–383.

60. At the end of the account of the first heaven in chapter 12.5, this much longer narrative contains a brief reference that apparently offers a summary of the exact same narreme that chapter 4.6 recounts in greater detail. Compare *Liber Denudationis*, 4.6, from Burman, *Religious Polemic*, 266–267; and *Liber Denudationis* 12.5, from Burman, *Religious Polemic*, 380–381: "And he saw one angel weeping, and he asked about the cause of his weeping, and he answered, 'sins are [the cause.]' He then prayed for him."

61. *Liber Denudationis*, 4.6, from Burman, *Religious Polemic*, 266–267, with a slightly adapted translation here.

62. *Liber Denudationis*, 4.7, from Burman, *Religious Polemic*, 268–269.

63. Tieszan, *Christian Identity*, 220.

64. Vuckovic, *Heavenly Journeys,* 12.

65. Vuckovic, *Heavenly Journeys*, 14–15.

Chapter Three.

1. Qāḍī ʿIyāḍ, *al-Shifāʾ bi-taʿrīf ḥuqūq al-muṣṭafā* (Beirut: Dar al-Kutub al-ʿIlmiyya, n.d.); cited by Aisha Abdurrahman Bewley, *Muḥammad: Messenger of Allah, Ash-Shifāʾ of Qadi Iyad* (hereafter a source referred to simply as "Bewley") (Inverness: Madinah Press, 2011), 302–303.

2. Qāḍī ʿIyāḍ, 1:117; Bewley, *Muḥammad*, 91–92.

3. Qāḍī ʿIyāḍ, 1:117; Bewley, *Muḥammad*, 93.

4. Translated in full in my dissertation, "Constructing an Islamic Ascension Narrative," 117–118.

5. This composite approach is one that Asín, in *La escatalogía musulmana*, considers the sign of the third and most advanced "cycle" of the development of the ascension narrative. Unfortunately, he cites only one report from Ṭabarī's *Tafsīr* (that of Abū Hurayra) as the sole attestation of this cycle, completely neglecting to discuss this and many other key early reports that harmonize the two portions of the journey.

6. Qāḍī ʿIyāḍ, 1:116; Bewley, *Muḥammad*, 92 (where Bewley unfortunately relegates this key paragraph from the main text of the Arabic into a footnote in her English translation).

7. Qāḍī ʿIyāḍ, 1:115; Bewley, *Muḥammad*, 91.

8. Qāḍī ʿIyāḍ, 1:115; Bewley, *Muḥammad*, 91.

9. Qāḍī ʿIyāḍ, 1:117; Bewley, *Muḥammad*, 93.

10. Qāḍī ʿIyāḍ, 1:117; Bewley, *Muḥammad*, 93.

11. Qāḍī ʿIyāḍ, 1:117; Bewley, *Muḥammad*, 93. Note that Qāḍī ʿIyāḍ never defines precisely the criteria of usefulness in this section, nor states clearly the presumed context in which some points may be more "useful" (in terms of . . . X; for the purpose of . . . Y) than others.

12. On the Abu Hurayra ascension report, see Colby, *Narrating Muḥammad's Night Journey*, 96–101.

13. Qāḍī ʿIyāḍ, 1:118; Bewley trans., 93–94. I discuss this scene from the Abu Hurayra hadith in *Narrating Muḥammad's Night Journey*, 98, where I label it the "eulogy contest." A parallel scene appears in Thaʿlabī's Qurʾān commentary; see *Narrating Muḥammad's Night Journey*, 109.

14. The "Seals of Sūrat al-Baqara," the final two verses of this longest chapter of the Qurʾān that complete it with a "seal" in the form of a petitionary prayer, are often interpreted in the Ibn ʿAbbās ascension narratives as presenting one of the key passages revealed to Muḥammad (sometimes spelled out in the form of an actual dialogue between Muḥammad and God) during the intimate colloquy. On this trope, see Colby, *Narrating Muḥammad's Night Journey*.

15. Qāḍī ʿIyāḍ, 1:118–119; Bewley trans., 94–95; compare the author's reference to a similar "favor of the prophets" narreme in Bewley, *Muḥammad*, 87.

16. Qāḍī ʿIyāḍ, 1:118; Bewley, *Muḥammad*, 94. Notice the parallel passage in the Ibn ʿAbbās ascension narrative presented in Madrid Real Academia MS Codera 241, fol. 8v.

17. Qāḍī ʿIyāḍ, 1:118; Bewley, *Muḥammad*, 94.

18. Qāḍī ʿIyāḍ, 1:119; Bewley, *Muḥammad*, 94.

19. Qāḍī ʿIyāḍ, 1:119; Bewley, *Muḥammad*, 95. Although these titles are not explained in the passage, "opener" presumably is a reference to the Muslim idea about the "light of Muḥammad" as being first in creation, rivaling Christian claims about Jesus, for instance, in the beginning of the Gospel of John: "In the beginning was the Word, and the Word was with God, and the Word was God. He was in the beginning with God. All things came into being through him." (John 1:1–3, NRSV).

20. Rev. 1:8, 21:6, 22:13. These references in turn could be seen as echoing the passages in Isaiah (e.g., Isa. 41:4, 44:6, 48:12).

21. Qāḍī ʿIyāḍ, 1:119; Bewley, *Muḥammad*, 94–95.

22. Madrid Real Academia MS Codera 241, fol. 8v, a reference coming at the end of the folio just as this fragmentary manuscript ends abruptly.

23. Madrid Real Academia MS Codera 241, fol. 8v.

24. Qāḍī ʿIyāḍ, 1:117; Bewley, *Muḥammad*, 93. The full text of this brief narreme is as follows: "In the report of Mālik b. Ṣaʿṣaʿa: When I passed him — meaning Moses — he wept. A voice called out to him, 'What makes you weep?' He replied, 'Lord, you sent this boy after me, yet more of his community than of mine will enter the Garden.'"

25. Qāḍī ʿIyāḍ, 1:119; Bewley, *Muḥammad*, 95.

26. Qāḍī ʿIyāḍ, 1:117–118; Bewley, *Muḥammad*, 93.

27. Qāḍī ʿIyāḍ, 1:119; Bewley, *Muḥammad*, 95.

28. Qāḍī ʿIyāḍ, 1:120; Bewley, *Muḥammad*, 95.

29. This report may be found in the large *Musnad* collection of hadith ascribed to Ahmad b. ʿAmr al-Bazzār.

30. Qāḍī ʿIyāḍ, 1:14; Bewley, *Muḥammad*, 3; compare the later citation of the same narreme in Qāḍī ʿIyāḍ, 1:217; Bewley, *Muḥammad*, 85. This report was related in select reports not only by Bukhārī and Muslim but also by al-Tirmidhī in his *Jāmiʿ al-Ṣāḥīḥ*.

31. Qāḍī ʿIyāḍ, vol. 1, part 1, chap. 1, Bewley, *Muḥammad*, 3; Qāḍī ʿIyāḍ, vol. 1, part 1, chap 3, Bewley, *Muḥammad*, 85.

32. Suhaylī, *al-Rawḍ*, 1:430.

33. Suhaylī, *al-Rawḍ*, 1:432–433.

34. Suhaylī, *al-Rawḍ*, 1:460.

35. Suhaylī, *al-Rawḍ*, 1:466.

36. Suhaylī, *al-Rawḍ*, 1:465.

37. Suhaylī, *al-Rawḍ*, 1:465.

38. Suhaylī, *al-Rawḍ*, 1:466.

39. Suhaylī, *al-Rawḍ*, 1:450–452. This same anecdote will later be transmitted at length by Suhaylī's student known as Ibn Diḥya al-Kalbī (d. 633/1236) in his book dedicated wholly to the theme of the Prophet's ascension titled *al-Ibtihāj fī aḥādīth al-miʿrāj* (Cairo: Maktabat al-Khānjā, 1996), 103–106.

Chapter Four.

1. On the life, works, and legacy of Ibn Barrajān in particular, and on this mystical exegetical technique drawn from Ibn Masarra's concept of *iʿtibār* in particular and the Andalūsī esoteric path more generally, one that grew in development parallel to the growth of eastern Sufism, see the extremely important study by Yousef Casewit, *The Mystics of al-Andalus: Ibn Barrajān and Islamic Thought in the Twelfth Century.* My own situating of Ibn Barrajān's life and approach to interpretation is very much indebted to Casewit's analysis in this particular work of his.

2. Ibn Barrajān, excerpt from his "major" commentary titled *Tanbīh al-afhām*, ed. Aḥmad Farīd al-Mazyadī (Beirut: Dar al-Kutub al-ʿIlmiyya, 2013), 3:365–366 (commentary on Q 17:1), with numbers inserted into the text of this list of "signs" for clarity and for the purpose of subsequent reference. The list continues with enumerating some of the other "signs" witnessed, including the angels, Burāq, and the "signs in the heavens" such as the prophets in their stations, the "Frequented House," the Garden and the Fire, al-Kawthar, the upper kingdoms (al-Malakūt), the Lote Tree of the Boundary, etc. (Ibn Barrajān, *Tanbīh*, 366).

3. How Muḥammad is able to encounter the previous prophets on the way to Jerusalem, in Jerusalem itself, as well as up in the levels of the heavens, gets explained by Ibn Barrajān with recourse to the idea of there having been multiple "night journeys," not just one. See Ibn Barrajān, *Tanbīh*, 3:364, just preceding this anecdote. Later in the same work, he describes a report in which the Prophet proceeds directly to the highest heavens without encountering the prophets in the different lower heavens (see Ibn Barrajān, *Tanbīh*, 5:209, commentary on Q 53:6–8). Here and elsewhere, Ibn Barrajān insists that there were *at least* two "night journeys," if not more (Ibn Barrajān,

Tanbīh, 5:209). Other commentators sometimes provide different explanations for how/why the prophets seem to appear in multiple locations. Some insist that the prophets appear only as spirits in the heavens, for instance, while their physical bodies remain on Earth.

4. See al-Qurṭubī, *al-Jāmiʿ li-aḥkām al-qurʾān*, vol. 10 (Cairo: Dār al-Kitāb al-ʿArabī, 1967), 212–213 (commentary on Q 17:1), translated and discussed in Vuckovic, *Heavenly Journeys*, 29–30.

5. See the many sources cited in Ibn Barrajān, *Tanbīh*, 3:365–366 (commentary on Q 17:1), near the end of note 1 on 365 and the entirety of note 1 on 366.

6. Casewit, *Mystics of al-Andalus*, 238–244. Note that while it is possible that such "proximity" could be detected in the oral recitation of the text of the Qurʾān, it seems to me to be more likely a technique arising out of the scholarly engagement with verse-by-verse written textual commentaries on the entirety of the sacred text, for the concept of "proximity" between the end of one sura and the beginning of the next presumes a deep engagement with the specific ordering of the written codex.

7. This is the translation of the title as rendered into English by Yousef Casewit and Gerhard Böwering in their edition of this work: *A Qurʾān Commentary by Ibn Barrajān of Seville* (d. *536/1141*): *Īḍāḥ al-ḥikma bi-ʾaḥkām al-ʿibra* (*Wisdom Deciphered, the Unseen Discovered*), ed. Gerhard Böwering and Yousef Casewit (Leiden: Brill, 2016). All references to *Īḍāḥ al-ḥikma* that follow in this work refer to this edition, with the English translations of the Arabic being my own unless otherwise specified.

8. Ibn Barrajān, *Īḍāḥ al-ḥikma*, 389, par. no. 561, exegesis of Q 17:1.

9. It should be noted that this approach to Qurʾān interpretation of key passages related to the night journey via the Qurʾān's "structure" (*naẓm*) receives less attention in Ibn Barrajān's earlier "major" *tafsīr*, titled *Tanbīh al-afhām*, than the more thorough attention he devotes to it in his later "minor" (i.e., shorter) commentary, titled *al-Īḍāḥ al-ḥikma*.

10. Ibn Barrajān, *Īḍāḥ al-ḥikma*, paragraphs 878–902, spanning pp. 630–643 in the edition of Casewit and Böwering.

11. This fact is particularly interesting given the way Casewit demonstrates Ibn Barrajān's unacknowledged indebtedness to Ṭabarī's *Jāmiʿ al-bayān* (see *Mystics of al-Andalus*, 169). The indebtedness becomes especially evident, however, in Ibn Barrajān's grammatical and etymological discussions, as Casewit points out, and as we shall see examples of below.

12. Ibn Barrajān, *Īḍāḥ al-ḥikma*, paragraphs 878–879.

13. Casewit, *Mystics of al-Andalus*, 288–291, wherein he cites the author's work *Sharḥ asmāʾ Allāh al-ḥusnā*, 1:109–110, as evidence for the following numerological idea: "Ibn Barrajān explains that 6 is a perfect number since 1 + 2 + 3 = 6, just as 1 x 2 x 3 = 6, while the number 7 recapitulates the wholeness of the six-fold sequence, encapsulating what comes before it in its entirety" (Casewit, *Mystics of al-Andalus*, 291).

14. On Ibn Barrajān's cosmology, and the use of phrases surrounding *al-ḥaqq* in his thought, see Casewit, *Mystics of al-Andalus*, especially chapter 5, 171–205. For example, Casewit helpfully summarizes the idea that for Ibn Barrajān, "The qurʾānic *ḥaqq* is 'protological'; it stands at the origin of things (*makhlūq bihi*). Yet . . . it is also eschatological, for it stands at the end [of] all things (*al-ḥaqq al-ladhī ʿilayhi al-maṣīr*)

and is the final manifestation of God who was there from the beginning" (Casewit, *Mystics of al-Andalus*, 183).

15. Ibn Barrajān, *Tanbīh*, 3:364.

16. I here follow Casewit, *Mystics of al-Andalus*, 37, who states that as a technical term, *tanbīh* stands for "caveats or explanations of particular points." Elsewhere, he explains that when this technical term appears as an organizational unit, especially in this earlier "major" Qur'ān commentary that draws part of its title (*Tanbīh al-afhām*) from this term, it might be best understood as connoting a "reminder" (Casewit, *Mystics of al-Andalus*, 162n116).

17. Ibn Barrajān, *Tanbīh*, 3:364–366; see some discussion of this idea earlier in this chapter, above, note 3.

18. Ibn Barrajān, *Tanbīh*, 3:365–366.

19. Ibn Barrajān, *Tanbīh*, 3:366. The qur'ānic reference at the end of this quotation is from Q 53:10, "he revealed to his servant what he revealed."

20. On his use of the term *naẓm* to explore the range of meaning for the term *subḥān* from the beginning of Q 17:1, see above.

21. Ibn Barrajān, *Tanbīh*, 5:207–208.

22. Ibn Barrajān, *Tanbīh*, 5:209. This phrase is not qur'ānic but rather is taken from an ascension hadith, a small fragment from which Ibn Barrajān quotes in the paragraph that follows this citation in Ibn Barrajān, *Tanbīh*, 5:209. See the discussion of the "scratching of the pens" reference below.

23. Ibn Barrajān, *Tanbīh*, 5:210.

24. Ibn Barrajān, *Tanbīh*, 5:212–213.

25. Remember that, as Casewit explains, Ibn Barrajān and his mystical contemporaries in al-Andalus and North Africa in the fifth/eleventh century did not think of themselves as "Sufis" but rather as Muʿtabirūn, "contemplators," or those who use the technique of *iʿtibār* ("crossing over" through "contemplation"). Casewit traces this technique and its role in the spread of mysticism in the region to the earlier figure, Ibn Masarra. See Casewit, *Mystics of al-Andalus*, 36–41.

26. Ibn Barrajān, *Tanbīh*, 5:209.

27. Ibn Barrajān, *Tanbīh*, 5:209.

28. "Sacred saying" (*hadith qudsī*) stands for separate utterances transmitted from the angel Gabriel to the Prophet but whose ultimate source, according to Muslim belief, is the divinity speaking outside the context of the qur'ānic revelations.

29. Ibn Barrajān, *Tanbīh*, 5:209–210.

30. Casewit, *Mystics of al-Andalus*, 253; parallels to this report appear in Muslim and Ibn Ḥibbān's collections.

31. Ibn Barrajān, *Tanbīh*, 5:210.

32. Ibn Barrajān, *Tanbīh*, 5:210.

33. A similar structure of four sections to the journey, here each categorized as a world or "realm," appears in Ibn Barrajān's other commentary, *Īḍāḥ al-ḥikma*, paragraph 875.

34. Casewit, *Mystics of al-Andalus*, 166–167.

35. Ibn Barrajān, *Īḍāḥ al-ḥikma*, paragraph 560.

36. Casewit, *Mystics of al-Andalus*, 171–205.

37. The human being in this passage is likely a stand-in for the "universal servant" (*al-*ʿabd *al-kullī*), even though he does not employ that phrase in this instance.

38. Ibn Barrajān, *Īḍāḥ al-ḥikma*, paragraph 561.

39. Beyond the aforementioned reference in *Mystics of al-Andalus,* see the introduction by Böwering and Casewit to *Qurʾān Commentary*, 36–37.

40. See Ibn Barrajān, *Īḍāḥ al-ḥikma*, paragraphs 877, 880, 884, 885, and 901. For one instance, paragraph 885 begins with evoking Muḥammad's state of ritual purity on his ascension and quickly shifts to talking about how each Muslim believer "ascends" by making ritual purifications before praying *ṣalāt.* See the discussion of this particular idea in what follows.

41. E.g., see Alī b. Usmān Hujwirī, *Kashf al-maḥjūb*, ed. Valentin A. Zhukovski (Tehran, Iran: Kitābkhānah-i Ṭahūrī, 1997), 389; compare the translation by Nicholson, *The Kashf al-Maḥjūb: The Oldest Persian Treatise on Sufism* (Leiden: Brill, 1911), 302.

42. Ibn Barrajān, *Īḍāḥ al-ḥikma*, paragraphs 877 and 901, the second of which provides one of the few chains of transmission that Ibn Barrajān prefixes to any report, this one from Muḥammad Bāqir and ultimately transmitted on the authority of ʿAlī b. Abī Ṭālib. This same report was included at the end of the ascension section in Qāḍī ʿIyāḍ's *Shifāʾ*, where he does not so much dispute the authenticity of the report and its "usefulness" as he questions the way it treats certain theological matters, for instance the approach to the divine — as if God physically resided in a specific place — as well as the hearing of God's voice. See Qāḍī ʿIyāḍ, *al-Shifāʾ*, 120–121, and the discussion in the previous chapter in this study in the section dedicated to Qāḍī ʿIyāḍ's work.

43. Ibn Barrajān, *Īḍāḥ al-ḥikma*, paragraph 880; the same idea is repeated in paragraph 884.

44. Ibn Barrajān, *Īḍāḥ al-ḥikma*, paragraph 885.

45. Ibn Barrajān, *Īḍāḥ al-ḥikma*, paragraph 885.

46. Ibn Barrajān, *Īḍāḥ al-ḥikma*, paragraph 900. Compare the reference to Jesus's second coming in the discussion of "one of the three, between two" in Ibn Barrajān, *Īḍāḥ al-ḥikma*, paragraphs 878–879, discussed above.

47. Ibn Barrajān, *Īḍāḥ al-ḥikma*, paragraph 896. Compare this passage to one that Casewit describes from Ibn Barrajān's *Sharḥ asmāʾ Allāh al-ḥusnā*, 2:14–15, cited in *Mystics of al-Andalus*, 176n20, where the "Universal Servant" (*al-ʿabd al-kullī*) is compared to "a man standing in prayer (*rajul qāʾim yuṣallī*) of perfect adoration and submission before God," a metaphor that Casewit also detects in the way that the parallel concept of the "Universal Human Being" (*al-insān al-kullī*) is described in a treatise associated with the esoteric group known as the "Brethren of Purity" (*Ikhwān al-ṣafā*).

48. Ibn Barrajān, *Īḍāḥ al-ḥikma*, paragraph 897.

49. The base report of this hadith appears in Bukhārī, the first report included in the night journey section, that ascribed to the companion Abu Dharr: "Ibn Shihab said: Ibn Hazm informed me that Ibn ʿAbbās and Abu Habba al-Ansari used to say that the Prophet said, 'Then he ascended with me until I reached the level in which I heard the scratching of the pens.'" This same reference is excerpted by Qāḍī ʿIyāḍ in his *Shifāʾ* as one of the first additional "useful details" that he cites: "In the transmission of Ibn ʿAbbās: 'Then I was made to ascend until I appeared at the level in which I heard the scratching of the pens.'" The reference is also given in the note to Ibn Barrajān, *Īḍāḥ*

al-ḥikma, paragraph 896. See also those selections from *Īḍāḥ al-ḥikma* that will be analyzed below (paragraphs 876 and 895).

50. Ibn Barrajān, *Īḍāḥ al-ḥikma*, paragraph 896.

51. I draw the concept of "boundary moment" here from Michael Sells, "Sound, Spirit, and Gender in the Qur'ān," in *Approaching the Qur'ān*, 2nd ed. (Ashland, OR: White Cloud, 2007), 199–223. In this important piece he defines these boundary moments as "points of contact between the eternal and the temporal realms, in which the structures of language . . . are transformed through contact with a realm beyond temporality" (Sells, "Sound, Spirit, and Gender," 201), and highlights the examples of such moments in the times of prophecy, creation, and reckoning.

52. These three entities, the two mentioned in the previous sentence (angels and spirit) and the two mentioned in this sentence (the spirit and the command), appear together in one key qur'ānic verse that Ibn Barrajān cites later in this same quotation, from the chapter of the Qur'ān known as "Destiny" (*al-qadr*) and describing the "night of destiny": "The angels descend, the spirit upon them [i.e., the angels], by the permission of their lord from every command" (Q 97:4). The three terms also appear together in Q 16:2, as follows shortly in the quotation.

53. Here the language of "breathing out" of the spirit into the mind parallels the language that the Qur'an uses for the breathing of the spirit into both Adam (e.g., Q 15:29 and 38:71–72) and Jesus (e.g., Q 21:91) at the moment of their creation. See Sells, "Sound, Spirit, and Gender," especially 208–213.

54. For a nuanced understanding of different layers of meaning in this pivotal verse from the Qadr chapter of the Qur'ān (Q 97), see Sells, "Sound, Spirit, and Gender."

55. See the note above with regard to this phrase "the scratching of the pens," drawn from a hadith report appearing in Bukhārī's collection.

56. Ibn Barrajān, *Īḍāḥ al-ḥikma*, paragraphs 894–895 (combined together here in this block quotation).

57. For two examples out of Ibn ʿAbbās reports, one earlier and the other later in terms of development, see *Narrating Muḥammad's Night Journey*, appendix A, 185; and appendix B, 221–222.

58. See "3 (Hebrew Apocalypse of) Enoch (5th–6th century AD)," trans. P. Alexander, in *The Old Testament Pseudepigrapha*, ed. James Charlesworth (New York: Doubleday, 1983), 268.

59. Ibn Barrajān, *Īḍāḥ al-ḥikma*, paragraph 895.

60. Again, see examples in 3 Enoch, e.g., chapters 38–39, 290–291.

61. In this fashion, while some hadith reports identify the Lote Tree as the furthest point that any created being can ascend, in contrast, many of the widespread ascension reports circulated in the name of Ibn ʿAbbās depict the Prophet as leaving Gabriel behind at the Lote Tree and ascending higher and higher on a "green *rafraf*" past numerous seas, veils, and other exalted realms. The way Ibn Barrajān depicts the realm of the "scratching of the pens" here, or the exalted "place of sitting" in the next anecdote, shows how he shares the presuppositions of these other narratives that do not see the Lote Tree as a boundary for the Prophet Muḥammad in the way that it serves as a more definitive boundary for the angel Gabriel.

62. Ibn Barrajān, *Īḍāḥ al-ḥikma*, paragraphs 875–876.

63. Ibn Barrajān, *Īḍāḥ al-ḥikma*, paragraph 876.

64. See Ibn Barrajān, *Īḍāḥ al-ḥikma*, paragraph 874, that invokes Surat Yā Sīn (Q 36) for proof of the hidden knowledge that the Prophet descended with and brought to the community of the elect:

> Since three characteristics of perfection of the prophecy are sound for the Prophet — namely [1] not to go astray from the straight path of God; [2] not to be deluded by Satan; [3] not to say what he said from his own selfish desire, but rather to [speak] from the inspiration inspired in him from the esoteric knowledge possessed (*ladun*) by the [divine] dear merciful one, [God] gathered this together in his saying, "*Ya sin / by the wise Qur'an / indeed you are among those sent / on the straight path / a sending down from the dear merciful one / in order to warn the folk what their fathers warned*" (Q 36:1–6). They [i.e., the "folk," *al-qawm*] are the ones meant when he [i.e., the Prophet Muḥammad] arrived" (Ibn Barrajān, *Īḍāḥ al-ḥikma*, paragraph 874).

The concept of the esoteric knowledge that God possesses (so-called *ʿilm ladunnī*) and conveys to only the most elect of his servants is a familiar trope that springs from a mystical interpretation of the knowledge of the unseen possessed by God's servant (which tradition commonly comes to associate with the mysterious saint known as Khidr) mentioned in the Cave chapter (Q 18), in which the source of this idea appears from a mystical reading of the qurʾānic phrase, expressed in the divine voice regarding this chosen servant of God, "he taught him knowledge from what we possess" (*ʿallamahu min ladunnā ʿilman*, Q 18:65).

65. Note that in some of the later Ibn ʿAbbās ascension narratives one encounters the idea that at the highest point of the ascension, God grants the Prophet knowledge of all things, "from the first to the last," and this idea could be partially behind what Ibn Barrajān says here. See a discussion of this theme in my "Constructing an Islamic Ascension Narrative" (PhD diss., Duke University, 2002).

66. Ibn Barrajān, *Īḍāḥ al-ḥikma*, paragraph 895.

67. Again, see 3 Enoch, chapter 11, 264.

68. Ibn Barrajān, *Īḍāḥ al-ḥikma*, paragraph 875. He argues again for this same connection in paragraph 898, without repeating the explanation of why the difference between the two distinct *s* letters in Arabic should not make a difference when exploring the mystical connection between these words.

69. Ibn Barrajān, *Īḍāḥ al-ḥikma*, paragraph 898.

70. Böwering and Yousef, *Qurʾān Commentary*, 33, where they identify Q 14:48 as one of a handful of what Ibn Barrajān treats as "privileged verses" that he returns to repeatedly throughout his *tafsīr*.

71. The edited version by Böwering and Casewit offers the name "the Nile" here, but this river has already been named as one of the two "apparent" rivers (see above). While it is possible that Ibn Barrajān could have included the Nile in the category of both "apparent" and "hidden" rivers flowing from under the Lote Tree, were that the

case, one would have expected him to say something about that duplication in the commentary that follows this second mention. He does not, but instead after "al-Kawthar" he discusses its companion river "al-Salsabīl," which thus seems much more likely to have been the original reference in this opening statement about the two hidden rivers.

72. This list sounds a lot like the roots of jurisprudence (*uṣūl al-fiqh*) as taught by Mālik b. Anas, eponymous leader of the school of jurisprudence that predominated in al-Andalus and North Africa, especially since the time of the al-Murābiṭūn (Almoravids), understanding the "teachings of good people" to stand for the "teachings of the people of Medina" which Mālik and his school held in high esteem.

73. Ibn Barrajān, *Īḍāḥ al-ḥikma*, paragraph 898.

74. Ṭabarī, *Tafsīr*, 8:11 (commentary on Q 17:1). See also Reuven Firestone, trans., "Muḥammad's Night Journey," in *Windows on the House of Islam*, ed. John Renard (Berkeley: University of California Press, 1998), 343; Renaud, "Le Récit du miʿrāj," 284.

75. See Ṭabarī, *Tafsīr*, 11:517–518 (commentary on Q 53:16).

76. See Ṭabarī, *Tafsīr*, 11:518.

77. The phrase "no one can describe it because of its beauty" is common to several early reports transmitted by Ṭabarī, *Tafsīr*, 11:516.

78. This phrase is commonly collated into reports of Muḥammad's ascension, and it can be found independently in hadith reports. It also appears in the Christian New Testament, 1 Cor. 2:9, using an identical turn of phrase as that found in this Muslim version.

79. Ibn Barrajān, *Īḍāḥ al-ḥikma*, paragraph 899.

80. See Sulamī, *The Subtleties of the Ascension*, 73 (saying number twenty) and 81 (saying number twenty-three); Sulamī, *Ṭabaqāt al-ṣufiyya*, 463 (hadith transmitted in a chain including Ibn Khafīf Shīrāzī, with variants ascribed to ʿAbd Allāh Ibn Masʿūd and other hadith transmitters).

81. See Vuckovic, *Heavenly Journeys*, 61–72.

82. Casewit, *Mystics of al-Andalus*, 166.

83. Casewit devotes a special section to Ibn Barrajān's use of biblical material (see *Mystics of al-Andalus*, chapter 7, 245–265). He also describes in particular how in Ibn Barrajān's later commentary *Īḍāḥ al-ḥikma*, the author's image of "the tree" as a symbol becomes more biblically oriented (Casewurt, *Mystics of al-Andalus*, 167). While connections to the "tree of life" or the "tree of the knowledge of good and evil" do not play a role in his discussions of the qurʾānic "Lote Tree" in the context of the Islamic ascension narratives, as one might expect from Casewit's statement, nevertheless, other biblical ideas serve as an inspiration for select aspects of his mystical commentary on Muḥammad's otherworldly journey, as I have attempted to show above.

Chapter Five.

1. See Michael Ebstein in "Was Ibn Qaṣī a Sufi?" *Studia Islamica* 110 (2015): 196–232, where he states, "Ibn Qaṣī's political-religious project was shaped by the specific historical conditions in al-Andalus of the 6th/12th century: the fragmentation and

disintegration of political unity; economic crises and social tensions; the invasion of foreign dynasties (the Murābiṭūn and Muwaḥḥidūn); and the Christian Reconquista" (Ebstein, "Was Ibn Qaṣī a Sufi?" 225).

2. See Alexandre Herculano, *História de Portugal*, 8 vols. (Paris: Livraria Bertrand, n.d., 2:170–173 and 204–213; 3:52–55 and 64–65; Francisco Cordera, *Decadencia y desaparición de los Almorávides en España* (Zaragoza, Spain: n.p., 1899); Abū'l-ʿAlā' ʿAfīfī, "Abūlqāsim Ibn Qaṣī wa kitābuhu *Khalʿ al-naʿlayn*," *Majallat kulliyat al-ādāb, Iskandariyya* 11 (1958): 53–87; David Goodrich, "A Sufi Revolt in Portugal: Ibn Qaṣī and his *Kitāb Khalʿ al-naʿlayn*," PhD diss, Columbia University, 1978; Josef Dreher, "Das Imamat des islamischen mystikers AbūlQāsim Aḥmad ibn al-Ḥusain Ibn Qaṣī (gest. 1151)" (PhD diss., Rheinischen Friedrich-Wilhelm University, 1985).

3. Goodrich, based on a study of Istanbul Suleymaniye K. MS Şehid Ali Paşa 1174.

4. See Dreher, based on the aforementioned Istanbul MS Şehid Ali Paşa 1174 as well as a second copy, Istanbul Suleymaniye K. MS Veliyuddin 1673. Note that between the two dissertations of Goodrich and Dreher was yet another by William Elliott, "The Career of Ibn Qaṣī as Religious Teacher and Political Revolutionary in 12th Century Islamic Spain" (PhD diss., University of Edinburgh, 1979), but it does not add significantly to the other two previously mentioned dissertations, and merely offers an English summary of chapters and an elaboration of a number of general concepts.

5. See above, chapter 4, especially in its analysis of Ibn Barrajān, *Īḍāḥ al-ḥikma*, paragraphs 560, 875–876, and 896.

6. Dreher, "Das Imamat," 23–24; see Ibn Qaṣī, *Khalʿ al-naʿlayn*, ed. Aḥmad ibn Farīd Mazyadī, 23. Unless otherwise specified, all references to the Arabic text of *Khalʿ al-naʿlayn* in the analysis that follows will cite page numbers in this Mazyadī edition.

7. Dreher, "Das Imamat," 25.

8. See especially Goodrich, "Sufi Revolt," 45–48.

9. Ebstein, "Was Ibn Qaṣī a Sufi?"

10. Ebstein, "Was Ibn Qaṣī a Sufi?," 201–202.

11. Ebstein, "Was Ibn Qaṣī a Sufi?," 202; compare the elaboration of these "spheres" as described in Dreher, "Das Imamat," 25–27.

12. Dreher, "Das Imamat," 25–27.

13. Ebstein, "Was Ibn Qaṣī a Sufi?," 202–203 and 208. Ebstein asserts that "the ontological status of each echelon in the universe is relative, in the sense that it is higher in relation to the level situated below it and lower in relation to the one located above it" ("Was Ibn Qaṣī a Sufi?," 208). See Ibn Qaṣī, part 1, "al-Malakūtiyya," 55–58.

14. See Ali Humayun Akhtar, "Identifying Mysticism in Early Esoteric Scriptural Hermeneutics: Sahl al-Tustari's (d. 283/896) Tafsīr Reconsidered," *Journal of Islamic and Muslim Studies* 2, no. 2 (2017): 46–47.

15. See Q 20:12; compare in the Hebrew Bible, Exodus 3:5 forward.

16. See Walid Saleh, *The Formation of the Classical Tafsīr Tradition: The Qur'ān Commentary of al-Thaʿlabī (d. 427/1035)* (Leiden: Brill, 2004), 198–199; see also Pieter Coppens, *Seeing God.*

17. Ibn Qaṣī, *Khalʿ al-naʿlayn*, 99–108. The title of this section draws on the title of the work as a whole, implying a deepening of the process, extricating oneself from the material world a step further.

18. Ibn Qaṣī, *Khalʿ al-naʿlayn*, 109. Both of the words in the title of this section are common synonyms used for the qurʾānic revelation itself. From this point forward, our working hypothesis will take both "The Removing of the Removing" and "The Criterion and the Making-Plain" as part of the same single thematic section of the larger work by Ibn Qaṣī, *The Removing of the Sandals*, setting aside for the time being the question of whether they may reflect a later interpolation into this work. One should note that "The Criterion and the Making-Plain" brings the discussion of the two qurʾānic "horizon" passages full circle, suggesting that these two "chapters" from *Khalʿ al-naʿlayn* should be treated together, as I have argued here. One should bear in mind a potential counter argument, however, that the brief references in "The Criterion and the Making-Plain" might have served as a pretext for the insertion of the later teaching, which does end with formulaic expressions that suggest the conclusion of an independent work.

19. Coppens, *Seeing God*, 229–230.

20. They include Ibn Masʿūd, Anas b. Mālik, Ibn ʿAbbās, Muḥammd b. Kaʿb, Abū Saʿīd al-Khudrī, and Kaʿb b. ʿAjra, as well as two of the descendants of ʿAlī that come to play important roles for different groups among the "partisans of ʿAlī" (Shīʿat ʿAlī): Ḥasan b. ʿAlī al-Riḍā [al-ʿAskarī] (d. 260/873), the eleventh *imam* for Imāmī Shīʿites; and [Muḥammad] Ibn al-Ḥanafiyya (d. ca. 81/700), son of ʿAlī and al-Ḥanafiyya (rather than Fāṭima, the Prophet's daughter), who was a leader followed as a Shīʿī *imām* by al-Mukhtār and his compatriots.

21. Ibn Qaṣī, *Khalʿ al-naʿlayn*, 99.

22. This phrase appears only in one of the two manuscript versions of the text, but it fits well within the context of the discussion. What's more, all of these various positions appear together in the early Qurʾān commentary of al-Ṭabarī, so the author was well aware that each had some backing by at least some subgroup of early traditionists.

23. Ibn Qaṣī, *Khalʿ al-naʿlayn*, 99.

24. Ibn Qaṣī, *Khalʿ al-naʿlayn*, 100.

25. He also later appends the adjective "life-giving" (*al-aḥyā*) to this highest spirit, complicating the temptation to identify it with an epithet for Gabriel. See, for instance, Ibn Qaṣī, *Khalʿ al-naʿlayn*, 101.

26. Ibn Qaṣī, *Khalʿ al-naʿlayn*, 100–101. Recall that this "highest place of sitting" (*mustawā al-aʿlā*) received direct praises from Ibn Qaṣī at the opening of his *Khalʿ al-naʿlayn*, after praises to God and blessings to Muḥammad (see above).

27. Or "second" (*al-thānī*); see Dreher, "Das Imamat," 204.

28. Ibn Qaṣī, *Khalʿ al-naʿlayn*, 101–102. Compare the German translation in Dreher: "So manifestiert sich das Höchste zu dem Höchsten hin, das unter diesem Höchsten liegt. Dann manifestiert sich dieses Höchste zu dem zweiten Höchsten, das unter diesem Höchsten steht. So wird verfahren von Pleroma zu Pleroma bis zum Pleroma des Himmels über dem Diesseits. Daher manifestiert sich der zuverlässige Geist (Gabriel) auf dem klaren Horizont erst, wenn sich ihm das höchste Schreibrohr auf seinem glänzendsten Ort manifestiert hat, das höchste Schreibrohr manifestiert sich

erst von diesem glänzendsten Ort her, wenn sich ihm der Heilege Geist auf dem höchsten Horizont manifestiert hat. Der Heilege Geist manifestiert sich auf dem höchsten Horizont erst, wenn ihm die höchste Majestät in dem heiligsten und lebenerfülltesten Schleier erschienen ist. Alle diese Stationen sind Schleier vor der Majestät des (göttlichen) Wesens un die Lichter der genannten Namen und hohen Eigenshaften" (Dreher, "Das Imamat," 26–27).

29. It is interesting to note that the temporal chronology of this process does not align neatly with the chronology that comes to be established for these qurʾanic verses in the biography of the Prophet (*Sīra*) attributed to Ibn Isḥāq via Ibn Hishām, for in this *Sīra* tradition the vision of Gabriel blocking the horizon comes to be associated with the very start of his prophetic career and the night of the ascent associated with the year just before the end of the Meccan period. Nevertheless, Ibn Qaṣī's model need not follow the *Sīra* model, nor from a mystical perspective need it make logical sense in the temporal world of creation given that (1) Ibn Qaṣī is describing here a model of disclosures from the divinity who is beyond time and space; and (2) for Ibn Qaṣī the process of flowing out and flowing back is not a onetime occurrence but a continually repeating cycle.

30. Ibn Qaṣī, *Khalʿ al-naʿlayn*, 102.

31. To be consistent with the distinction he made at the beginning of this section, it seems the reference here should be to "the clear horizon" (Q 81:23) instead of "the highest horizon" (Q 53:7). That being as it may, since Ibn Qaṣī will go on to talk about how, from a different level of perception, both of these visions involved a vision of Gabriel, whom Muḥammad saw in his true form twice, and since these two experiences are ultimately just different veils that describe/cover the exact same experience, perhaps insisting on terminological consistency in this way misses the broader point.

32. Ibn Qaṣī, *Khalʿ al-naʿlayn*, 102.

33. Ibn Qaṣī, *Khalʿ al-naʿlayn*, 104.

34. This theory of vision can be traced back to Aristotle, if not before. Goodrich discusses how vision as this "active" process dependent on the faculties of the viewer gets developed by Ibn Qaṣī in his broader theory of perception (see Goodrich, "Sufi Revolt," 39–40).

35. Ibn Qaṣī explains further, "The Dihyan form was an outer veiling upon an inner veiling that sight cannot comprehend and the imaginations of humanity cannot encompass. When the revelation was sent down, it was the faithful spirit Gabriel, no other, and the encompassing form [of Gabriel] was an outer veiling upon an inner, essential, sacred, encompassing veiling that '*sight does not encompass*' (Q 6:103)" (Ibn Qaṣī, *Khalʿ al-naʿlayn*, 102).

36. Ibn Qaṣī, *Khalʿ al-naʿlayn*, 103.

37. Ibn Qaṣī, *Khalʿ al-naʿlayn*, 103.

38. Ibn Qaṣī, *Khalʿ al-naʿlayn*, 103.

39. Goodrich, "Sufi Revolt," 40.

40. Ibn Qaṣī, *Khalʿ al-naʿlayn*, 34. See some discussion of this short passage in Goodrich, "Sufi Revolt," 74; Dreher, "Das Imamat," 28.

41. In Mazyadī's edition of Ibn Qaṣī, *Khalʿ al-naʿlayn*, the "*Malakūt*" portion spans in the printed text from pages 55 to 136.

42. Life = *al-ḥayāt*, the first emanation from the divine essence.
43. Ibn Qaṣī, *Khalʿ al-naʿlayn*, 103.
44. Ibn Qaṣī, *Khalʿ al-naʿlayn*, 104.
45. Ibn Qaṣī, *Khalʿ al-naʿlayn*, 105.
46. Ibn Qaṣī, *Khalʿ al-naʿlayn*, 105–106.
47. Goodrich, "Sufi Revolt," 44 and 47–48.
48. See the discussion of this theme in Goodrich, "Sufi Revolt," 41–42.
49. Ibn Qaṣī, *Khalʿ al-naʿlayn*, 107. On various elaborations of this report, see the discussion by Rustomji, *Garden and the Fire*, 89–91; see also Lange, *Paradise and Hell in Islamic Traditions*, 101.
50. Ibn Qaṣī, *Khalʿ al-naʿlayn*, 107–108.
51. Ibn Qaṣī, *Khalʿ al-naʿlayn*, 108.
52. The section title "The Criterion and the Making Plain" offers a complementary detailed interpretation of the climax of the ascension vision, as we shall see in the discussion below (Ibn Qaṣī, *Khalʿ al-naʿlayn*, 109).
53. Ibn Qaṣī, *Khalʿ al-naʿlayn*, 108; compare Ibn Qaṣī, *Khalʿ al-naʿlayn*, 100: "The assembly of what was in their sayings served to connect what they had in their hands to what was in their deeds"; and again, Ibn Qaṣī, *Khalʿ al-naʿlayn*, 105: "He informed his companions who were reliable of transmission, and each carried all that one [could] carry."
54. Ibn Qaṣī, *Khalʿ al-naʿlayn*, 108.
55. Ibn Qaṣī, *Khalʿ al-naʿlayn*, 108.
56. Different printed editions of *Khalʿ al-naʿlayn* treat the final approximately twenty lines differently, some seeing it as a separate section and presenting the title "The Criterion and the Making-Plain" at its head, with others not dividing it from the rest of "The Removing of the Removing" and not inserting a new section heading at this point. It is because of this ambivalence in the textual tradition itself, and because of the related subject matter found in this passage, that I have chosen to treat "The Criterion and the Making-Plain" as inseparably connected to the rest of "The Removing of the Removing" that precedes it.
57. Following Mazyadī here with *takthīr*, as opposed to Goodrich, who reads *takbīr*.
58. From the section "The Criterion and the Making Plain," Ibn Qaṣī, *Khalʿ al-naʿlayn*, 109.
59. Madrid MS Real Academia de Historia MS Olim CCXLI Codera 241, 7r–7v. See the full translation in the appendix and the analysis in chapter 1.
60. Madrid MS Real Academia de Historia MS Olim CCXLI Codera 241, 7r–7v. For a different example, compare the developed version of the Ibn ʿAbbās ascension tale translated in appendix B of my *Narrating Muḥammad's Night Journey*, especially 225–226.
61. Ibn Qaṣī, *Khalʿ al-naʿlayn*, 109.
62. Ibn Qaṣī, *Khalʿ al-naʿlayn*, 99, the very beginning of the "Removing of the Removing" treatise, Q 81:23 and 53:7 being the two key verses that the above section discusses at length.
63. Ibn Qaṣī, *Khalʿ al-naʿlayn*, 109.

64. Ebstein, "Was Ibn Qaṣī a Sufi?," 207.

65. There is no question that Ibn Qaṣī remained firmly in the Sunnī camp theologically, whether or not he comes to draw on Ismāʿīlī or other Shīʿī valenced tropes. See Ebstein, "Was Ibn Qaṣī a Sufi?," 224.

66. Ibn ʿArabī, *Sharḥ kitāb khalʿ al-naʿlayn li'l-shaykh al-akbar muḥyī'ddīn ibn ʿarabī al-ḥātimī*, ed. Muḥammad al-Amrānī (Marekesh: Muʾassasat Āfāq, 2013). On the surviving manuscripts of the work from which this edition was published, see Ibn ʿArabī, *Sharḥ kitāb*, 114–115. Most trace their origin to Istanbul MS Shahīd ʿAlī Pasha 1174 (Süleymaniye Kutuphanesı), according to its title page (Ibn ʿArabī, *Sharḥ kitāb*, 114) representing a work dictated by Ibn ʿArabī to one Shams al-Din b. Shudakīn (d. 640/1242), and dated in its colophon to the month of Jumāda I in the year 741 AH (Ibn ʿArabī, *Sharḥ kitāb*, 122), corresponding to October of 1340 CE.

Conclusion.

1. See Ebstein, *Mysticism and Philosophy in al-Andalus.*

2. See Casewit, *Mystics of al-Andalus*, 299–306.

3. For shorter studies to date, see James Morris, "The Spiritual Ascension: Ibn ʿArabī and the Miʿrāj, Part 1," *Journal of the American Oriental Society* 107, no. 4 (1987): 629–652; James Morris, "The Spiritual Ascension: Ibn ʿArabī and the Miʿrāj, Part II," *JAOS* 108, no. 1 (1988): 63–77; Brooke Olson Vuckovic, appendix to *Heavenly Journeys, Earthly Concerns*, 125–134; Suʿād al-Ḥakīm, scholarly introduction to her addition of *Kitāb al-Isrā ilā al-maqām al-asnā* (Beirut: Dandara lil-Ṭibāʿa wa'l-Nashr, 1988), 9–45.

4. For a model to such an approach, see ʿAlī ʿAbd al-Fattāḥ Muḥammad ʿAbduh, *al-Miʿrāj ʿinda Ibn ʿArabī* (Beirut: Kitāb al-Nāshirūn, 2017). See also Michel Chodkiewicz, *Seal of the Saints: Prophethood and Sainthood in the Doctrine of Ibn ʿArabī*, trans. Liadain Sherrard (Cambridge: Islamic Texts Society, 1993); see also James Morris, "Ibn ʿArabī's Spiritual Ascension," in Ibn ʿArabī, *The Meccan Revelations*, vol. 1, ed. Michel Chodkiewicz, trans. William C. Chittick and James W. Morris (New York: Pir, 2002).

5. Ibn ʿArabī is said to have composed the work in the city of Fez during the month of Jumada in the year 594/1198, when the author would have been in his early thirties.

6. Ibn ʿArabī, *Kitāb al-isrā'*, 54.

7. Such an appropriation of Muḥammad's heavenly journey as an allegorical teaching tool is not unique to Ibn ʿArabī, of course: within the Islamic intellectual tradition one recalls from about two centuries earlier the *Miʿrājnāmeh* (*Book of the Ascension*) ascribed to the famous Muslim philosopher Ibn Sīna (Avicenna, d.428/1037), on which see Peter Heath, *Allegory and Philosophy in Avicenna* (Ibn Sīnā). Mention also should be made of the literary masterwork describing an imagined journey to the Paradise and Hellfire by the poet al-Maʿārrī (d. ca. 1033), *Risālat al-ghufrān* (*The Treatise of Forgiveness*); see the recent English multivolume translation as *The Epistle of Forgiveness or, a Pardon to Enter the Garden*, by G. J. H. van Gelder and Gregor Schoeler, 2 vols. to date (New York: New York University Press, 2013–). See also the

edition of *Risālat al-ghufrān* edited by Aishah ʿAbd al-Rahman (Bint al-Shati), 7th ed. (Cairo: Dar al-Maʿārif, 1981).

8. See Ibn Diḥya al-Kalbī's work *al-Ibtihāj fī aḥādīth al-miʿrāj*, ed. Fawzī ʿAbd al-Muṭṭalib (Cairo: Maktabat al-Khānjā, 1996).

9. Since the discovery of multiple manuscripts of this work in the mid-twentieth century, the bibliography has grown immensely, yet much scholarly work remains to be done in determining its provenance. See, however, the commentary and articles accompanying the following translations and editions of the work: *Le Livre de l'Échelle de Mahomet*, new ed., trans. Gisèle Besson and Michèle Brossard-Dandré (Paris: Librarie Générale Française, 1991); Jamel Eddine Bencheikh, *Le Voyage nocturne de Mahomet* (Paris: Imprimerie Nationale, 1988); and Reginald Hyatte, *The Prophet of Islam in Old French: The Romance of Muhammad (1258) and the Book of Muhammad's Ladder (1264)* (Leiden: Brill, 1997). See also Daniel Gimaret, "Au cœur du miʿrāǧ, un hadith interpolé," in *Le voyage initiatique en terre d'Islam*, ed. Mohammad Ali Amir-Moezzi (Louvain-Paris: Peeters, 1996), 67–82; and Jean-Patrick Guillaume, "'Moi, Mahomet, Prophète et Messager de Dieu . . .': Traduction et adaptation dans le *Liber scale Machometi*," in Guillaume, "'Moi, Mahomet," 83–98.

10. See *Tafsīr Ibn ʿArabī*, 2 vols. (Beirut: Dār al-Ṣādir, 1968), especially its commentary on the Night Journey verse (Q 17:1), 1:370; and the beginning of the Star chapter (Q 53:1–18), 2:271–271. The proper title of this work appears to have been *Taʾwīlat al-qurʾān*.

11. ʿAbd Allāh Ibn Abī Jamra, *Bahjat al-nufūs*, 2nd ed., 4 vols. in 2, followed in the last volume by the appended work *Kitāb marāʾī al-ḥisan* (Beirut: Dār al-Kutub al-ʿIlmiyya, 2007). See my preliminary comparative study of this work in "Ascension Visions of Sufi Masters: The Rhetoric of Authority in Visionary Experiences of Ibn Abī Jamra (d.ca. 699/1300) and Rūzbihān Baqlī (d. 606/1209)" in *Words of Experience: Translating Islam with Carl W. Ernst*, ed. Ilyse R. Morgenstein Fuerst and Brannon Wheeler, 94–111 (Sheffield, UK: Equinox, 2021).

12. In particular, I am thinking here of the dream manual of Ruzbihan Baqlī, *Kashf al-asrār* (*The Unveiling of Secrets*), trans. Carl W. Ernst (Chapel Hill, NC: Parvardigar, 1997); Ruzbihan Baqlī, *The Unveiling of Secrets* (*Kashf al-asrār*): *The Visionary Autobiography of Ruzbihan al-Baqlī (1128–1209)*, ed. Firoozeh Papan-Matin (Leiden: Brill, 2005).

13. Jonathan Katz, "Visionary Experience, Autobiography, and Sainthood in North African Islam," *Princeton Papers in Near Eastern Studies*, 1992 (1): 85–118; Jonathan Katz, *Dreams, Sufism, and Sainthood: The Visionary Career of Muḥammad al-Zawāwī* (Leiden: Brill, 1996).

Appendix.

1. Madrid, Real Academia de la Historia MS Olim CCXLI / Codera 241 (Gayangos Collection).

2. Context clear from comparing the comparable passage in the Primitive Version of the Ibn ʿAbbās ascension narrative. See Suyuti, *al-Lālī al-maṣnūʿa*, 1:63; Colby, *Narrating Muḥammad's Night Journey*, appendix A.

3. The meaning of this phrase becomes clear in what follows shortly after this introduction where the "enormous tablet" that the Angel of Death scrutinizes continually is described.

4. Tear in the upper right, the beginning of fol. 1v, line 1, making all but "*bi-ma*" of the first three to four words of the line absent from the manuscript.

5. After the folios missing from the beginning of the text (which makes it "acephalous"). here begins one or more additional missing folio(s) from the middle of the text, following 1v and preceding 2r, containing the account of the visit to the fifth heaven that is cited at the end of 1v but then not ever described. One could conjecture that the missing folios describing the fifth heaven may have originally included an encounter with the angel Mālik and a subsequent tour of Hellfire (see Frederick Colby, "Fire in the Upper Heavens: Locating Hell in Middle Period Narratives of Muḥammad's Ascension").

6. Compare the throne room scenes of Jewish apocalyptic texts known by the general title of "Hekhalot," for example 3 Enoch (Sefer Hekhalot) or the Greater Hekhalot (Hekhalot Rabbati), in which one commonly finds long lists of the names and qualities of the divinity, the recitation and/or participation of which often forms part of the heavenly angelic liturgy, together with the Qedushah (Isa. 6:3). For one brief instance, see 3 Enoch (Sefer Hekhalot), chapters 39 to 40.

7. Fol. 8r, line 10, unclear because the beginning of the lines from here on down is obscured because of an inner seam rip, the paper folding up.

8. Fol. 8r, line 11, word missing because of rip in middle of folio but understood from the context. While there is no "hanging sword" trope in the Hekhalot texts, for the idea of the fear of God's "sword of judgment," see 3 Enoch (Sefer Hekhalot), chapter 32.

9. This reflects my best guess at trying to read the inside seam (torn) at the beginning of fol. 8r, line 13, its meaning illuminated by the later attestations of what I have called the "hanging sword" narreme (diverse instances of which are discussed in *Narrating Muhammad's Night Journey*, e.g., 76, 143, 147, 155, 230).

10. Q 4:125. The missing words here and in what immediately follows in the defective final folio of the manuscript have been supplied from parallel passages of the same narreme in other works. For instance, for the opening lines of the "Favor of the Prophets" trope, al-Qāḍī ʿIyāḍ has the following phrase: "His Lord answered him: [Though I took Abraham as an intimate friend,] I took you as both an intimate friend and a beloved, as it is written in the Torah, '*Muḥammad, beloved of the Most Merciful*' " (see Qāḍī ʿIyāḍ, *al-Shifāʾ*, 118–119, translated above).

11. Q 4:164.

12. From the difficult-to-read end of fol. 8v, line 1, which neglects to insert the word "and" before "Idrīs," leaving no conjunctive "*wa*" between the names of Abraham and Enoch.

13. Q 19:57, usually associated with Enoch only, as can also be seen in God's answer that follows. Perhaps Abraham has been added here on account of the fact that Abraham is the prophet who typically appears in the highest heaven in mainstream narratives of Muhammad's ascension.

14. Obscure at the beginning of fol. 8v, line 3, but understood from the context.

15. Q 38:35.

16. This word might also be "*al-ḥayawān*," although that reading appears unlikely. It is difficult to know for sure, since significant fading appears here in fol. 8v, line 12. A cleansing "river of fire" appears in 3 Enoch (Sefer Hekhalot), chapter 36, and the idea that it is from such a body of water that angels are created and to which they precede when destroyed, see 3 Enoch (Sefer Hekhalot), chapters 40 and 47.

17. The "*Fātiḥa*" of the Qur'ān, which is Q sura 1.

18. End of fol. 8v, line 13 almost totally obscured, but from context in comparison with parallel versions, one expects this reference to be to the "Seals" of the second sura, Q 2:285–286.

Bibliography

ʿAbduh, ʿAlī ʿAbd al-Fattāḥ Muḥammad. *al-Miʿrāj ʿinda Ibn ʿArabī.* Beirut: Kitāb al-Nāshirūn, 2017.

Adamson, Peter. *The Arabic Plotinus: A Philosophical Study of the Theology of Aristotle*. London: Duckworth, 2002.

ʿAfīfī, Abū'l-ʿAlā'. "Abūlqāsim Ibn Qaṣī wa kitābuhu *Khalʿ al-naʿlayn.*" *Majallat kulliyat al-ādāb, Iskandariyya* 11 (1958): 53–87.

Ahmed, Shahab. *What Is Islam? The Importance of Being Islamic* (Princeton, NJ: Princeton University Press, 2015

Akhtar, Ali Humayun. "Identifying Mysticism in Early Esoteric Scriptural Hermeneutics: Sahl al-Tustari's (d. 283/896) Tafsīr Reconsidered." *Journal of Islamic and Muslim Studies* 2, no. 2 (2017): 38–52.

Amir-Moezzi, Mohammad Ali. *Le voyage initiatique en terre d'Islam: Ascensions célestes et itinéraires spirituels*. Louvain-Paris: Peeters, 1996.

Anonymous. "[*Kitāb al-miʿrāj*]." Real Academia de Historia, Madrid. MS Olim CCXLI / Codera 241 (Gayangosm Collection). Madrid, Spain.

Arbel, Vita. *Beholders of Divine Secrets: Mysticism and Myth in the Hekhalot and Merkavah Literature*. Albany: State University of New York Press, 2003.

Asín Palacios, Miguel. *Abenmassara y su escuela*. Translated by Elmer H. Douglas and Howard W. Yoder as *The Mysticial Philosophy of Ibn Masarra and his Followers*. Leiden: Brill, 1978.

Asín Palacios, Miguel. *La escatalogía musulmana en la Divina Comedia*. 2nd ed. Madrid: Consejo Superior de Investigaciones Cientificas, 1943.

Baffioni, Carmela, trans. *Epistles of the Brethren of Purity: Sciences of the Soul and Intellect.* Part 3, *An Arabic Critical Edition and English Translation of Epistles* 39–41. Oxford: Oxford University Press and Institute of Ismaili Studies, 2017.

Baqlī, Ruzbihan. *Kashf al-asrār / The Unveiling of Secrets*. Translated by Carl W. Ernst. Chapel Hill, NC: Parvardigar, 1997.

Baqlī, Ruzbihan. *The Unveiling of Secrets* (*Kashf al-asrār*): *The Visionary Autobiography of Ruzbihan al-Baqlī (1128–1209)*. Edited by Firoozeh Papan-Matin. Leiden: Brill, 2005.

Bencheikh, Jamel Eddine. *Le Voyage nocturne de Mahomet.* Paris: Imprimerie Nationale, 1988.

Bewley, Aisha Abdurrahman, editor and translator. *Muḥammad: Messenger of Allah, Ash-Shifāʾ of Qadi Iyad.* Inverness, UK: Madinah Press, 2011.

El-Bizri, Nader, general editor. Foreword to *Epistles of the Brethren of Purity*. Oxford: Oxford University Press and Institute of Ismaili Studies, 2008–.

Böwering, Gerhard. "From the Word of God to the Vision of God: Muḥammad's Heavenly Journey in Classical Ṣūfī Qurʾān Commentary." In *Le voyage initiatique en terre d'Islam*, edited by Mohammad Ali Amir-Moezzi, 205–222. Leuven: Peeters, 1996.

Böwering, Gerhard. "The Qur'ān Commentary of al-Sulamī." In *Islamic Studies Presented to Charles J. Adams*, edited by Wael B. Hallaq and Donald P. Little, 41–56. Leiden: Brill, 1991.

Brockelmann, Carl. *Geschichte der Arabischen Litteratur*. Leiden: Brill, 1943–1949.

Brown, J. Vahid. "Andalusi Mysticism: A Recontextualization." *Journal of Islamic Philosophy* 2 (2006): 69–101.

Buckley, R. P. *The Night Journey and Ascension in Islam: The Reception of Religious Narrative in Sunnī, Shī'ī, and Western Culture*. London: I. B. Tauris, 2013.

Bukharī, Abū 'Abd Allāh. *Ṣaḥīḥ Bukharī*. Edited by Muḥammad Nizār Tamīm and Haytham Nizār Tamīm. Beirut: Sharikat Dār al-Arqam, n.d.

Burman, Thomas E. *Religious Polemic and the Intellectual History of the Mozarabs, c. 1050–1200*. Leiden: Brill, 1994.

Casewit, Yousef. *The Mystics of al-Andalus: Ibn Barrajān and Islamic Thought in the Twelfth Century*. Cambridge: Cambridge University Press, 2017.

Chodkiewicz, Michel. *Seal of the Saints: Prophethood and Sainthood in the Doctrine of Ibn 'Arabī.* Translated by Liadain Sherrard. Cambridge: Islamic Texts Society, 1993.

Colby, Frederick. "Ascension Visions of Sufi Masters: The Rhetoric of Authority in Visionary Experiences of Ibn Abī Jamra (d. ca. 699/1300) and Rūzbihān Baqlī (d. 606/1209)." In *Words of Experience: Translating Islam with Carl W. Ernst*, edited by Ilyse Morgensein Fuerst and Brannon Wheeler, 94–111. Sheffield, UK: Equinox, 2021.

Colby, Frederick S. "Constructing an Islamic Ascension Narrative." PhD diss., Duke University, 2002.

Colby, Frederick. "Fire in the Upper Heavens: Locating Hell in Middle Period Narratives of Muḥammad's Ascension." In *Locating Hell in Islamic Traditions*, edited by Christian Lange, 124–143. Leiden: Brill, 2016.

Colby, Frederick. *Narrating Muḥammad's Night Journey: Tracing the Development of the Ibn 'Abbās Ascension Discourse*. Albany: State University of New York Press, 2008.

Collins, John J., and Michael Fishbane, eds. *Death, Ecstasy, and Other Worldly Journeys.* Albany: State University of New York Press, 1995.

Coppens, Pieter. *Seeing God in Sufi Qur'an Commentaries: Crossings between This World and the Otherworld.* Edinburgh: Edinburgh University Press, 2018.

Cordera, Francisco. *Decadencia y desaparición de los Almorávides en España.* Zaragoza, Spain: n.p., 1899.

Culianu, Ioan. *Experiences de l'extase: Extase, ascension et recit visionnaire de l'hellenisme au Moyen Age*. Paris: Payot, 1984.

Culianu, Ioan. *Out of This World: Otherworldly Journeys from Gilgamesh to Albert Einstein.* Boston, MA: Shambhala, 1991.

Dan, Joseph. "From Hekhalot Rabbati to the Hekhalot of the Zohar: The Depersonalization of the Mysticism of the Divine Chariot" [in Hebrew]. In *Jewish Studies* [*Kavod*] (2017): 143–162.

Dan, Joseph. *The Heart and the Fountain: An Anthology of Jewish Mystical Experiences*. Oxford: Oxford University Press, 2002.

Davila, James. *Hekhalot Literature in Translation: Major Texts of Merkavah Mysticism*. Leiden: Brill, 2013.

Dreher, Josef. "Das Imamat des islamischen Mystikers Abūlqāsim Aḥmad ibn al-Ḥusain Ibn Qasī (gest. 1151)." PhD diss., Rhenishen Friedrich-Wilhelm University in Bonn, 1985.

Ebstein, Michael. *Mysticism and Philosophy in al-Andalus: Ibn Masarra, Ibn al-ʿArabī, and the Ismāʿīlī Tradition*. Leiden: Brill, 2014.

Ebstein, Michael. "Was Ibn Qaṣī a Sufi?" *Studia Islamica* 110 (2015): 196–232.

Elliott, William. "The Career of Ibn Qaṣī as Religious Teacher and Political Revolutionary in 12th Century Islamic Spain." PhD diss., University of Edinburgh, 1979.

Ess, Josef van. "Vision and Ascension: Surat al-Najm and Its Relationship with Muḥammad's *miʿrāj*." *Journal of Qur'anic Studies* 1 (1999): 47–62.

Fierro, Maribel. "Batinism in al-Andalus." *Studia Islamica* 84 (1996): 87–112.

Fierro, Maribel. "Between the Maghreb and al-Andalus." In *The Almohad Revolution Revolution: Politics and Religion in the Islamic West during the Twelfth-Thirteenth Centuries*. Farnham, UK: Ashgate, 2012.

Firestone, Rueven, trans. "Muḥammad's Night Journey and Ascension." In *Windows on the House of Islam*, edited by John Renard, 336–345. Berkeley: University of California Press, 1998.

Gardiner, Eileen, ed. *Visions of Heaven and Hell before Dante*. New York: Italica, 1989.

Garrido Clemente, Pilar. "Edición crítica de la *Risālat al-Iʿtibār* de Ibn Masarra de Córdoba." *Miscellanea de estudios árabes y hebraicos, Sección árabe-Islam* 56 (2007): 81–104.

Gatti, Maria Luisa. "Plotinus: The Platonic Tradition and the Foundations of Neoplatonism." In *The Cambridge Companion to Plotinus*, edited by Lloyd P. Gerson, 15–36. Cambridge: Cambridge University Press, 1992.

Gilliot, Claude. "Le commentaire coranique de Hūd B. Muḥakkam/Muḥkim." *Arabica* 44, no. 2 (Apr. 1997): 179–233.

Gimaret, Daniel. "Au cœur du miʿrāǧ, un hadith interpolé." In *Le voyage initiatique en terre d'Islam*, edited by Mohammad Ali Amir-Moezzi, 67–82. Louvain-Paris: Peeters, 1996.

Goldziher, Ignaz. "Le ʾAmr ilāhī (ha-ʾinyan ha-ʾelohi) chez Juda Halevi." *Revue des etudes juives* 50 (1905): 32–41.

Goodrich, David. "A Sufi Revolt in Portugal: Ibn Qasī and his *Kitāb Khalʿ al-naʿlayn*." PhD diss., Columbia University, 1978.

Gramlich, Richard, trans. *Das Sendschreiben al-Qusayrīs uber das Sufitum*. Wiesbaden, Germany: Franz Steiner Verlag, 1989.

Gruber, Christiane, and Frederick Colby. *The Prophet's Ascension: Cross-Cultural Encounters with the Islamic Miʿrāj Tales*. Bloomington: Indiana University Press, 2010.

Gruenwald, Ithmar. *Apocalyptic and Merkavah Mysticism*. Leiden: Brill, 1980.

Guillaume, Jean-Patrick. "'Moi, Mahomet, Prophète et Messager de Dieu . . .': Traduction et adaptation dans le *Liber scale Machometi*." In *Le voyage initiatique en terre d'Islam*, edited by Mohammad Ali Amir-Moezzi, 83–98. Louvain-Paris: Peeters, 1996.

Halperin, David. *The Faces of the Chariot*. Tübingen, Germany: J. C. B. Mohr, 1988.

Halperin, David. "Hekhalot and Miʿrāj: Observations on the Heavenly Journey in Judaism and Islam." In *Death, Ecstasy, and Other Worldly Journeys*, edited by John J. Collins and Michael Fishbane, 269–288. Albany: State University of New York Press, 1995.

Hawwārī, Hūd b. Muḥakkam. *Tafsīr Kitāb Allāh al-*ʿazīz. 4 vols. Beirut: Dar al-Gharb al-Islamī, 1990.

Heath, Peter. *Allegory and Philosophy in Avicenna (Ibn Sīnā): With a Translation of the Book of the Prophet Muḥammad's Ascent to Heaven*. Philadelphia: University of Pennsylvania Press, 1992.

Herculano, Alexandre. *História de Portugal*. 8 vols. Paris: Livraria Bertrand, n.d.

Himmelfarb, Martha. "The Practice of Ascent in the Ancient Mediterranean World." In *Death, Ecstasy, and Other Wordly Journeys*, edited by John J. Collins and Michael Fishbane, 123–154. Albany: State University of New York Press, 1995.

Hodgson, Marshall G. S. *The Venture of Islam*: *Conscience and History in a World Civilization*. 3 vols. Chicago, IL: University of Chicago Press, 1974.

Horovitz, J. "Muhammeds Himmelfahrt." *Der Islam* 9 (1919): 159–183.

Hughes, Aaron. "Miʿrāj and the Language of Legitimation in the Medieval Islamic and Jewish Philosophical Traditions: A Case Study of Avicenna and Abraham ibn Ezra." In *The Prophet's Ascension*, edited by Christiane Gruber and Frederick Colby, 72–91. Bloomington: Indiana University Press, 2010.

Hughes, Aaron. *The Texture of the Divine: Imagination in Medieval Islamic and Jewish Thought*. Bloomington: Indiana University Press, 2004.

Hujwirī, Alī b. Usmān. *Kashf al-maḥjūb*. Edited by Valentin A. Zhukovski. Tehran, Iran: Kitābkhānah-i Ṭahūrī, 1997.

Hujwirī, Alī b. Usmān. *The Kashf al-Maḥjūb: The Oldest Persian Treatise on Sufism*. Translated by Reynold Nicholson. Leiden: Brill, 1911.

Hyatte, Reginald. *The Prophet of Islam in Old French: The Romance of Muhammad (1258) and the Book of Muhammad's Ladder (1264)*. Leiden: Brill, 1997.

Ibn Abī Jamra, ʿAbd Allāh. *Bahjat al-nufūs*. 2nd ed. 4 vols. as 2 vols. Beirut: Dār al-Kutub al-ʿIlmiyya, 2007.

Ibn ʿArabī, Muḥyī al-Dīn. *Kitāb al-Isrā ilā al-maqām al-asnā*. Edited by Suʿād al-Ḥakīm. Beirut: Dandara lil-Ṭibāʿa waʾl-Nashr, 1988.

Ibn ʿArabī, Muḥyī al-Dīn. *Sharḥ kitāb khalʿ al-naʿlayn liʾl-shaykh al-akbar muḥyīʾd-dīn ibn ʿarabī al-ḥātimī*. Edited by Muḥammad al-Amrānī. Marrakesh, Morocco: Muʾassasat Āfāq, 2013.

Ibn ʿArabī, Muḥyī al-Dīn [attributed; likely written by ʿAbd al-Razzāq al-Kashānī]. *Tafsīr Ibn ʿArabī*. 2 vols. Beirut: Dār al-Ṣādir, 1968.

Ibn Barrajān, Abū al-Ḥakam ʿAbd al-Salām. *A Qurʾān Commentary by Ibn Barrajān of Seville d. 536/1141*: *Īdāḥ al-ḥikma bi aḥkām al-ʿibra*: *Wisdom Deciphered, The Unseen Discovered*. Edited by Gerhard Böwering and Yousef Casewit. Leiden: Brill, 2016.

Ibn Barrajān, Abū al-Ḥakam ʿAbd al-Salām. *Tanbīh al-afhām*. Edited by Aḥmad Farīd al-Mazyadī. 5 vols. Beirut: Dar al-Kutub al-ʿIlmiyya, 2013.

Ibn Hishām, ʿAbd al-Malik. *The Life of Muḥammad*. Translated by Alfred Guillaume. Oxford: Oxford University Press, 1955; Karachi, Pakistan: Oxford University Press, 1967.

Ibn Khallikān, Abū al-ʿAbbās Shams al-Dīn. *Wafayāt al-Aʿyān*. Edited by Iḥsān ʿAbbās. 8 vols. Beirut: Dār al-Ṣādir, 1977.

Ibn Qaṣī, Abū al-Qāsim. *Khalʿ al-naʿlayn wa-iqtibās al-nūr min mawḍiʿ al-qadamayn*. Edited by Mazyadī, Aḥmad Farīd. Cairo, Egypt: Dār Rītāj liʾl-Nashr waʾl-Tibāʿa waʾl-Tawzīʿ, 2011.

Ibn Saʿd, Muḥammad. *Tabaqāt al-kubrā*. Vol. 1. Beirut: Dār al-Sādir, 1985.

al-Ikhwān al-Ṣafāʾ. *Rasāʾil*. 3 vols. Beirut: Dār al-Ṣādir, 1957.

Ivry, Alfred. "Ismāʿīlī Theology and Maimonides' Philosophy." In *The Jews of Medieval Islam: Community, Society, and Identity*, edited by Daniel Frank, 271–300. Leiden: Brill, 1995.

ʿIyāḍ, Qāḍī Abū al-Faḍl. *al-Shifāʾ bi-taʿrīf ḥuqūq al-Muṣṭafā*. Beirut: Dār al-Kutub al-*ʿIlmiyya*, n.d.

ʿIyāḍ, Qāḍī Abū al-Faḍl. *al-Shifāʾ bi-taʿrīf ḥuqūq al-Muṣṭafā*. Translated by Aisha Abdurrahman Bewley. See above, s.v. Bewley.

Jaʿfar, Muḥammad Kamāl Ibrahīm. *Min qaḍāya al-fikr al-islāmī: Dirāsa wa nuṣūṣ*. Cairo: Maktabat Dar al-ʿUlūm, 1978.

Jarrar, Maher. *Die Prophetenbiographie im islamischen Spanien*. Frankfurt, Germany: Peter Lang, 1989.

al-Kalbī, Ibn Diḥya. *al-Ibtihāj fī aḥādīth al-miʿrāj*. Edited by Fawzī ʿAbd al-Muṭṭalib. Cairo: Maktabat al-Khānjā, 1996.

Kappler, Claude. "L'Apocalypse latine de Paul." In *Apocalypses et voyages dans l'au-delà*, edited by Claude Kappler et al., 237–266. Paris: Les Éditions du CERF, 1987.

Katz, Jonathan. *Dreams, Sufism, and Sainthood: The Visionary Career of Muḥammad al-Zawāwī*. Leiden: Brill, 1996.

Katz, Jonathan. "Visionary Experience, Autobiography, and Sainthood in North African Islam." *Princeton Papers in Near Eastern Studies* (1992) 1:85–118.

Kaufmann, David. *Geschichte der Attributenlehre in der judischen Religionsphilosophie von Saadia vis Maimuni*. Gotha, Germany: F. A. Perthes, 1877.

Khargūshī, Abū Saʿd. *Manāḥil al-shifā wa-manāhil al-ṣafā bi-taḥqīq kitab Sharaf al-muṣṭafā taṣnīf. . . Khargūshī*. Edited by Abū ʿĀṣim Nabīl b. Hāshim al-Ghamrī. Makkah, Saudi Arabia: Dār al-Bashāʾir al-Islamiyya, 2003.

Knysh, Alexander, trans. *Al-Qushayrī's Epistle on Sufism: 'Al-Risāla al-Qushayriyya fī ʿilm al-taṣawwuf'*. Reading, UK: Garnet, 2007.

Krinis, Ehud. *God's Chosen People: Judah Halevi's "Kuzari" and the Shīʿī Imām Doctrine*. Translated by Ann Brener and Tamar Liza Cohen. Turnhourt, Belgium: Brepols, 2014.

Le Livre de l'Échelle de Mahomet [in French]. New ed. Translated by Gisèle Besson and Michèle Brossard-Dandré. Paris: Librarie Générale Française, 1991.

Lobel, Diana. *Between Mysticism and Philosophy: Sufi Language of Religious Experience in Judah Ha-Levi's* Kuzari. Albany: State University of New York Press, 2000.

al-Ma'ārrī, Abū al-'Alā'. *The Epistle of Forgiveness or, a Pardon to Enter the Garden.* Edited and translated by G. J. H. van Gelder and Gregor Schoeler. 2 vols. [to date]. New York: New York University Press, 2013–.

al-Ma'ārrī, Abū al-'Alā'. *Risālat al-ghufrān*. Edited by Aishah 'Abd al-Rahman [Bint al-Shati]. 7th ed. Cairo: Dar al-Ma'ārif, 1981.

Morewedge, Parviz, ed. *Neoplatonism and Islamic Thought*. Albany: State University of New York Press, 1992.

Morris, James. "Ibn 'Arabī's Spiritual Ascension." In Ibn 'Arabī, *The Meccan Revelations*, vol. 1. Edited by Michel Chodkiewicz. Translated by William C. Chittick and James W. Morris. New York: Pir Press, 2002.

Morris, James. "The Spiritual Ascension: Ibn 'Arabī and the Mi'rāj, Part 1." *Journal of the American Oriental Society* 107, no. 4 (1987): 629–652.

Morris, James. "The Spiritual Ascension: Ibn 'Arabī and the Mi'rāj, Part II." *Journal of the American Oriental Society* 108, no. 1 (1988): 63–77.

Nguyen, Martin. *Sufi Master and Qur'an Scholar: Abū'l-Qāsim al-Qushayrī and the "Laṭā'if al-Ishārāt."* Oxford: Oxford University Press, 2012.

Pines, Shlomo. "Shi'ite Terms and Conceptions in Judah Halevi's Kuzari." *Jerusalem Studies in Arabic and Islam* 2 (1980): 165–251.

Qāḍī 'Iyāḍ. See s.v. 'Iyāḍ, Qāḍī Abū al-Faḍl.

al-Qurṭubī, Muḥammad b. Aḥmad. *al-Jāmi' li-aḥkām al-qur'ān*. 3rd ed. 20 vols. Cairo: Dār al-Kitāb al-'Arabī, 1967.

Qushayrī , Abū al-Qāsim. *Kitāb al-mi'rāj*. Edited by Ali Ḥasan 'Abd al-Qādir. Cairo: Dār al-Kutub al-Ḥadītha, 1964.

Renaud, Étienne. "Le Récit du mi'rāj." In *Apocalypses et Voyages dans l'Au-Delà*, edited Claude Kappler, 27–290. Paris: Les Éditions du CERF, 1987.

Rowland, Christopher, and Christopher R. A. Morray-Jones. *The Mystery of God: Early Jewish Mysticim and the New Testament*. Leiden: Brill, 2009.

Rubin, Uri. "Muhammad's Night Journey (Isra') to al-Masjid al-Aqsa: Aspects of the Earliest Origins of the Islamic Sanctity of Jerusalem." *Qantara:Rrevista de estudios árabes* 29, no. 1 (2008): 147–164.

Saleh, Walid. *The Formation of the Classical Tafsīr Tradition: The Qur'ān Commentary of al-Tha'labī (d. 427/1035)*. Leiden: Brill, 2004.

Sands, Kristin Z. "On the Subtleties of Method and Style in the *Laṭā'if al-ishārāt* of Qushayrī." *Journal of Sufi Studies* 2 (2013): 7–16.

Schäfer, Peter. *Hekhalot-Studien*. Tübingen, Germany: J. C. B. Mohr, 1988.

Schäfer, Peter. *The Hidden and Manifest God*. Albany: State University of New York Press, 1992.

Schäfer, Peter. "The Ideal of Piety of the Ashkenazi Hasidim and Its Roots in Jewish Tradition." *Jewish History* 4 (1990): 9–23.

Schäfer, Peter, ed. *Wege mystischer Gotteserfahrung / Mystical Approaches to God*. Munich, Germany: Oldenbourg, 2006.

Scholem, Gershom. *Major Trends in Jewish Mysticism*. New York: Schocken, 1946.

Segal, Alan. "Paul and the Beginning of Jewish Mysticism." In *Death, Ecstasy, and Other Wordly Journeys*, edited by John J. Collins and Michael Fishbane, 95–122. Albany: State University of New York Press, 1995.

Sells, Michael. "Sound, Spirit, and Gender in the Qur'ān." In Michael Sells, *Approaching the Qur'ān*. 199–223. 2nd ed. Ashland, OR: White Cloud, 2007.

Stern, S. M. "Ibn Masarra, Follower of Pseudo-Empedocles — an Illusion." In *Actas IV congress de estudios árabes e islamicos: Coimbra-Lisboa, 1 a 8 Setembro de 1968*, , 325–337. Leiden: Brill, 1971.

Stroumsa, Sarah. "Ibn Masarra and the Beginnings of Mystical Thought in al-Andalus." In *Wege mystischer Gotteserfahrung / Mystical Approaches to God*, edited by Peter Schäfer, 97–112. Munich, Germany: Oldenbourg, 2006.

Stroumsa, Sarah, and Sara Sviri. "The Beginnings of Mystical Philosophy in al-Andalus: Ibn Masarra and His *Epistle on Contemplation*." *Jerusalem Studies in Arabic and Islam* 36 (2009): 201–253.

Suhaylī, ʿAbd al-Raḥmān ibn ʿAbd Allāh. *al-Rawḍ al-unuf fī sharḥ al-sīra al-nabawiyya*. Edited by ʿAbd al-Raḥmān Wakīl. 7 vols. Cairo: Dār al-Kutub al-Ḥadītha, 1967–1970.

Sulamī, Abu ʿAbd al-Raḥmān. "Bayān laṭā'if al-miʿrāj." In *Sufi Treatises of Abū ʿAbd al-Raḥmān al-Sulamī (d. 412/1021)*, edited by Gerhard Böwering and Bilal Orfali, 21–30. Beirut: Dar El-Machreq, 2009.

Sulamī, Abu ʿAbd al-Raḥmān. *The Subtleties of the Ascension*. Translated by Frederick Colby. Louisville, KY: Fons Vitae, 2006.

Sulamī, Abu ʿAbd al-Raḥmān. *Ṭabaqāt al-ṣufiyya*. Edited by Nūr al-Dīn. Cairo: Maktabat al-Khānjā, 1986.

Suyūṭī, ʿAbd al-Raḥmān. *Lāʾālī al-maṣnūʿa fī aḥādīth al-mawḍūʿa*. 3 vols. Beirut: Dār al-Kutub al-ʿIlmiyya, 1996.

Ṭabarī, Abū Jaʿfar Muḥammad. *Jāmiʿ al-Bayān fī taʾwīl al-qurʾān* [*Tafsīr al- Ṭabarī*]. 12 vols. Beirut: Dār al-Kutub al-ʿIlmiyya, 1992.

Thibon, Jean-Jacques. *L'oeuvre d'Abū ʿAbd al-Raḥmān al-Sulamī (325/937–412/1021) et la formation du soufisme*. Damascus: Institut français du Proche-Orient, 2009.

"3 (Hebrew Apocalypse of) Enoch (5th–6th century AD)." Translated by P. Alexander. In *The Old Testament Pseudepigrapha*, edited by James Charlesworth, 1:225–315. New York: Doubleday, 1983.

Tieszan, Charles L. *Christian Identity amid Islam in Medieval Spain*. Leiden: Brill, 2013.

Tottoli, Roberto. "Muslim Eschatology and the Ascension of the Prophet Muḥammad: Describing Paradise in *Miʿrāj* Traditions and Literature." In *Roads to Paradise*, edited by Sebastian Gunther and Todd Lawson, 1:858–890. Leiden: Brill, 2017.

Vuckovic, Brooke Olson. *Heavenly Journeys, Earthly Concerns*. New York: Routledge, 2005.

Walker, Paul E., trans. *Epistles of the Brethren of Purity: Sciences of the Soul and Intellect*. Part 1, *An Arabic Critical Edition and English Translation of Epistles*, 32–36. Oxford: Oxford University Press and Institute of Ismaili Studies, 2015.

Watt, Montgomery. *A History of Islamic Spain*. Edinburgh: Edinburgh University Press, 1965.

Wasserstrom, Steven. *Between Muslim and Jew: The Problem of Symbiosis under Early Islam*. Princeton, NJ: Princeton University Press, 1995.

Wasserstrom, Steven. "*Sefer Yeẓirah* and Early Islam: A Reappraisal." *Journal of Jewish Thought and Philosophy* 3 (1993): 1–30.

Wolfson, Eliot. "Merkavah Traditions in Philosophical Garb: Judah Halevi Reconsidered." In *Proceedings of the American Academy for Jewish Research* 57 (1990–1991): 179–242.

Zaleski, Carol and Philip Zaleski, eds. *The Book of Heaven: An Anthology of Writings from Ancient to Modern Times*. Oxford: Oxford University Press, 2000.

Index

Abraham, prophet, 54, 55–56, 63, 65, 124, 134n51, 155n13; mentioned, 53, 68–69, 139n56
Almoravids. *See* al-Murābiṭūn
Almohads. *See* al-Muwāḥḥidūn
angel: at the gate of each heaven, 61–62; cannot ascend beyond the Lote Tree, 86–87; of Death (Azrā'īl), 23, 30, 64, 119; demonstrating postures of liturgical prayer (*ṣalāt*), 31, 109, 123, 134n49; Gabriel, 27, 39, 40, 45–46, 53–54, 58, 60, 68–69, 82, 86, 88–89, 102–103, 108–110, 119-121, 133n45, 150n28, 151n35; Guardian of Hellfire (Mālik), 23, 31, 63, 68, 119, 155n5; Half-Fire Half-Ice, 23; Isrāfīl, 31, 121–122; Guardian of the veils, 123; polycephalous (i.e. many-headed), 31, 45, 120, 122; Michael (Mikā'īl), 31, 63, 121; resembling Jesus, 72; Rooster, form of, 23, 31, 122; seated and forced to stand, 23–24, 27, 131n18, 132n33, 132n35; seeking Muḥammad to intercede on its behalf, 47, 139n52, 140n60; teaches the call to prayer, 58, 81
Brethren of Purity. *See* Ikhwān al-Ṣafā
Burāq, 25, 59–61, 74, 78, 82, 88; mentioned, 62, 103–104, 142n2
cold hand of God, 46, 139n54
colloquy scene (Muḥammad speaks to God face to face in heavens), 31–32, 55–57, 105, 123–124, 141n14
command (*amr*), divine, its cosmic role, 43, 79–80, 85–86, 138n41, 146n52; its role during the ascension, 80, 85, 92
contemplation, 37–39, 67, 75, 83, 94, 95, 112, 125n1, 142n1, 144n25
explorative authority, 3–4
Enoch (Idrīs), 6, 30, 63–65, 89, 119, 124, 155n13; mentioned, 8, 139n56
favor of the prophets, 32–33, 55–57, 124, 141n15, 155n10
Fāṭimids, 11, 12, 35–36, 114, 116; mentioned, 73
Gabriel, angel. *See under* angel, Gabriel
Halevi, Judah, 43–44, 138n44; mentioned, 18, 36, 42
Hanging Sword anecdote, 32
Hawwārī, Hūd b. al-Ḥakam tafsīr, 25–27
heavenly host debate, 24, 31, 124
Hekhalot, 6, 21–22, 23, 27, 43, 87, 89, 108, 132n34, 137n29, 155n8, 156n16
Ibn 'Abbās ascension narratives, 9–10, 23, 28–33, 42–43, 45–48, 86, 108–109, 113–114, 130n13, 133n45, 134n51, 139n54, 139n56, 145n49, 147n65; mentioned 17–18, 27, 40
Ibn 'Arabī, 111–112, 115–117, 129n54, 153n66; and his *Kitāb al-isrā'*, 115–117, 153n5; mentioned, 2, 3, 14, 17, 19, 96, 125n1
Ibn Barrajān, 67–94, 143n14, 145n47; biography of, 14–15; exegesis from his major (longer) commentary *Tanbīh al-afhām*, 74–79; exegesis from his minor (shorter) commentary *Īḍāḥ al-ḥikma*, 70–74, 79–82, 87–93; his prediction of the fall of Jerusalem, 28, 114; mentioned, 37
Ibn Ezra, Abraham, 40–43; mentioned, 6, 17, 18, 38
Ibn Masarra, 37–39, 136n12, 136n17; mentioned, 98
Ibn Qaṣī, 95–112; biography of, 15–16, 148n1; commentary on the ascension in his treatise *Khal' al-khal'*, 99–111; 152n56
Ibn Sīnā, 39–40, 153n7; mentioned, 38, 44
Ikhwān al-Ṣafā, 35–37, 96–97, 111, 116, 135n5, 145n47; mentioned, 11, 14, 15, 19, 106

imām, 114; Ḥasan b. ʿAlī, 150n20; Ibn Qasī's claim to office of, 96; Ibn al-Ḥanafiyya, 150n20; Ismāʿīlī leader known as, 35; Jaʿfar, 25; Muḥammad serving during liturgical prayer as, 30, 52, 58–59, 83, 90
Iyāḍ. *See under* Qāḍī ʿIyāḍ
Jesus, prophet, 6, 55–56, 65, 68, 72–73, 83, 134n51, 141n19, 145n46; mentioned, 29, 52, 53, 69, 139n56
Khargūshī, 22–23
Khudrī ascension hadith report, 24–27
Liber Denudationis, 45–48, 138n47; mentioned, 18, 44
Liber Scalae Machometi, 116, 154n9; mentioned, 48
Lote Tree of the Boundary, 7, 26, 55, 75, 79, 83, 85, 88, 134n51, 146n61, 148n83; mystical interpretation of, 90–93, 103, 110, 142n2
Mahdi, 12, 15, 71–73, 96, 114
Mālikī jurisprudence, 9, 11–12, 13, 16, 91, 148n72; mentioned, 49, 113
Moses, prophet, 26, 46, 55–57, 64–65, 68, 92–93, 105–106, 124, 137n33, 138n44, 141n24; mentioned, 29, 52, 53, 69, 134n51, 139n56
al-Murābiṭūn, 10, 11–12, 13, 15–16, 72, 95, 112, 113, 128n23
al-Muwāḥḥidūn, 10, 11, 12, 13, 15, 16, 72, 96, 112, 113–115
nearness to God, 76–78, 84, 88, 145n42
Neoplatonism, 6, 14, 36, 38, 79–80, 85–86, 90, 94, 96–98, 101, 103; mentioned, 37, 44, 100, 107, 111–112, 126n11
Party Kings, 10, 11; mentioned, 36
place of sitting (in divine proximity), 78–79, 83–84, 88–89, 96–97, 101, 146n61, 150n26
prayer, liturgical (*ṣalāt*) and its intimate connection to ascension, 80–85, 145n40. *See also under* angels, demonstrating postures of liturgical prayer (*ṣalāt*); imām, Muḥammad serving during liturgical prayer as
Qāḍī ʿIyāḍ: biography of, 13; *al-Shifā*, 44–45, 51–59, 81, 127n18, 134n51, 141n11
Qummī tafsīr, 25
Qushayrī, 22–23; mentioned, 30
rafraf, green, 31, 76, 121
scratching of the pens heard in the highest heavens, 76, 83–84, 86–89, 101, 104–105, 145n49, 146n61
seals of Surat al-Baqara (i.e. Qurʾān 2: 285–286), 24, 55–56, 141n14, 156n18
seas and oceans, heavenly, 31, 120–121
snake, wrapped around heavenly throne, 31, 122–123, 134n47
throne, divine, 97–98, 122–124; sword hanging from, 32, 124, 155n8, 155n9
Suhayli: biography of, 16; commentary on the *Sīra*, 59–66
vision of God, 100–107; in the heart, 42, 43, 62, 100, 105, 107, 124; possibility of, 31, 75, 151n35; with physical eyes, 17, 62, 92, 100, 107, 124; mentioned, 52, 97

INDEX OF QURANIC VERSES

2:143	54
2: 285–286	24, 55, 56
3:36	55
3:48	55
3:49	55
3:110	56
4:125	55, 155n10
4:164	55, 155n11
5:54	71–72
7:143	92, 106
14:48	90, 147n70
15:33	70
15:87	55, 56
16:2	85, 146n52
16:32	91
17:1	7, 8, 14, 24, 25, 52, 67, 70, 75, 79–80
17:85	85
18:65	147n64
19:57	64, 155n13
21:20	108
21:107	54
24:55	71–72
25:1	54
27:3	83
32:9	79
34:28	54
34:38	55
36:1–6	147n64
36:26	91
37:165–66	86
38:35	55
42:11	83
50:16	77
51:21–23	107
53:1	75–76
53:1–18	8, 14, 52, 67, 70–71, 75, 88, 104
53:5	88–89
53:6	84, 88–89
53:7	89, 99, 102, 104, 110
53:8–9	76–78, 84, 88, 104
53:10	58, 75, 76, 79, 83, 89

53:11	104–105
53:12	43
53:13–18	7, 38, 108
53:14	79, 104, 110
53:15	79
53:16	76, 92, 109
53:17	104, 109
53:18	38, 108
53:19–28	51
55:76	31
77:20	79
81:22–24	99, 110
94:1-2	54
94:4	54
96:19	84
97:4	79, 85, 146n52

www.ingramcontent.com/pod-product-compliance
Lightning Source LLC
Chambersburg PA
CBHW061123040425
24518CB00002B/7